Naked

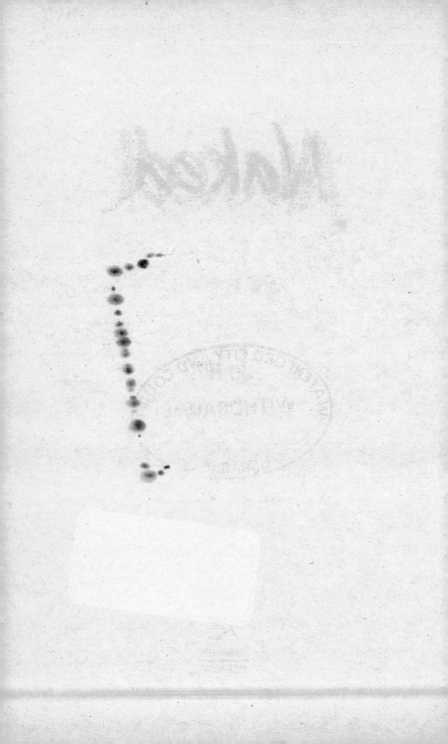

Naked

Jo Hill

headline
review

First published in 2008 by
HEADLINE REVIEW
An imprint of Headline Publishing Group

1

Cataloguing in Publication Data is available from the British Library

Paperback 978 07553 1809 4
Trade paperback 978 0 7553 1814 8

Typeset in Dante by Avon DataSet Ltd,
Bidford-on-Avon, Warwickshire

Printed and bound in Great Britain by
Mackays of Chatham plc, Chatham, Kent

Headline's policy is to use papers that are natural, renewable and recyclable
products and made from wood grown in sustainable forests. The logging and
manufacturing processes are expected to conform to the environmental
regulations of the country of origin.

HEADLINE PUBLISHING GROUP
An Hachette Livre UK Company
338 Euston Road
London NW1 3BH

www.headline.co.uk
www.hachettelivre.co.uk

Jo Hill is married with two children and lives in the country.

Prologue

'I'M NOT TAKING MY CLOTHES OFF.'

I stood rigid in front of my mum, my words bouncing off the walls of the empty changing room.

Mum turned away, and when she looked back at me her eyes were watering. 'Don't be silly. You're just a little girl.'

I was ten years old. I folded my arms tightly across my chest. I'd seen them outside. Naked. I closed my eyes tight, trying to block out all the people we'd just walked past. What were we doing in this place?

Mum tried a smile. 'Nobody minds here.'

But I minded. I'd never seen strangers naked before. Men with their penises showing. Mum had always said to be careful about things like that. Like the man I'd told her about once who'd asked me directions from his car but was touching himself. It made me feel sick.

Mum turned to me. 'Come on, Jo . . .'

I edged back from her into the corner.

She gave me one of those smiles, like the one I'd seen in her bible, the one of Jesus looking down from the cross. 'There's nothing to it at all. Look.'

She slipped off her shoes and started to undo her suspenders. I'd seen her do this lots of times before. I usually liked to watch the way she rolled her nylons down – perfectly – slipping each one over her foot and then holding the two toes together to wind them up into a soft ball. But not now. I knew what was coming next.

'Please, Mum . . . ?'

She turned her back to me and pulled off her jumper. Then slid off her skirt.

'Please, Mummy, I want to go home.'

She took a deep breath and turned to face me in that 'Simon-Says-do-this,' way and I fixed my eyes on her bra.

'Come on, Jo. Just take off your top. Like me.'

I prayed I could get away with just my vest and knickers, even though I'd seen them all outside.

Perhaps Mum thought she was setting a good example by doing what she did next. She looked right at me and lifted down the shoulders of her bra, undoing the hooks at the back, swinging it off and letting her breasts hang loose.

I put my hands up to my face and peeped through my fingers. Her breasts were flattened and lay slightly to each side like empty saddlebags.

I looked away as she wriggled out of her girdle and turned, trying to hide myself in the corner next to the lockers. Then, from the corner of my eye, I saw her pink,

Bri-Nylon knickers on the bench. Mum put her hands on my shoulders and turned me, slowly, around.

I was looking down. There's a certain age when you don't want to see the fuzz of your mum's pubic hair. I felt sick because I knew what was coming.

Mum let go of my shoulders then spread her arms out like a crucifix. 'See? Nothing to be ashamed of.'

'Please, Mummy, please . . .' The tears were beginning to sting at the back of my nose.

I heard Dad's voice outside. 'What on earth's going on in there? Hurry up. We're waiting.'

Mum tried a smile. 'Come on, Jo, your turn.'

I shook my head.

Mum's mouth went tight. 'Take your clothes off! Now!'

'No.'

'Just do as I say.'

'You can't make me.'

'Take them off!'

Suddenly she was at me – her temper was up. She prodded me on the chest. 'Off.'

'Please . . . ?'

'Do it or you'll be sorry . . .'

She made a grab for my jumper. I tried to dodge her but she was too quick for me and we struggled together. I didn't want to touch my mum with no clothes on. There were certain places where I couldn't put my hands. I closed my eyes. She came at me from behind and although she was small, she was strong. With spiteful, slapping hands she tugged and pulled at my jumper. I tried to hold it at the neck. I could feel her nails scratching at my bare skin. I'd never seen her as cross as this before, not since the time when I'd been playing in the garden and got dog dirt all over my party dress and she'd slapped my legs so hard they stung like nettle rash.

'No, Mum, no.'

'Mary-mother-of-God give me strength.'

I could feel the jumper straining, the pop of wool snapping. Suddenly it turned inside out as she wrenched it over my head, but the neck stuck. I was in darkness, struggling for breath as she pulled and pulled. My neck was stretching. The jumper was tightening around my throat, throttling me.

'Mu-um.' My voice muffled. 'Please . . .'

It was hot under the jumper. I could feel the tears welling up from my chest, I tried to swallow them down, to be strong. We twirled round and round in a mad dance. I was in darkness, sobbing loudly now, holding on to the neck of my jumper as hard as I could. My fingers were aching as I tried to dig my nails in. I felt it pulling away from me, bit by bit, as she strained to drag it over my head.

'Let go or you'll be sorry. God help me . . .'

Suddenly, I lost my grip on the jumper, heard her release a breath as it burned and scraped over my ears.

'There!'

It came off, with my vest at the same time.

I sucked in a huge mouthful of air. White lights spun all around. I felt sick.

'Please, Mum, don't. Mummy . . . Please?'

She made a grab for my trousers and caught me off balance. We tumbled to the floor and I could feel the heat of her naked body, damp with sweat. The smell of Palmolive soap mixed with Estée Lauder. She held me down, gasping, and unhooked my Dr Scholl's sandals. I tried to crawl away on the dusty floor but she was on me. I could feel her bare skin all over me. Then she flattened herself against my back. The weight of her pushed the breath from my body and I went limp.

Slowly and firmly Mum peeled off my trousers. I tried to hold on to my knickers but she'd got them in her strong hands. It was a tug of war and I was losing my grip. The elastic stretched as she pulled them down my legs. I struggled and struggled but couldn't hold on any longer. I made a last feeble attempt by pulling my foot up into a right angle. She wrenched the elastic taut, looked at me quickly – and let it go. It snapped back on my skin and I winced with the shock. I felt her nails dig deep as she snatched the pants off.

Mum was panting. Her hair was all messed up. 'There now, what was all the fuss about?'

I rolled into a small ball, feeling like a plucked chicken, white and cold with goose bumps all over. I was crying now, my nose running.

Mum straightened her hair, bouncing her curls back into place. 'See? Just as God made us.'

Yes, God had made us like that. But as I was about to find out, we were not in the Garden of Eden.

Chapter 1

As we came out of the changing rooms, I had pulled down my hair to cover my front and clasped my hands down below. It was cold and I started to shiver. I kept my head lowered, watching the tiny blond hairs rise on my arms, and then followed the goose bumps appearing all over my legs and stomach. The summer sun shone, but the wind blew up from the sea, lifting my hair as I tried desperately to keep it in place.

I couldn't remember being outside without clothes on before. Never in this way, where everyone could see, and there was no Mum standing there ready with a towel to save my blushes. The sides of my cheeks began to burn. I kept my eyes down and tried to stifle the choking feeling that was rising up from the back of my throat. For a moment, I swayed on the step of the changing rooms, my head dizzy. I had to breathe in deep to steady myself.

Dad had his back to us, hands on hips. He was talking to a woman who was so tanned that she didn't actually look naked. I'd seen him talking like this with women before, one hand on his hip, and leaning back, laughing.

He slapped his hand on his thigh and turned around. I'd never seen him naked, and as if in freeze frame. I didn't want to look at him down there. It seemed wrong. He was my dad, after all, and I'd passed the point where I would happily share a bath with my mum. There was something wrong about all this, yet I could see that he wasn't bothered at all.

I wanted my dad with his trousers on, like when I'd crawl up on his knee and maybe he'd tell me a story. I didn't want to have to see what was underneath. But I looked anyway. I tried not to, in the same way that I tried not to look at the scary bits in films, knowing that I was going to see something I didn't want to, but not being able to help myself. So I found myself looking at my dad's penis. I closed my eyes. I don't know what I was hoping for but when I opened them again nothing had changed.

Dad threw back his head again, laughed and gave his thigh another slap as he looked in our direction.

'Here they are – the lovely ladies in my life – my wife Elizabeth and my daughter Jo.'

I didn't like the way he introduced us like he owned us, but then here we were doing exactly what he wanted us to do, like we always did.

The brown-skinned woman stretched out her hand and Mum shook it meekly. I went to shake it but our fingers banged clumsily.

'Say hello, Jo!'

'Hello.' My voice had gone hoarse.

I pulled my hair further over my shoulders and clasped my left hand over my right wrist to cover myself.

The woman smiled. She seemed totally relaxed – just as if she were chatting at the corner shop. There was no real difference in the colour of nipples or her pubic region, her all-over suntan was like a dark body stocking. And I thought, if only I could get that brown then, perhaps, no one would notice me?

The brown woman was glamorous. She was tall, her body athletic, and she had short, curly hair. As she showed us around I tried to keep my eyes on the neat stone path, watching my bare feet, feeling the cold stone as we wound through meticulously kept gardens. From time to time I'd look up and catch a glimpse of someone, then quickly turn away.

It's largely a blur in my memory, that first day. A woman lying on a sunlounger with her legs wide apart. A man bending down to reveal a darkened anus. An old man sauntering along, his private parts swinging like wrinkled prunes in a bag. There was lots of smiling and nodding in our direction as Dad said hello to everyone. Allowing Dad to take centre-stage, Mum and I stood quietly on the sidelines, out of the way. People seemed to leave us alone as we settled in.

*

I was thankful when the sun started to slip lower in the sky. I was given my shorts and T-shirt to wear as I helped Dad put up the tent. Dad braved the chill, as did Mum, wearing not a stitch. It was getting late and I could tell by the way he was clanging the tent poles around that Dad was getting cross. Over a series of rainy camping holidays the canvas of the tent had shrunk and Dad had sawn down the tent poles so that it still fitted. This, however, had made the whole business of putting up the tent extremely stressful.

'You two,' he shouted at Mum and me. 'Take a corner each and twist the poles together.'

I didn't like to look at him as he barked orders, naked. The tent poles had been colour-coded with stripes of nail varnish. We worked silently though the puzzle, my mind in a jumble. What were we doing here? Why weren't people wearing any clothes?

'Dad . . .I don't understand . . .'

'Bloody hell, it's simple . . .'

I wanted to tell him that it wasn't simple for me – I just didn't understand what we were doing here.

'Dad, I . . . I can't . . .'

'Of course you can, you just twist the two yellow ones together.'

'No . . . I . . . That's not what I meant.'

Mum turned and, seeing I was about to cry, gave me a warning look. It was never a good idea to cry in front of my father. I pushed my tongue hard against the back of my front teeth to try and stop the tears forming.

'Stop snivelling,' Dad shouted, as I tried to twist the tent poles.

Mum took the poles from me. 'Here, Jo, give them to me.'

She twisted and twisted them, her small, strong hands white at the knuckles.

'It's so difficult.'

There, seeing my mum against the darkening sky with no clothes on, I knew exactly what she meant.

Dad sniffed and told us both we were useless. He snatched the poles from her and said that if he wanted a job doing properly he had to do it himself. He carried on, clanging the poles, while Mum set up the primus stove and heated some soup. She stirred it around slowly in the pan and, without looking at Dad, said, 'It's not easy for her . . .'

I blew up the lilos with a foot pump and fetched the cushion that I slept on when we were camping from the back of the car. You didn't try to reason with my dad when he was getting cross. You just stayed quiet. As we ate our soup, I thought about the journey here and I remembered how excited I'd been and immediately felt sick. Perhaps I'd wake up in the morning and it would all have been a bad dream?

It was the first time I'd seen my mother drink like this. She sat on one of the blue folding camp chairs and poured beer into a large glass. Strange, I thought, surely beer was a man's drink? And ladies drank from delicate glasses – I'd seen them on the adverts. Ale glasses belonged in masculine hands and in beer cellars where men sang noisy drinking songs. Mum didn't sip her drink, either. Instead, she lifted it to her lips, stretched her mouth wide, tilted back her head and opened her throat – swilling rather than drinking. I watched her Adam's apple pump quickly, heard the smack of her lips as she put the glass on the table, half empty, and noted the frothy moustache above her top lip. She looked over to where my dad was and topped up her drink quickly. 'Cheers.'

Dad had taken quite some time to readjust the tent pegs and stamp them well into the ground. Finally, he sniffed deeply and pulled up a chair. He stared at the mass of empty bottles under the camping table.

'Hang on a minute, Elizabeth. How come you got through all that beer?'

'What d'you mean?'

'How many bottles have you drunk?' He ran his fingers through his hair.

'What's it to you?'

Mum stuck out her bottom lip at him and pulled a silly face.

'Just pull yourself together, Elizabeth. You've had far too much to drink.'

'Rubbish.'

'Come on now, just slow down.'

Mum banged her empty glass on the table. 'I was thirsty, that's all.'

'All I can say is, you've got one hell of a thirst.'

Mum's speech was slurring. 'What are you trying to insinuate?'

'Look, I just . . . How many have you had?'

'This is a party, and I'm on my holidays. Who's counting?'

Unable to sleep, later that night in the tent's tiny bedroom compartment I drew a deep breath to speak but what I said came out in a whisper.

'I want to go home.'

My whisper met with silence.

I pushed the tent's thin yellow lining against the outer skin – trying to make patterns. This wasn't like the times we'd go camping and Dad would tell stories until I fell asleep. Now, while the sound of his snoring grew louder and louder the worries of the day formed like words on my brow. Then I did what I always did when things seemed to be getting too much – I wiped my hand across my forehead and cleaned all the words away.

I heard my mother's voice, quietly, in the dark.

'Jo, don't forget your prayers.'

I wondered if I said my prayers as though I really meant them, whether God would reach down his great hand from heaven and take me out of here. Mum said that you should always call on God in times of need. She was always calling on Him, or Our Lady – she'd look up like they were hovering close above her.

'Hail-Mary-mother-of-God, hallowed be thy name . . .'

It was my cue to join in. Even though I didn't want to say the words, I squeezed my eyes tight shut and prayed as hard as I could. Then, in my head, I added a prayer of my own:

'Dear God, I promise I'll always be good, always, if you could just stop all this. I'll never be naughty again, I'll never forget to clear out my guinea pig's cage or tidy my bedroom or to say my prayers every night, and morning. If only you could make it all stop, please . . . ? . . . For ever and ever. Amen.'

I crossed myself in the way Mum had taught me.

'Night-night Jo, sleep tight.'

And I was tight. My hands were clenched into tight fists as if I was going to punch someone. I didn't say goodnight to my mum. I didn't want anything to do with her. She must have agreed to come here and at that moment I hated her – and my dad. One day I'd run away and hide somewhere they'd never find me. I didn't know, yet, how I'd do that. I was too little. I would just have to wait until I was old enough to find a way to escape. Then I'd show them. I'd run away and never come back.

I turned over and over in my sleeping bag, not wanting to fall asleep because that would mean having to face it all again when I woke up. Mum had stopped praying. She lay on her side, asleep, mouth open, muttering, her breath smelling of stale beer.

I don't know when I first noticed that my parents didn't get on. It seemed to me that they had always argued and their arguments became part of the background noise of the house – mostly just an insistent grinding away but every now and again there would be a crackle of gunfire. I'd had nothing to compare their behaviour to until I visited other people's homes. When I went round to my friend Sue's house, I noticed that her parents didn't scream at each other and that however many times I saw Sue's mum, I never saw her cry.

We played a game at school called 'paper, scissors, stone'. You'd clap your hands and, on the third clap, form your hand into a plane for paper, a 'V' for scissors or into a fist for stone. We played at home, too, and I always used to try and guess what Mum and Dad would do. They tended to have a favourite, so over time you could beat them at it.

Dad liked to be scissors. I can't remember how many times I watched him cut up Mum's paper. I liked to be the stone. It wasn't the obvious choice – dull, even – but stone could blunt scissors. It was only a game, but I thought of the three of us like that. My dad flashing those scissors at Mum, with me, quietly there, waiting for a chance to blunt them.

Chapter 2

Life had felt relatively normal before the nudist camp holiday. We lived in Warrington, in an ordinary house in an ordinary street of identical houses built shoulder to shoulder. 'It's semi-detached,' Mum would say, in the same posh voice she used to answer the telephone. Warrington was always grey: grey skies blocked out the sun, grey houses huddled together for warmth, grey pavements wet and shiny with rain. A favourite activity at primary school was to trace the River Mersey from textbooks and I used to love adding a large blob and, in neat handwriting, 'Warrington'. All relatively normal.

However, after the visit to the camp, everything felt weird. Sitting at my school desk, watching the teacher Miss Masters scan the class in case of disorder, I scribbled a sketch of her wearing nothing but her little half-moon glasses and drew arrows pointing to her large stomach and big breasts. When I slipped the picture to my friend Sue it made her clasp her hand over her mouth and start to shake with laughter, and that really set me off.

Miss Masters rapped a ruler on her desk.

'You again, Jo! Now there's a surprise. Get on with your work.'

She turned to the blackboard and started writing down the names of towns while meantime, as my drawing of her was passed around, the giggling in class grew louder. Sue handed me back the drawing just as the teacher turned to face us.

'Stop that at once.' Miss Masters clapped her hands then looked straight at me. 'What have you got there?'

'Nothing.' The word was tight in my throat.

'Well you can come up here and bring this "nothing" to me.'

Panicked, I stuffed the piece of paper into my mouth.

'Is that chewing gum, Jo?'

I nodded.

'Come and spit it into the bin.'

I walked to the front, deposited the drawing and returned to my desk. I found on the map where we'd been on holiday and nudged Sue.

'That's where we went,' I whispered. 'Sussex.'

Then Sue pointed to the Isle of Man which was where she went on holiday every year. I wished I could tell her what had happened on our holiday in Sussex. But I was afraid of what she would think.

Miss Masters peered over the top of her half-moon

glasses. 'Enough talking. Any more trouble and you'll be outside the door, at opposite ends of the corridor.'

We were silent; the last thing I wanted was to be split up from my best friend.

I stared out of the high classroom window at the clouds and thought about my holiday, that trip that had changed everything. The really strange thing was that there'd been no talk beforehand about where we were going: no family discussion to prepare me; no gentle introduction to taking your clothes off in the company of like-minded strangers; no talk about the benefits of 'getting back to nature'. No explanation at all.

I certainly wasn't brought up as a naturist: there are a few old black-and-white photographs of me, aged about two and completely naked, standing in the garden or braving the wind and rain on some beach holiday. I clearly remember the itch of wet sand in a swimming costume and getting changed on that beach with my mum holding a towel up around me and saying, 'There now, Jo, I'll hold it, no one's looking.'

There was a sense of propriety, even from a very early age. I knew that being naked was rude. 'Get yourself decent,' Mum would tut if she came into my bedroom when I was dressing for school.

I was encouraged to sit with my knees held together,

my skirt pulled over them so no one would see my knickers. I was told to keep my skirt from flying up in the wind – a petticoat was something to be hidden. Indeed, my mum used to say, 'It's snowing down south,' when your petticoat was showing. And if Dad should ever forget to do up his flies that, too, was referred to in code – 'You've got egg on your chin,' Mum would whisper, blush and look away.

On the whole, it was my mother who put me right on such matters. Being ladylike was something she taught me, much as she helped me learn how to read or to tell the time. I knew that bottoms were not to be talked about and definitely not to be shown. I also knew that, later, I'd develop breasts and they'd be rude, too, and must be hidden away in a bra. I understood that a man had a penis that he didn't show to anyone except his wife and only then if it was time to make a baby (unless he was a bad man and then you had to stay well away from him). We had no central heating at home: in cold weather we wrapped up, stoked coals on open fireplaces and filled hot water bottles to slide between cold, damp sheets. The last thing you thought about, other than when you changed quickly into your winceyette nightie, was being naked.

I thought I had it clear in my head. Being naked was for being on your own. No one said anything about taking all my clothes off and stretching out stark naked in front of complete strangers. No. There was nothing about that in the 'How to grow up into a Polite Young Lady' manual.

Perhaps, when Dad decided to take us on holiday to a nudist camp, my parents thought that at ten years old I was still young enough to forget everything they had, up until then, drummed into me. Whatever their thinking, that summer afternoon we rolled into that Sussex campsite and I climbed out of the car with my dad, eager to look around. He behaved perfectly normally as we walked around the camp and I trailed behind with a feeling that perhaps I was dreaming.

We walked past naked bodies spread eagled in the sun, people playing a strange version of tennis – miniten – with round wooden bats and men in straw hats balancing newspapers on their knees. It could have been an ordinary campsite anywhere – except that everyone was naked.

I had the feeling that I was the one who'd got it all wrong. But it soon became clear that there was nothing normal about this holiday – where your mum marched you into a changing room and wrestled your clothes from you. There was nothing normal about any of it.

Chapter 3

Our house was on what Dad called 'the good side of the crescent'. The road was shaped like a moon, and around the other side – the dark side of the moon – was the place I was not allowed to go.

'Don't you ever let me catch you around the other side of the crescent,' Dad warned me. 'The children there are good-for-nothings, all their fathers are in prison.'

Nevertheless, I was drawn to the 'dark side'. Limping caravans in driveways, cars powdery with rust, smashed windows, peeling paint. More than anything I wanted to be in the good-for-nothings' gang – making wobbly crates on wheels, kicking battered tin cans, breaking the windows of empty houses. One day, when Dad wasn't around, I tried to make friends with those children.

When Dad found out where I'd been, he built a big gate; not to stop me from running across the road but to keep the other children out. Once, he caught me with a foot on the bottom rail of the gate. 'Just stay behind that,' he shouted, and looked towards the garage. He kept a hickory stick in there. Even the, to me, curious name of that stick was enough to terrify me and with Dad's temper I didn't have to do much to be threatened with it.

Sometimes, he would sometimes bend an imaginary stick in the air and I'd feel my stomach go tight. I never actually saw the hickory stick – I'd searched the darkest corners of the garage, among the rusting tools, but never found it – yet I always thought that the day would come when I'd do something and he'd really get it out and hit me with it.

I didn't want him to be angry but it was hard to avoid because I was never quite sure what would set him off. There were times I'd do something to make him cross and he'd get up quickly and head for the garage, then I'd wait, stomach clenched . . . Would this be the time he'd hit me? Then he'd peer around the door and offer me the chance to be good.

Often it was something really simple that would spark his anger. One day, for example, I was turning the handle of the little toy washing machine that I'd get out when Mum was doing her laundry and she'd fill it with handkerchiefs.

'Go and take your dad his tea,' Mum said. 'Be careful now you don't spill it in the saucer.'

I hated it when she told me to take in Dad's cup of tea. He couldn't stand any kind of mess. He'd told me that if

I moved the cup and saucer round in a circle as I walked the tea wouldn't spill, but I couldn't get the hang of it. Now, the cup wobbled on the saucer and the tea slopped out. It was only a drop and I hoped he wouldn't notice. Dad picked up the cup and tea dripped from its bottom. He sniffed in hard and his cheeks bulged.

'What's that in the saucer?'

I didn't want to say as that would set him off and this might be the time he'd go and get that stick.

'Can't you do a simple job properly without making a mess?' He stared at me long and hard until I had to look away. I wanted to tell him that I didn't mean to spill his tea, that I'd carried it as carefully as I could, but it was too late.

'Just watch it, Jo, or I'll get the hickory stick.'

'Please don't . . . Please . . . It was an accident.'

'Oh, just get out of my sight.'

Dad took off his glasses and his eyes went small like a rat's. I knew it was time to go and I took off quickly, skidded through the kitchen door and slammed it behind me. Mum had overheard and was already fixing him another cup of tea. She handed me some freshly laundered hankies and nodded to my toy ironing board.

'Just get on and play now, Jo.'

My waking hours were spent tip-toeing around Dad's moods. In a word, I was scared: scared of doing the wrong thing; of saying the wrong thing. Sometimes, scared to exist, even. I was certainly too scared to ask him any questions about the nudist camp, including, most importantly, if we'd be going back.

I'm sure that Mum felt the same; she had long ago stopped trying to stand up to her husband about things that were important to her – although when it came to going to church she did, for a while, still try. She especially loved dressing me up in my Sunday best but when she did, it was always the same: rows.

'All good Catholics go to church on a Sunday.'

'But I want to go and play.'

'Hush now, you can wear your special jacket and your new black patent shoes.'

I loved it when Mum brushed my hair: 'All young ladies brush their hair a hundred times a day,' she insisted, 'to make it shine.'

We'd be all dressed up ready to go then Dad would appear at the door.

'Where d'you think you're off to?'

Mum would put her hand on my shoulder. 'It's Sunday, I'm taking her to church.'

While Dad didn't approve of religion or churchgoing, I noticed – more and more – that my mum seemed to need it. Dad had agreed to become a Catholic when he married Mum but, after the wedding, there'd apparently been no mention of him following through with the faith.

'Brainwashes children, that's what religion does – tells them what to think. I don't want that for my child.' And so, eventually – just as she gave up on so many other things in her marriage – Mum stopped taking me to church, though she did still try to bring me up as a Catholic.

Mum used to say that opposites attracted each other but, like magnets turned the wrong way around, they also repelled: Mum was a devout Catholic, Dad had reverted to atheism; Mum was quiet, Dad was loud; Mum was submissive, Dad was dominant. How they ever got together in the first place, I could never imagine. Mum said she never felt it was a real wedding because the priest had only married them at a side aisle.

The mother I knew was different from the woman who looked out of the old black-and-white photographs on the sideboard. The woman in the photographs wore strapless evening gowns like the glamorous movie stars did in those old films Mum called 'the weepies'. Even now, with her oval face, soft eyes, curved lips and hair coiled up, Mum could still look beautiful. Occasionally, when Dad took her to a dinner dance and, dressed up, she'd twirl and turn in front of her long mirror then briefly, very briefly, I'd see how lovely my mum once was. She'd go out in a rustle of silk then, late at night when she came home, I'd wake to the smell of her perfume when she'd kiss my cheek and leave me a silver party hat, a tasselled horn or some other little trinket from the ball.

My parents didn't have a fairytale romance. Like so many other couples back then during the forties, they'd met at a dance and very soon were married. They were both getting on a bit in their thirties and, also, it was just after the war when people were anxious to make up for lost time. But as it turned out, 'marry in haste – repent at leisure' was what my mum came to say.

Mum quickly became the perfect housewife. In the early years of marriage, when I was little, she stayed at home and cleaned and cooked. Her role was very clear: keep the house tidy, be a mother and have a meal ready on the table when Dad came home from work. It was understood that my father made all the important decisions and, when she became his wife, my mother had promised to love, honour and obey him. And obeying meant just that – no discussion. Mum would do anything to avoid Dad flying into a temper.

Dad always got his own way and I knew, even without being told, that it would have been his decision to go to the nudist camp. Dad decided on everything. The nudist camp hadn't been mentioned since we came home. Dad hadn't spoken a single word about the people we'd met, or the camp and that was rare because his views overwhelmed just about every family discussion.

One evening, while the three of us were watching the news on television – a rare moment of family unity – I noticed the way Mum's hands were clasped together, almost in prayer and it made me wonder: how could she have agreed to the nudist camp? How could she have been naked with people she'd never met? Then I remembered how mad Dad would get whenever she dared to disobey him or question his word, and I realised that my mum had as little choice as I did.

Despite the fact that she always did as Dad said, she must have known going to nudist camps was wrong – especially when it involved taking a ten year old. Mum was religious; surely the local priest wouldn't approve? Anyone who wore a long black cassock and stiff white collar could hardly condone such a public display of nudity. There was probably something about it in the Bible. I wondered if she had mentioned her nudity in confession, sitting in that little wooden box.

'Forgive me, Father, for I have sinned.'

'Tell me, my child . . .'

'I took my clothes off in front of strangers on holiday and . . .'

Suddenly, the priest's nose would be up against the lattice divide for sure. 'You did what . . . ?'

However Mum and I might have felt, Dad's rules were there to be obeyed and our lives were plagued by some very strange ones. Dad ran the house rather like a military camp; sometimes we even had an inspection parade – heralded by a sharp, two-tone whistle. There was never any time to tidy up myself or my belongings, the whistle meant I had to report immediately. The parades were held in a jokey fashion but there was always a chance that Dad might get cross, especially if I'd left a heap of my gear in the hall. Sometimes the inspection focussed on me: 'Hands out,' he'd say, then he'd examine my fingernails. He'd shake his head and I'd know I'd missed a bit. I also knew I couldn't get away with that too often or it wouldn't be a joke anymore.

Mealtimes were another battlefield. Normally, I ate alone at my tiny table in the kitchen where sometimes Dad stood over me, ensuring I completed my meal as efficiently and quickly as possible. Then, one Sunday lunchtime, out of the blue, I was promoted to a seat at the big dining table – though it was made clear that other than for Sunday lunches, I should continue to eat at my table in the kitchen. The dining table was covered with a stiff white cloth and set with the best china. I think Dad was trying to make more of an effort to spend time with me, but I found it very difficult being watched as I ate.

Mum stared into space and Dad just cut up his food and ate. I tried to break the silence with conversation but 'Don't speak with your mouth full,' Dad tutted. I had to eat every last scrap on my plate – even if I'd had enough. We would just sit there in silence while I finished, the gravy congealed on my plate.

Despite this, it soon became clear that Sunday lunch was also to be used as a forum for discussion.

'Jo, now you're ten, you must learn how to make some conversation,' Dad began.

'What about?' I asked as I started to cut up my meat, taking care that the knife didn't scratch on the plate.

'Just go ahead.' His eyes fixed on me through his glasses.

I wondered what on earth I could say that my dad would want to listen to. Mum nodded at me to start me off.

'We did Chinese skipping at school today. She'd never done it before – Sue I mean – you have to get your foot under the elastic, only it caught in her buckle. She fell over, and when she fell everyone saw her knickers, and she cried so much so I showed them my knickers, too, so she wouldn't be on her own 'cos I'd made her do the Chinese skipping in the first place and it was like really hard, like and . . .'

'Jo, go to your room.'

As I walked upstairs to my bedroom it all seemed so unfair. He was cross with me for showing my knickers, yet he'd taken me to that holiday camp where nobody had any clothes on at all.

I picked up my llama and held him close. He was what I held on to, tight under the covers, when Mum and Dad were arguing or when I would hear Mum crying. I had hugged him so much that he was almost bald. What was left of his fur was short and wiry but I still got some kind of comfort when I rubbed it hard on my face, and it helped to stop me from crying. I took my diary from the plastic safe, in a drawer under the bed where I kept all my secret stuff, then I started to write; hard, angry lines, in capitals, all about that horrible camp. I wrote and wrote until my hand was aching and the paper was starting to tear. Then I closed the diary and put it back under my bed.

No matter how I tried, I couldn't block out how miserable I'd been at the camp. Would we be going back? Why hadn't Mum or Dad mentioned it since we'd been home? It was almost as if by not talking about it, it wasn't real. But it was all too real for me.

Chapter 4

Every morning on that nudist-camp holiday, I'd woken to the sound of pots and pans clattering outside the tent as my mum made our breakfast and for a moment, as I lay in my cosy sleeping bag, I'd forget where I was. Then I'd see the yellow tent lining, my stomach would jolt and I'd remember.

One morning, Dad popped his head through the tent flap.

'Come on, up you get and enjoy the lovely day!' Then he broke into song – *'The sun has got his hat on . . .'*

'*. . . Hip-hip-hip hooray,*' Mum chimed in, squinting at the sunlight.

I hated the way Mum was joining in and singing that stupid song with Dad. And at the thought of having to see my parents naked, again, I crawled deep into my sleeping bag and pulled it over my head. My stomach churned at the thought of having to take off my pyjamas and step outside the tent naked. My legs felt heavy. The longer we stayed at the nudist camp, the more it seemed that I would never get used to it.

The first thing I saw on that bright summer's day was Mum bending over a primus stove. I tried not to notice how her breasts swung forward as she jiggled the pan, and the way her nipples had stretched to the size of saucers. She half turned away and picked up the breakfast plates to shield herself; I knew that was what she was doing because that's the way I felt myself.

Dad swung a towel over his shoulder. 'Time for the toilet block.' We walked together in silence to the shower block and split up as I joined the ladies' queue. Some new people had arrived in camp and I couldn't help noticing the shapes of the white bits where they'd been wearing swimsuits. It looked as if they were still wearing their costumes but someone had added rude graffiti, like the drawings I'd seen on toilet walls.

Dad had gone by the time I'd showered so I walked back to our tent with my towel wrapped tightly around me and tried to keep looking straight ahead as people nodded and said 'hello'. Holidaymakers were breakfasting naked, and I saw a man's private parts sticking out from under his newspaper.

Mum looked up. 'Come on, Jo, boiled eggs and soldiers, your favourite.' But I'd lost my appetite. Some bacon fat spat from the frying pan onto her bare skin. 'Ow!' she screeched, rubbing her stomach. I couldn't tell her I was sorry she'd burned herself, I could only think that it would never have happened if she'd been wearing clothes.

We sat round the blue folding camp table. My bare backside stuck to the plastic camping stool as I picked at my egg, my concentration focussed on removing each small piece of shell from the top. Mum was hot from standing over the stove and I could see a channel of sweat running down between her breasts. When she noticed me looking, she avoided my gaze. Dad breathed in the air deeply.

'Isn't this glorious?'

His question hung in the air along with the smell of the bacon and I started to retch.

'What's the matter with you, Jo? Look at the face on you. I don't know, I bring you all this way on holiday and you sit there dull as ditchwater.'

'I . . . I . . .'

'For God's sake cheer up.'

'I think I'm going to be sick.'

'Quick, take her away from the breakfast, for Christ's sake.'

'Mum . . . I . . .'

I stood over the washing up bowl and just managed not to vomit.

'Sorry, Dad.'

Suddenly, his voice was all charm. 'Come on, Jo, let's go and play boules.'

'Don't feel like it.'

'Less of your lip, young lady! Boules is a French game – I'm trying to broaden your horizons.'

I didn't want to have any more of my horizons broadened and I didn't want to take part in anything that would involve standing close to other naked people; feeling their sticky skins as they brushed past, never knowing where to look when someone spoke to me. This was the worst place I'd ever been to.

'Come on, Jo, don't be so sulky, we're on holiday,' said Dad, then he gave me that look, the look that meant 'Watch it, stop ruining things'. I followed him down the twisty path, my eyes fixed on the back of his heels, trying not to notice anyone. A large man pushed past me with his shoulders back – he reminded me of the *Emperor's New Clothes* in my storybook. A woman smiled at me, wearing nothing but red lipstick and matching nail polish on her fingers and toes and I wondered why she bothered.

The sun was burning and I felt raw. I'd never had sun on my chest before and noticed it was turning bright pink. I pulled my hair across my chest and folded my arms to keep it there. Was I the only one here who was embarrassed? I glanced around: a woman was sitting on a towel with her legs wide open, rubbing in suntan lotion; the man lying by her side had private parts so dark that I wondered if that part of you went brown in the sun, too. There were people sitting around in camping chairs chatting, men with their legs apart – everyone naked. No one seemed shocked by the nudity and I kept thinking: What's wrong with me? Could they see that I was trying to hide myself?

As Dad and I walked up the hill I noticed a group of old men wearing hats and I couldn't figure out why they'd gone to the trouble of protecting their heads when their bodies were exposed. Dad slowed down and in his booming voice swept his hand in my direction.

'This is my lovely daughter Jo.'

I kept my arms tightly folded as they all looked at me.

'Say "hello", Jo.'

Hoping Dad wouldn't make me shake hands, I smiled and nodded, trying as best as I could to look at their faces. I tried not to notice their wrinkled bodies and how their skin sagged in folds, like the bags of boules they were holding. A man standing next to me unzipped his bag and handed me a shiny silver ball.

'Here, you can use one of mine.'

I knew he was trying to be kind, but I didn't want to join in – and not just with the boules game but with anything in this weird place. Wishing, somehow, that I could hide behind the heavy boule, I held back my tears while Dad chatted intently with the men.

'Come on then, dearie.' One of the men touched me lightly but I drew back from the heat from his hand on my shoulder.

'She's just thinking about how to beat you,' said another.

While my Dad was distracted, one of the men ruffled up my hair, 'Quite happy to be beaten by a pretty young lass like her.' And they all sniggered.

A man with popping, bloodshot eyes put his face close to mine. 'You got a boyfriend yet?'

I shook my head and looked down but it was too late. As he came closer, I couldn't help noticing that he had wiry grey pubic hair with bald patches.

'She's blushing now,' and he rubbed my arm.

I pulled back; I didn't want this naked man, whose private parts I'd just seen close up, touching me when I, too, was naked.

Dad turned from his conversation and came back to join me.

'Come on now, Jo, show them what you can do . . .'

I wanted to show them that I could turn around and run down the path, and the naked, doddering old men would never be able to catch me. But Dad looked down at me and drew a deep breath so, instead, I rolled the boule towards the little wooden jack.

'She's good, you sure this is her first time?'

I stood, arms folded, pretending I was cold. How could I ever tell my friend Sue that I'd been to this place? What would she think?

'Just beginner's luck, I'm sure,' Dad was telling them.

I waited patiently while Dad finished the game, watching a bluebottle settle, again and again, on his skin. The game over, the men started arranging another match for the following day and, as usual, Dad just couldn't help taking control. I watched him organising the men's teams and then, like the persistent bluebottle, the realisation settled on me: it was my dad who'd wanted this awful holiday. He'd decided to bring us here. He decided everything.

I often looked around at the other children at the camp, who played games and joined in with the adults and wondered if their dads made them come, or if they liked it here and somehow I was the weird one.

Chapter 5

Dad had an important job in a warehouse – that's how I remembered it, later. It meant he got to wear a brown coat and order people about. He walked upright and proud in that coat, like a soldier in uniform, which made his decision to take a holiday at a nudist camp still harder to understand. Sometimes, he'd take me around the warehouse and I'd wear a hard hat, and a coat just like his but with the cuffs turned up. The warehouse was so noisy that you couldn't hear yourself talk. Perhaps that's where my dad learned how to shout, yelling orders at the men in overalls. I was there when one of the machines had broken down and there was an urgent order waiting to be packed: 'Get down there and have a look at it,' Dad barked. Later, when I was helping out in the office, one of the men shook his head.

'That dad of yours, he's a right so and so . . .'

And I knew just what he meant. You should try living with him, I thought. What would they think if they knew what he got up to on holiday? They probably wouldn't take him half so seriously. But as I looked round the dusty warehouse, I wondered, perhaps, if Dad chose to get away from it all in a nudist camp in order to feel fresh air on his skin after spending so much time surrounded by noise and machines. Whatever the reason, I hoped that feeling the air on his bare skin once would be enough.

The house changed when Dad came home from work, it came to life. He seemed to entirely take over the small hallway when he came through the door. It was not just that he was tall, and had a voice that could make the walls vibrate – it was his sheer energy. He would swing me up, almost banging my head on the ceiling. Sometimes he would let me ride high on his shoulders and I'd see the world as if I were as tall as him. He'd talk about work, and about the machines.

There were times he'd come home with rolls of old paper from the control room and make up stories about weird monsters, bringing them to life with drawings so realistic you could imagine they'd crawl across the page. He'd put music on, and I'd step on his metal toe protector shoes while we danced around the room. He'd make giant balloons and draw on them pictures of the neighbours he didn't like, then float them up into the dark sky where we'd watch them until they got mixed up with the stars. At times such as these he was the most exciting father I could have wished for. But it wasn't always like that when he came home . . .

Mum was always flustered at teatime. During the week, she had to feed me before Dad came in from work because, then, everything had to be just so. One time, I was sitting at the kitchen table eating my tea and watching Mum peel potatoes. She slid a knife under the skin.

'Your father has a lot on his plate, Lord help him.'

Mum liked to have a sherry when she made the evening meal. She always called it her 'cooking sherry', but I never saw her cook with it. She made me a potato man – with two eyes, a nose and a smiley mouth – and balanced him on the window ledge. I watched her peel the rest of the potatoes, working her tongue well down in between her bottom teeth as she stripped them of their muddy coats. I hoped she wouldn't peel the skin off my potato man – he was so happy in his skin, sitting on the windowsill.

I always had a different tea from Dad. My favourite was boiled egg with soldiers.

'Why can't I have boiled eggs all the time?'

'Too many eggs bind you up.'

'What does that mean?'

'Stop asking questions,' Mum said and she took another sip from her glass of sherry.

Mum drew a face on my egg and I stood on a chair and watched it sink into the bubbling water. She handed me the timer and I turned it upside down, watching the tiny stream of sand piling up into a perfect pyramid. I liked my special jobs in the kitchen.

Mum handed me a knife, 'Careful now,' and I cut crosses on the bottom of the sprouts then watched her lower the metal cages into the steamer and waiting for the steam to hiss from the pressure cooker.

'Hurry up now, Jo, and get that egg finished before your dad gets home.'

I perched the egg in the eggcup and started to sing *Humpty Dumpty*. Then I looked at his egg face and cracked his head. I felt a burst of cold air from the front door.

'I'm ho-ome.'

Dad always announced himself like this, though we knew perfectly well that the only person to come in at a quarter past five, with a key, was my dad.

Mum struggled to discard her pinny, caught the curls at the bottom of her hair and bounced them quickly back into place, then switched the pressure cooker to high to hurry up his meal.

'Mary-mother-of-God, there's your father home and his tea not ready.'

Mum drained her glass, washed it, popped a mint in her mouth and started muttering for God to give her strength. I dipped my bread soldier into the yolk of my boiled egg so it burst and spilled out, then mopped up the mess with my bread and ran my finger round the plate. Mum used her soft voice.

'Jo, you're all messy. You know your father won't like that. Go on now and take your plate and sit on the stairs while you finish.'

I watched the steam begin to rise from the pressure cooker. It was easier to see now, pushing out from the tiny hole in the centre of the lid. I lifted my plate as carefully as I could but the egg in its cup was wobbling and sliding. And there was my dad, filling up the doorway.

'Can a man not come home to some peace? Look at the state of you. What a mess.'

'Sorry Dad.'

'Why can't you eat nicely?'

He averted his eyes from the mess on my plate. I knew better than to upset him, particularly when he'd just got in from work. Sometimes, like today, you could tell by his face that it'd been a bad day. His face was covered in lines like someone had tried to cross him out. I did my best to skirt past him to the stairs, concentrating, my tongue pressed to my top lip, on keeping my egg balanced. Then I saw it go. I reached to catch it but too late, the egg was in pieces, the yolk all over the carpet.

The rhyme was going through my head: 'All the King's horses, And all the King's men, Couldn't put Humpty together again.' And the pressure cooker was going off, squealing high as Dad took off his glasses and started shouting. And Humpty's broken face lay close to mine as I crouched on the floor. I closed my eyes and wished hard that I could be the little girl Dad wanted me to be. That little girl would never have sticky fingers so she'd be allowed to eat with him at the big dining table all the time. She'd never spill her food. She'd be tidy and neat, with clean fingernails, and never speak unless she was spoken to.

Dad sent me straight to my room. Mum came up a little while later to see if I was OK, as she often did when Dad shouted at me or punished me for being clumsy. We sat in silence then Mum spoke.

'Jo, you must try harder to do as your father says, to make him happy. Try and keep quiet and don't question him. Just try for me. I beg you.'

'I hate the way he bosses me round all the time, makes me do things I don't want to do, like going to that horrible camp place . . .'

'I'm not going to talk about it.'

'Why?'

Mum stayed quiet. I held her hand tight.

'Promise me, we'll never go back there?'

She looked away.

'Promise? Cross your heart and hope to die.'

No matter how I begged, she wouldn't promise.

'Stay up here for a while, I'll let you know when you can come down,' she whispered.

Dad's voice rang out. 'Jo, you can stay up there until you've learned your lesson. Elizabeth, the kitchen's full of steam, you need to come down here and serve up dinner.'

I sat in my room thinking, sadly, how I'd secretly hoped that Mum would be on my side, especially as she could see how upset the camp had made me.

Dad was a man of extremes; for him there were no half measures. Despite his temper, for example, he also had a gentle side. He would leave out saucers of sugar for wasps who'd been chased out of the nest at the end of the year and I'd watch their feeble antennae waving as they sipped the sweet liquid. He seemed to quite like animals – even my guinea pig. On the other hand, I once thought he might be going to kill our neighbour's dog on account of my guinea pig.

Mrs Gilmore had a dog called Jackson. 'He's a standard poodle,' she told me, although I wasn't sure why Jackson was called 'standard' when he was as big as a Great Dane. He liked to come over and play in our garden. It was a little secret I shared with Mum because we knew Dad would never allow it.

'Let's give him some scraps,' Mum said, tipping some leftovers onto an old plate.

'Mrs Gilmore only ever gives him vegetables – the Gilmores are vegetarians, you know. She says you should never eat anything with a face, and that goes for poor Jackson too.'

After Mum told me that, I was always a bit funny about meat. I'd look at a lamb chop on my plate, wondering which part of the body it fitted into.

One day, when Dad came home from work I was playing in our back garden, throwing sticks for Jackson.

'What's that thing doing here?' Dad shouted, and then he saw that Jackson had messed on our lawn.

'What's that?'

I didn't want to say the word because I knew I'd get into even more trouble. Dad picked up a shovel that was leaning on the wall and turned on Jackson. I closed my eyes and held my breath. Jackson whimpered. Dad took the shovel and scooped up the mess then pulled me down the road with the dog barking behind us and knocked on Mrs Gilmore's door.

'Excuse me, I think this belongs to you.' And he threw the dog shit down on her path. Jackson didn't come round to our house much after that.

Not long afterwards, when I came home from school, Mum stopped me on the drive.

'Don't go in the garden, Jo, please.'

'Why?'

'Jackson's been.'

'Oh . . . He hasn't made another mess has he?'

'It's your guinea pig...'

I ran out to the back garden where Dad had made a temporary run with four planks of wood for my guinea pig. I could hear terrible squealing as I turned the corner and there he was, writhing with a gaping red bite in his back. I stood there, numb, knowing that I had to find a way to put him out of his misery, but I couldn't move.

Then, with a twitch, he was still.

'Thanks be to God,' Mum murmured.

The next day, by way of compensation Mrs Gilmore came round with a colouring book. When Dad came home from work I heard him shouting at Mum in the kitchen, then he grabbed my hand again and marched me down the street.

'She can stick her bloody colouring book!' And he stuffed it right back through Mrs Gilmore's door.

Chapter 6

When the brown woman at the camp had shown us around, she'd pointed out a little log cabin called a sauna where she said we could escape and relax. I'd never seen a sauna before, and immediately thought it would be a good place to hide. So whenever I had the chance, I took the path down the hillside to where the sauna stood. Inside, it smelled of warm wood and had slatted benches where you could stretch out. In the corner were some hot coals and the lady had shown us how to put on water from a bucket. I closed the door and sat down. The sauna was rarely used by anyone else at the camp and there, inside, enveloped in the smell of warm wood, I felt safe and hidden.

In my steamy refuge, I thought about the old men outside playing boules – their smiling faces, their all-over suntans and their wrinkly bodies. I thought about how I hated my parents and how I didn't understand what was going on: why we were here, pretending it was normal to go about daily life with no clothes on? I couldn't wait to get home, back to wearing clothes, back to my friends.

But then, when I thought about Sue, I knew she'd just think it was weird; why wouldn't she when I didn't even understand what I was doing here?

I ladled water onto the hot coals and watched it bubble, filling the room with intense heat. Then I lay down, wrapped in my towel, feeling the heat bake through me while the sweat dripped out of my body. I stayed in there for hours, imagining that everything bad I felt about this place would ooze out from me like sweat.

I stayed in that little room until it had all completely filled up with steam. Now, no one could see me and, even if I tried, I couldn't see out.

When I got back to our tent, Dad was waiting for me.

'Where the hell've you been?'

'Oh, I just went down to the sauna. It was lovely in there, my skin's all nice and smooth.'

He gave me a half smile. 'You could have said . . .'

'I didn't want to interrupt you.'

It was my way of getting him off my back but as far as he was concerned, he was pleased that I was settling in.

Every day, I made my way down to the sauna. It was a way of hanging on to my towel.

'What are you doing with that?' Dad asked as I reached for a towel.

'Oh, just going off to the sauna – I love it there.'

'Wait till your breakfast's settled,' he ordered.

'She's all right.' Mum nodded at me.

'I said she had to wait. Five minutes to digest her food, that's all. What's the hurry?'

I sat and concentrated on counting away the minutes. If I counted up to sixty, five times over, then I didn't have to talk to him, and I didn't have to think about why I was sitting here on a little camping stool with no clothes on. I stood up to go, clasping my hands in front of me as I did so, then, casually, coiled the towel around me.

'I'm off for that sauna. See you later.'

He couldn't object to me taking a towel for that.

'Don't be long, being in there on your own is no good for you – you should be mixing with the other kids.'

I walked past a woman lying on the grass and saw a fly settle on her pubic hair, then past a row of sunbathers, stretched out so they could get brown all over – though I tried not to notice them. I made my way down the path, where I saw the brown woman playing volleyball with a group of men and women; their body parts took on a life of their own as the players jumped for the ball. The brown woman held the ball up high with both hands to steady herself, getting ready to serve. Stretched up, her oiled skin shining in the sun, she looked like one of those naked lady lamps I'd seen in antique shops – Mum had told me they were Art Deco. I couldn't get over how proud she seemed of her body, and I knew for certain that I'd never feel like that about mine.

Hurrying on, I passed a group of boys with wiry bodies and red-raw shoulders. I tried not to look at them down below, I didn't want to see. They weren't much older than me but when they called out to me I pretended not to hear. I didn't want to talk to a group of boys, or even be near a group of boys, in a place like this. 'Need some company?' they asked, then burst out laughing.

I kept walking, keeping my legs straight so it didn't look like I was going too fast. I thought they must have been making fun of me because I was hanging on to my towel as tight as I could. I looked back to check they weren't following, but they were. At each turn of the path, they came after me, calling, 'Aw, come on, don't be shy . . .'

I ran and, increasing my pace, sped down to the sauna cabin. I waited for a moment by the door, my breath coming in short gasps. The boys were nowhere to be seen, so I closed the door, put water on the coals and waited for the heat to have its desired effect. Slowly, I tried to relax. They were just a gang of boys. It was nothing to worry about. I shut my eyes and tried to dispel the images of the people I'd passed along the way, but I couldn't. The only way I could avoid being seen naked was to hide in this stifling heat. So, although I felt safe here, I also saw it as a kind of punishment, a torture almost, but one I could just about manage given the alternative.

I stretched out on the wooden bench. Through the steam, I caught a flash of something at the small, square window in the door. I watched carefully. There it was again. It was one of the boys I'd passed on the path. I moved quickly, pulling down the wooden bolt that secured the door from the inside. Then another face appeared at the window. The boys started knock, knock knocking on the door, pulling at the handle.

'Little piggy, little piggy, let me come in.'

I sat there trembling.

'Then I'll huff and I'll puff and I'll blow your house in.'

I hoped that, eventually, they would get bored and go away. I tried to stay calm but the more they shouted, the more I panicked.

'Open the door!'

Trapped, I huddled in the corner hugging my knees. The boys wouldn't go away. The cabin was getting hotter and hotter, filling with steam – I could hardly breathe. The air burned as it went up my nose. My eyes were stinging. Laughing and bashing on the window, the boys called and called, knocking on the door, screeching and circling the cabin like wolves.

In the end, I opened the door: I was close to tears, my face was burning and I could hardly breathe. I held my towel around me. The boys looked me up and down. 'We knew you'd come out in the end.' I turned away, not wanting to see their naked bodies close up.

'What's your name?'

I looked down at the gravel on the path.

'Why've you got your towel on?'

'None of your business.'

'Take it off.'

'No.'

'Why not?'

'I . . .'

'What've you got to hide?'

'Nothing.'

'You got tits yet?'

'No.'

'Come on, let's get her!'

Horrified, I turned and started to run. The boys came after me, half-heartedly chasing me up the hill, laughing and shouting, clearly not really trying to actually out-run me. 'Come on, let's have a look!' 'Get her! Get her!' I ran up the steep hill as they screamed after me, faster and faster. My legs were burning and I was crying, the sobs coming hard and fast. I ran towards our tent hoping, for once, that I might bump into my parents. Thankfully, I came upon a group of men playing boules and the shouting stopped, the boys scattered and were gone.

Looking back, I realise now that these boys were only playing; that they were only boys being boys. But at the time, horrified by my surroundings, everything felt dangerous. I felt hunted.

As an introduction to naturism, the holiday wasn't all bad. The sun shone and the gardens were beautiful. I kept my blue cotton shorts or my towel on whenever I could, and sometimes I'd escape to the far side of the campsite where I'd discovered a gazebo where nobody went. The gazebo was my thinking place. I was calm on the surface but angry that I had to suffer this place. I cried and ranted and questioned until I didn't really know how I felt.

At the gazebo, sometimes, I'd turn around to make sure no one was there, then I'd slowly and carefully take off my shorts and knickers. I'd lie with the sun beating down upon my bare, young body and try hard to be the uninhibited little girl my father wanted me to be. I'd try and feel comfortable without any clothes on, thinking that, if I did it for long enough, then maybe I'd get there. I might even get to like it.

If I'd had a choice, I would have stayed there, in my secret hideaway. I would have stayed there for ever and never come out.

Chapter 7

I kept the trip a total secret. It wasn't like our other holidays when Mum and I had searched the shoreline for special pebbles for her fossil collection.

'How can you tell which ones have got something inside?' I'd ask. And she'd pick up a smooth, round pebble that to me just looked like any other and weigh it in her hand. 'I can just tell,' she'd say.

I'd collect stone after stone and take them to her but she'd shake her head. Then, at the end of the day she'd set them on a flat rock and take a hammer and chisel to them. Crack! And there inside would be the perfect mould of a prehistoric creature. 'It's called an ammonite,' Mum would tell me, and I'd coil my finger around the ridged surface of its shell.

I thought of those stones when I tried to keep my secret – when I almost buckled and gave in to my wish to tell Sue all about it. But I decided to be brave and keep hold of my secret. I think I knew that, ultimately, my feelings didn't matter, that my dad's wishes would always come first. It's almost as if something switched off in me.

Once we returned home I tried to forget about the nudist camp. Despite that fact that my head was swimming in confusion, and I felt like my world and everything I knew and believed in had shifted on me, I shut it out of my mind and did my best to get back to the life I felt comfortable with, running and skipping with Sue. We would have spent every minute of the day together if we'd been allowed.

We'd play hopscotch as we ran between each other's houses. 'Jump on a crack, break your back,' we'd shout. I stepped on one as we ran and Sue caught my hand. 'Careful, Jo, that's bad luck . . .' And she was right.

As soon as I'd get home, Sue would ring me. 'Is that Sue on the phone again?' Dad would shout. 'Don't know why she phones as soon as you get home – she's been with you all day. What on earth d'you find to talk about?' Everything, I'd think to myself, other than the nudist camp.

I was always worried the truth might slip out, though I didn't tell a single person where I'd been on holiday. It was one of those secrets kept in a box, inside another box on a very high shelf. So, for release, I wrote about the visit in my diary, next to the bit that said I was a Catholic but having a secret from Sue felt really wrong.

I behaved differently at home from the way I did when I was at school and with Sue. At home I was always tip-toeing around, holding my breath, but at school I let that breath out, running wild at break times. Sue and I were always up to something – selling my mum's sweeteners to the boys at the school next door as 'love pills', joining in with all the new crazes. We swirled around and around that playground, laughing until our stomachs ached.

We had agreed to share everything with each other. Sue told me how bad she felt when she'd forgotten to take Fred, her tortoise, out of his winter hibernation box until she found his stiff, dried up body in the summer. Her mum had gone mad at her, and Sue had called her mum a 'fucking cow' in her sleep. Her mum had kept her in for a week after that.

I told Sue I was a Catholic, but she didn't mind – she said it was all one God at the end of the day, no matter which church you went to. I wanted so much to tell her that my parents had taken me to a nudist camp but I thought that if I did, she wouldn't want to be my friend anymore. I knew the nudist camp was something she'd never understand – she would think it was dirty and that I was weird, like a pervert – I mean, who stands naked in a field in front of their parents and a load of total strangers?

Apart from Sue, all the girls in my class hated Catholics. Ours was a Church of England school and had they found out I was a Roman Catholic, it would have led to a beating-up in the playground, at the very least. It'd been close when they'd found out I had only one god-mother and one godfather, which was different from the Protestant tradition where girls tended to have two godmothers and one godfather. I'd got away with it by saying I just got mixed up. But nothing would be as bad as if they'd found out that I'd been to a nudist camp.

At the start of the new term, Sue and I took places next to each other and sat whispering about whether or not Miss Masters was wearing a wig. The teacher always wore her hair in such tight curls that it looked like a judge's wig and, just like a judge, she was always trying to create order.

Miss Masters told us we'd be doing a project. 'Now, girls, the subject of your project, which you'll be working on over the next few weeks, will be "My Summer Holiday".'

I almost stopped breathing altogether. Images of laughing, naked people flashed through my mind.

'. . . You can paste in pictures from your summer holiday, or any break you've had this year. A weekend away, a half-term, that sort of thing . . .'

I remembered the wrinkled men playing boules.

'. . . maybe a map of where it was . . .'

I didn't want anyone to find out.

'. . . and the special things you did . . .'

And there I was, back in the sauna, hiding in the steam.

'. . . the people you met . . .'

The naked boys who chased me up the hill.

'. . . and whether or not you felt it was a good holiday destination . . .'

Never.

Miss Masters handed out small notebooks. 'Remember, girls, this is just to write down your first thoughts, we'll be copying it all out in your best handwriting later.'

I looked at the blank pages, wondering what I was going to write.

'The first section is to be entitled: "Where I Went on Holiday." Big writing now, just write down everything you can remember.'

I didn't want to remember anything about that holiday. As I looked around the class, everyone seemed to be scribbling away.

'Come on now, Jo, dreaming again?'

I wrote down, 'Sussex', spending ages over the large, neat letters. I was back there, remembering the horror of my mum ripping off my clothes, the brown woman, the old men and the boys. Then there was the naked image of my dad that I didn't want to think about at all. Slowly, I began to write: I wrote and wrote until my hand ached, writing about anything – anything other than the things that had really made an impression on me. It was a big lie.

Every day we worked on our holiday books. It was everyone else's favourite part of the day and they always talked about it at playtime. Sue couldn't understand why I wasn't joining in. I stood, alone, leaning against a wall in the playground, trying to make up a game for just me. Then, back in the classroom everyone would be sticking in photographs of themselves smiling with their families.

I had pulled out some old photographs of holidays from the family album and was terrified in case my dad saw the blank spaces left with corners of glue. I looked quite different in those pictures but I hoped no one at school would notice. I wished I'd been on holiday to the Isle of Man, like Sue.

'Oh, I forgot to give you this,' she said, handing me a twisted brown paper bag. 'Pressie from my hols.' Inside was a key ring.

'Thanks. What're the three legs on it for?'

'It's their symbol, see, same as like they have Manx cats there with no tails.'

'Sounds a strange place, the Isle of Man. Men with three legs and cats with no tails.'

I wanted to tell Sue that I'd been to a strange place. I wanted to tell her that I'd made up most of the things in my holiday book.

She smiled. 'Did you like where you were?'

'Oh, you know . . .' But she could never know, nobody could.

'What did you do then?'

I couldn't tell her the truth so, instead, I made things up, based on other holidays I'd been on.

'There was a maze . . . and an arcade . . . and . . .'

'Sounds dead good.'

Sometimes, walking to school with Sue, I'd look at someone passing by and instantly visualise them naked. It was worse at school – I didn't want to be chatting with my friends and suddenly see them in the flesh. And worst of all was the occasional time I had a flash of Miss Masters with her big stomach and breasts that hung right over it. People would never look the same to me again. It was as if I'd been given a gift of special sight – but I didn't want it.

After that week's holiday I'd come home suntanned all over. Now, my tan was a permanent reminder every morning I got dressed and every night I had a bath, of my holiday and of the shame.

Chapter 8

Dad had big ideas. As well as his job in the warehouse, he sometimes helped local children with extra tuiton. It was as if he was trying to get on twice as fast as anyone else and it made him twice as tired and bad-tempered, but he was desperate to move up from our semi-detached house and the crescent to something bigger and better.

Following Dad's lead, I worked hard at school, hoping he'd be proud of me if I did well. But, despite all the plays I performed in or prizes I won, he never came to witness any of my big moments. In fact, it seemed to me that all he ever had to say drew attention to my failures.

To improve my mind, he gave me complex arith-metical problems to solve and I'd sit on the stairs trying to work them out. I hadn't inherited his gift for figures, but found a way with a sharp pencil to draw a line down the division signs to make them look like additions; that way I got them all right. I felt for those who came to our house for extra tuition as he was short-tempered with them, too when they got things wrong. They still came though, and they came to thank him when he got them through their exams.

To help out with the housekeeping, Mum took a trial job as an Avon Lady, knocking on doors selling bits and pieces like make-up and jewellery. Dad wasn't too pleased but I thought it would be good for her to get out of the house a bit more. The job didn't last long, but it was fun for me whilst she did do it, especially when Mum got samples in advance and let me try on all the perfumes and creams and she'd paint my nails.

'There now, that's the way, three strokes only down the nail, that's how the manicurists do it.' And I'd blow on my nails.

After a while, it felt as though things were getting back to normal again, and everything that had happened at the camp seemed to fade away.

One morning, I was getting ready for school, cleaning my shoes on a piece of newspaper by the kitchen sink. There were two brushes with words on top, 'I put on polish', and 'I shine your shoes'. I opened the tin of Cherry Blossom wondering if Ox Blood was made from real animals. Mum had told me that pink icing was made with cockroaches and I'd never eaten a pink iced bun since.

I picked up the first brush and made fresh pricking marks on the perfect crust atop the polish, then dabbed it on my shoes. I liked cleaning my shoes, Mum had bought me a pair with my first little heel; it was only tiny but the important thing was that it sloped inward, like grown up shoes.

I remembered to put polish underneath on the instep and on the inside of the heel because Dad always checked that I'd done it properly. I tried not to drop any but some of the chunks fell and bounced off the newspaper onto the floor. I reached for the clean brush and tried to pick them up with it, but it only pushed the polish deeper into the lino. I tried to pick up the bits with my fingers but I couldn't manage. They squished like finger paint leaving giant red smudges on the kitchen floor. When I rubbed, it only made it worse.

The polish was all over my fingers, deep red under my nails. Without thinking, I ran my hands down my sides, remembering – too late – that this was my school dress, my clean school dress. I thrust my hands under the tap but the polish stayed, waterproofing my fingers. So I turned to the floor and took the polishing cloth to it, leaving clouds of Ox Blood all over the grey floor.

'Mum, Mum, I've had a bit of an accident. Mum?' But Dad was there first, catching me rubbing at the floor. I slid the newspaper to cover up the worst, but he'd seen.

'What're you trying to hide? What have you done?'

'I . . . I was trying to . . .'

And then Mum was there with her hands to her lips. 'She didn't mean to . . .'

As punishment, Dad made me get on my hands and knees to clean the floor. Mum watched as I scrubbed away at the Ox Blood polish.

'I'll do it, it's nothing, nothing at all,' she said.

I put my tongue firmly behind my front teeth and pressed hard so that the tears didn't come. But try as I might, I couldn't get it clean. It was red everywhere, like blood. Dad stood over me with his hands crossed over his chest as he watched me work away, and I tried so hard but I knew the floor would never be clean, that I'd ruined it for ever.

Often, when I came home from school Mum would be asleep. She called it her 'forty winks', I didn't know why. When I was little, she insisted that I have forty winks with her. She lay in the middle of the big double bed with me squashed up against her side. I used to close one eye and open it, staring at the sharp, cut-out figures on the curtains, trying to wink and count up to forty at the same time.

One day, I came home and let myself in through the back door. Mum was asleep so I went upstairs and sat at her dressing table, waiting for her to wake up, opening the drawers, searching through the cosmetics and the jewellery. The drawers smelled of soap and perfume. As I tucked one of her compacts in the corner behind the silky nylons, my fingers touched something hard and soft at the same time. I pulled out a black velvet box and carefully opened it, though the hinge was stiff. Inside was lined all in white, soft velvet and there were three small pills. I knew they weren't sweets. They were chalky and sort of triangular, not like sweets at all, so I knew they were dangerous and not to put them in my mouth. I closed the box gently, wondering why Mum was hiding them.

That weekend, I was playing in the garden when Dad called me into the kitchen and announced that we were moving.

'We're going up in the world.' Mum pushed up her hair at the back. 'A detached house on an estate. I'm having a through-lounge and a fitted kitchen.'

Sue and I cycled over to where the new estate was being built and played in the piles of bricks. When the builders had gone home, we climbed up the skeletons of the unfinished houses and balanced on roof rafters. Up high on those roofs nothing could touch us. We dared each other to jump onto the piles of sand below and afterwards, screaming, rode our bikes down neat roads trimmed with privet. I was so excited about moving there. Everything was going to be good.

'Will you still want to be my friend?' Sue asked. 'Even when you move here?'

'Don't be stupid . . . It's even nearer to your house.'

We moved from a crescent to a close. That made us posh. I thought with the move, that it would be a new beginning for my mum and dad. All that stuff at the nudist camp was behind us. Sometimes Dad would look at me and remark how well I'd looked after our trip but, apart from that, he and Mum never spoke to me about what had happened. I thought it was all over and done with.

Chapter 10

The new house smelled of fresh paint and Mum kept the windows open all the time. Once we were all settled in and had finally unpacked all the boxes, it felt really homely and life seemed to settle down a bit. Dad whistled a lot in his out-of-tune way, Mum seemed to be smiling more, singing in the kitchen – she sang opera songs that she fitted my name to: 'My Jo, – oh my Jo, – oh my Jo – darling girl . . .' I didn't see as many of those half-full glasses around the place that mum would take sly sips from when she thought I wasn't looking.

And then one Sunday, Dad said we were going for a drive. I hated those 'family' trips we'd started taking to the countryside, usually to Wales where we'd scramble up a mountain to eat squashed sandwiches on the top and drink warm water from yellowed, plastic bottles.

Although it was autumn, it was a sunny day. Dad was in a temper and was outside, packing the car, slamming doors.

'Get a move on, you two!'

I knew to stay away.

'Anything else to go in the car? For Christ's sake, where the hell are you?'

Mum hated it when Dad took the Lord's name in vain, she'd flinch and raise her eyes to heaven. She was busy in the kitchen, slapping meat paste into sandwiches. There was something different about her today, she had her eyes almost closed and was swaying as she made the sandwiches.

'Mum, are you all right?' I asked nervously.

'Fine, I'm just fine, Jo.'

She dug the knife firmly into the pot of sandwich paste and it went everywhere as she pulled it out.

'Silly me' she giggled – and she staggered around trying to hold on to the work surface. She stared slamming cupboard doors.

I knew something had happened between them. They would always take it out on inanimate objects when they'd had a row. Mum was still slamming around. I went to stand by her side.

'What's the matter?'

'Nothing.'

'But you look weird.'

Mum glanced at me and picked up a small bottle of pills, shutting them away again very quickly.

'Mum, aren't you feeling well?'

She looked at me, but her eyes couldn't quite focus.

'Perfectly well, Jo.'

'What are the pills for then?'

'Err. Nothing, nothing at all.' Mum started to cry again.

'What is it?'

'Just make yourself useful and give me a hand with this lot.'

She banged the knife down on the table and I went to stand by her side.

'Do we have to go?'

'Don't start me off now'

'I want to see Sue, I promised I'd go over.'

'Well you can't, not today.'

'Where are we going then, can Sue come?

'Just stop asking questions.'

'What shall I put on?'

She just looked at me and shook her head.

'Fetch me some cutlery, Jo, won't you?'

I opened the drawer and saw the doll next to a bottle of pills. Mum kept a voodoo doll of my dad in the kitchen drawer. There was no attempt at keeping it a secret – he knew all about it. Sometimes, after one of their rows, I'd come across it with a pin in its head. Dad would be nursing a migraine. 'You been sticking pins in me again?' he'd say. Mum would just smile.

I think he was terrified of that doll. Certainly he never attempted to remove it from the drawer, or even to take the pins out. Perhaps he thought if he threw it in the bin then he'd never know what would happen to it. This time I noticed it had two fresh pins in its head.

'Mum, what's Dad done this time?'

She slammed the kitchen drawer shut, narrowly missing my fingers.

'What is it, Mum?'

She turned to me and stroked my hair. 'My little Jo . . .'

'What?'

'Come on, we've got to go.'

Mum closed the Tupperware container and put it in a bag along with the rest of the things. Turning to me, she said 'Come on. Let's get a move on for your Father', and hurried out of the kitchen. I waited for a moment and then heard the front door close. Slowly, I opened the kitchen drawer again and took out the pill bottle, trying to read the long name on the front. What was wrong with her? What wasn't she telling me? Was that why she was spending more and more time in bed? I unscrewed the top of the bottle and shook one of the pills into my hand. It was made up of two halves. Carefully, I pulled it apart and white powder fell onto the kitchen side. Then I heard Mum at the front door, calling me, so I blew the powder away and put the pill case into the bin.

I sat in the back of the car. It was unusually quiet. Dad

had his head skewed to one side with a headache. I felt my stomach clench.

'Dad, where're we going?'

'Just for a day out.'

'But where?'

Mum looked at Dad. I knew something was up and it didn't take me long to guess what it was, given where we'd been last time we set off on a journey all together. Surely we weren't going back to that place? It was miles away. Surely you only went there on holiday, not for the day? But I knew we weren't climbing up mountains because Dad hadn't put the boots or anoraks in the car – in fact, there was very little in the car.

'Jo,' he shouted, 'can't you see that I'm trying to drive?'

'But you can drive and talk at the same time. When will we get there?'

'Hush now, it's just around the corner.'

It was always just around the corner.

'You always say that.'

Dad banged his hands on the steering wheel. 'That's enough of that, young lady.'

'But . . .'

'And there's no buts about it.'

'I was only asking.'

'Well don't.'

I watched my dad's face in half profile and saw him

tighten his jaw, ever so slightly, so that a dent appeared in his cheek. I knew he was hiding something. I felt a sudden flip to my heart that it might be a big surprise. Maybe we were going somewhere really special, but then it was nowhere near my birthday; or maybe to the fairground, or shopping – but of course it couldn't be that because it was Sunday and the shops weren't open. I knew it was something that Sue couldn't come to, so it had to be something special, it just had to. But then why had he been so nasty when I'd asked him? That had spoiled whatever surprise it was going to be. Why was Mum being so secretive, and why had she been crying?

Mum settled into sleep in the front, and after a long drive, we pulled up in front of a five-barred gate and Dad got out. I noticed he was fiddling with something on the side of the gate – it looked like a padlock. Once through the gate, he got out of the car again and locked the gate behind him.

'Where are we, Mum?'

Mum stirred in the front seat and sat up, keeping her head facing straight ahead, silent and rigid. 'Mum?' Why wouldn't she look at me? My stomach churned. We drove slowly along a bumpy dirt-track then into a small car park from where I could see a path leading into a mass of caravans and tents. And the funny feeling in my stomach got worse.

A man wearing Wellingtons was pushing a wheel-barrow into the car park. The wheelbarrow was stacked with hedge clippings and I could see that it was hot work because he had no shirt on. He put the wheelbarrow down, and I put my hand to my mouth. We were in a nudist camp.

There was something about the naked man in Wellingtons that made me want to laugh. He had a huge pair of shears resting on top of the wheelbarrow and I couldn't help thinking about how he must have felt, clipping away with those shears in close proximity to his manhood. He didn't seem at all bothered that his penis was swinging around as he walked over to welcome us with an outstretched hand. 'Hello. Welcome to Edendale, I'm Sid, the chairman.'

He led us down a path to a pavilion, the clubhouse, and showed us where to sign in and here I was, again, keeping my eyes down on the path while we were passing people with bare legs that led to bodies I just didn't want to see.

'First names only – we don't use surnames here. We, you know, keep private, no addresses . . . No questions.'

But I had lots of questions, like: What were we doing here? Why did people want to take their clothes off in secret? But most of all, what I really wanted to know was why I couldn't go home.

This time, I knew the drill. There were no tantrums or grappling on the floor. In the ladies' changing room there was an empty silence as my mother and I undressed. I kept my eyes down as I asked her if I could have a towel. She handed me one without a word and I wound it tightly around myself. I looked at her and felt the familiar sting in the back of my nose. We were back in one of these disgusting places. I'd thought that the holiday camp was a one-off; I didn't realise they had these places elsewhere, too.

Mum put her hand on my shoulder. 'Jo. It's your father's wish.'

I shrugged away from her. How could she let him do this to us? It was the same old question that I already knew the answer to: because she was his wife.

When I grew up I was never going to be a wife, because being a wife meant washing and ironing, shopping and cooking, sweeping and hoovering. I couldn't see the attraction of it, couldn't understand why you waited so long for your dream man to come along and then found yourself in a nightmare. Worst of all, being a wife meant doing what you were told, even if that meant being naked among complete strangers.

The changing rooms were in the front of the clubhouse. When we'd entered there was no one there but now, as we walked through, a few people were dotted around. As ever, I tried not to look at the sagging bodies on sagging armchairs but I couldn't help thinking about those bare bottoms on the chairs – like sitting on a toilet seat that never gets wiped.

Mum winced at me. 'Try to understand?'

But I knew I never would.

'I don't want to do it . . . Not again.'

She put her hand on my shoulder. I didn't like her touching my bare skin, not like this, then she bent down. Close up, her breath smelt sickly sweet.

'Mum . . . ? Mummy?'

Tears had collected in the bottom of her lids. 'Come on now.' She pushed me gently forward as she muttered a prayer under her breath. The layout of Edendale was similar to the first nudist camp, with a clubhouse – in this case a ramshackle building that looked like something put together by a group of over-enthusiastic DIY addicts. A series of pathways linked the main recreation areas. There were two tennis courts, a toilet block, a sun terrace and a swimming pool, some makeshift chalets and a playground. At the front and back the camping area was flanked by rows of caravans and in the nearby wood new plants were being raised for extra hedging.

I'd seen nudists before – but, still, I could not understand how they could seem so relaxed. I tried hard to be like them, to appear confident. If all these people could do it, then so could I, even if I didn't want to. I was stuck here, so I'd try and make the most of it. But it was harder here in this field in the middle of nowhere, and in the autumn chill.

Everywhere we went people were friendly, too friendly. It was the kind of friendliness that made everything seem so much worse. Nudists didn't have a special handshake and there was nothing to show they were any different from anyone else, apart from their all-over suntans. They seemed so proud it made me feel sick.

That Sunday at the camp was the day we met Terry. I wore my hair loose so that it hung around my shoulders and it reached almost to my waist as I walked slowly along a winding, muddy path. I kept my eyes on the ground ahead of me, and clasped my hands in front of my lower body like I was praying at church. If I walked slowly, my hair would stay where it was and cover my top half. Of course, anyone behind me would see I was naked but there was nothing I could do about that.

I tried not to look at my mother ahead of me; her body wobbled as she walked and her skin was puckered all over, like the craters on the moon. What would they think of me at school if they knew where I was? Dad marched ahead, slapping his thigh, leading our little troop through the gloom.

'Come on, you lot, we haven't got all day.'

I was cold. The path was damp under my feet and the trees hid the sun that struggled to pass on the last heat of the year. The wind blew through the wood, snatching the remaining leaves off the trees, leaving them twisted and bare. If I held my right elbow in my left hand, I could cover myself down there, and rub some warmth into my right side. With practice, I found I could swap over and rub my left side and still keep covered.

Abruptly, we came to a halt, almost falling like dominoes against each other.

'Well hello there,' Dad's voice boomed through the trees.

I heard a faint muttering as we arranged ourselves in a small huddle to meet the stranger.

'Good morning to you, sir. We're new here.'

I kept my eyes down. Then I saw a man's feet, stark white against the dark earth of the path, the bottom half of his legs sprouting curly, black hair. The feet moved apart and the man crouched down in front of me like a frog. As he did so, his penis came into view. I tried not to stare but I couldn't help it.

'So what's your name?' His voice was soft like my mum's.

Mum said you weren't supposed to speak to strangers, but then she and Dad were with me. I didn't want to speak to the man – didn't even want to look up – so I kept quiet.

'Come on now, don't be shy. Aren't you going to tell me your name?'

'I'm called Jo.'

'That's a beautiful name,' he whispered.

Chapter 11

Terry was large and fat with funny-coloured skin – his face and body were splashed red, as though he had something to be embarrassed about. I knew he was strange as soon as he said 'hello'. He had a way of looking at you while he talked that started at your face and then moved down, not in an obvious way, but with his eyes slightly to the left so he looked as if he was focussing on something else. Mum had always warned me about men like Terry, men with a 'wandering gaze', but she couldn't see it here. Here in this secret garden, she was just like all the rest of them.

'*Suivez-moi*,' Terry said, with a tight smile. I must have looked baffled as he repeated in English 'come on, follow me'. I was mesmerised by the swags of fat arranged on his back. His bottom would have been square if he hadn't been quite so fat and as he waddled, the rolls vibrated as each foot met the ground.

Terry turned. 'You all right there?'

Instinctively, I cupped my hand to cover myself. Terry looked at my awkward posture and smirked. I tried to look somewhere, anywhere away from the naked bodies of my father, my mother and this fat, balding stranger. For a place that was supposed to be promoting freedom, I felt trapped, and something began to rise up in me. At that moment, I'd had enough of the lot of them. I stood completely still.

'I want to go home.'

Dad raised his hand. 'Now stop that.'

'What?'

He sniffed loudly. 'I'm warning you.'

'I just want to go home.'

'That's the end of it.'

'Please, I'm only . . .'

'How many times do I have to tell you? Little girls should be seen and not heard. Shut it! Right now!'

I knew Dad was being serious. But, suddenly, his face broke into a big smile.

'What a lovely day. Let's go for a swim.'

Terry turned to me and bent down again so that his undercarriage swung low, almost touching the path.

'Come on, cheer up. The water's lovely and warm.'

I hesitated, thinking that at least under water I'd be covered.

The swimming pool was full of children playing, squealing and throwing a shiny striped beach ball. Terry dipped his toe in the water.

'Come on in, it's like a bath!'

I noticed that when he smiled, he had yellow teeth.

Dad made for the deep end and performed a perfect dive. Mum slowly lowered herself down by the steps and started a feeble breaststroke, her head held way out of the water so that she wouldn't get her face wet. The pool certainly looked inviting. In a flash, I threw off my towel, hoping no one would see me, and jumped in. The water went straight up my nose and I struggled, treading water and spluttering, looking over to Dad who was busy doing a serious crawl at the far side of the pool.

Someone tapped me on the shoulder and I turned around. It was Terry.

'Can you dive?' His curly hair was stuck flat to his head.

He turned himself upside-down and I closed my eyes to cut out the view of his backside as he disappeared into the water. I looked anxiously around me but couldn't see him anywhere. Then I felt a tickle on the back of my leg. He rose from the water and spat out a jet of it, laughing. He flicked some water at me, gently at first and then harder. I flicked back and soon we were into a full-scale water fight, laughing and screaming.

Dad swam over and joined in. Terry must have been all right if Dad thought so. Dad crashed his strong right arm down, creating the biggest splashes I'd ever seen. He had a way of shouting just as his head went underwater, making a sound like a roar. We splashed and splashed. It was ages since I'd seen Dad really enjoying himself like that. I suppose he must have been feeling relaxed. Maybe being naked gave him some sort of freedom; it certainly seemed to have put him in a good mood. He'd found a way of winding down from his work, far from the noise of the warehouse. I watched Dad climb out of the pool and stretch out to dry off on one of the sunloungers.

Now Terry decided to try out one of his diving tricks: 'Let's see if I can dive between your legs,' he announced. As he prepared to dive under, he gave me a little smile and held his tongue between his teeth in a way that made me feel very uncomfortable.

Before I could protest, he'd turned himself upside-down again. I thought of Terry under the water, between my legs. Did he have his eyes open? Could he see me? Instinctively, I pulled my legs together. Then I felt his hands, pulling them apart and holding them there, the wire of his hair between my legs as he went between them. He spat out water as he surfaced and started to laugh.

'Again!' shouted Terry and he duck-dived once more. The water around me went mysteriously still. I couldn't see him anywhere. Suddenly, I felt his hands on my legs again, only this time his grip was firmer. His hands were clenched around my ankles, hurting me. Terry was writing around beneath me, his body a hazy shape, when he pulled my legs wide open and held them there. I struggled to get away, but before I knew what was happening, he had his hands around my knees and was raising me up, up on his shoulders, out of the pool.

I wobbled unsteadily on Terry's shoulders. I was naked for all to see and, worse still, I had my legs wound around this man's neck. My private parts were grating on the back of his head.

I screamed and lost my balance, toppling backwards into the pool with my legs wide open. I felt hands around my waist, then hands running down me, slippery on my body. He was touching me all over – holding his breath for as long as he could. In the haze underwater, I saw his hair wild about his head and as he came at me, holding his breath, his face was bloated. I struggled to get away. This wasn't like when I went to the swimming baths with Sue and we'd hold our breath and dive down to look at the watery depths. I didn't want to see this strange man under the surface.

I came up for air, choking and coughing, swimming for the side, my eyes stinging. Trying to get away as fast as possible, I reached for where I had left my towel, but it had gone.

'You don't need that in here,' said Dad who was walking back towards the pool area from where the sunloungers were arranged. 'Just let yourself dry off in the sun.'

Perhaps if I'd told my dad what had gone on under the water he would have stopped it right there and then. But I didn't. I didn't have the words.

Chapter 12

Perhaps it was me? Perhaps I'd been wrong about what had happened in the swimming pool, or the way Terry had looked at me? Maybe I'd imagined it?

Then I remembered the feel of his rough hands on me under the water, and how he'd held my legs apart. I hadn't imagined that. Or had I? Wasn't he just diving underwater? I'd played that game so many times with Sue in the local baths, but this – naked with a man I didn't know – had been very different. I hoped he wouldn't play like that if we came back next Sunday. If I stayed away from the pool then I could avoid Terry completely. I felt totally sick at the thought of ever seeing him again, all I could think about were his disgusting hands all over me.

My bedroom at home was my haven. It was the only place I felt safe and could think it all through. There, among the old furniture and mismatched carpets and curtains, I felt right. Mum was always reusing things, it didn't matter that nothing matched – coordinating bedcovers and curtains were unheard of in our house. Curtains were just something to block out the light, my bedroom carpet used to be in our old dining room, and the furniture was inherited from my grandmother's house. The mixed up way I felt sat easily with that mishmash of my bedroom.

The night after we got back from the camp, I held my llama close and ran my fingernails around his eyes, enjoying the way the glass dug hard into my skin. It hurt in a good way. There, under the blue candlewick bedspread, I wrote my diary, twitching my feet so my toenails caught on the brushed nylon sheets. Recently, I'd started to tie my diary with a single, almost transparent strand of my long blond hair. I'd seen that trick in a spy film, so I would always know if Mum had read my diary. I wished she would read it, then she'd know how much I hated going to the nudist camp, and how I hated her for not standing up to Dad, for not putting me first. But most importantly, how much I hated Dad for taking me there in the first place.

At that moment I heard footsteps on the stairs and Mum tapped on the door.

'Jo love, fancy coming to watch a bit of television with me? *Little Women*'s on and you know how I love a weepie.'

I wiped my eyes on the bedspread and took a deep breath.

'OK, Mum, I'll be down in a sec.'

I put my diary back in its hiding place and made my way downstairs. I'd had enough of being on my own and liked my special times with Mum on the sofa, when it was just the two of us.

In the sitting room I found my dad in his chair and, instead of the old black-and-white film, he was watching some boring documentary about insects. I turned away from the close-up of a hairy tarantula biting into a butterfly, crushing its blue wings. Mum had her legs up on the sofa, leaving little room for me, so I squeezed on to the end and kept quiet. We watched what Dad wanted to watch. He never asked me if there was any programme I might like to watch; children weren't asked about anything.

That night, I lay awake waiting for the deep, rhythmic sound of my father's snore before switching on my bedside light. I crept out of bed and stood in front of the mirror then quickly, to the crackle of static, flicked off my Bri-Nylon nightie. I studied my reflection, trying to get used to the look of my naked body. If I could feel comfortable being naked in private then, maybe, I would feel more at ease being naked in public.

My dressing table mirror was quite small, so I could only look at myself in sections – like the game we played where people passed round a piece of paper and everyone added a section of a body. If I tilted the mirror at a certain angle I could study myself without seeing my head – it was less embarrassing that way.

My top half was thin, ribbed like a leaf and with the beginnings of breasts, which I hated. There was a flat, almost concave stomach with a sticking out belly button and a semi-circular scar like a smile beneath – Mum had told me I'd had an umbilical hernia. I'd always felt self-conscious about this scar and, unlike Sue, never wanted to wear a bikini when we went to the baths, but now this was the least of my problems.

I tilted the mirror down, took a deep breath and looked – though I found it difficult – at the section below. I wished I had hair down there, like the women I'd seen, to hide it. On the other hand, perhaps that would draw attention to it like the woman at the club with hair down there so dark it looked like an arrow pointing: 'Here it is!' I certainly didn't want hair like that.

I forced myself to look for a long time but no matter how long I stood there, I didn't feel any better about the way it looked. I stood and stood, getting colder and colder, while down the long corridor I could still hear my father snoring, deep in sleep.

I realised I'd never get used to being naked. I put my nightie back on and threw myself on the bed, holding my llama close, sobbing and sobbing, stifling the sound in my pillow.

Mum knocked on the door, 'Jo? Why is your light still on?'

I pushed my head deep in my pillow, I didn't want her to see me cry.

'What is it, my love?'

'Nothing.'

'I know it's not nothing. Now tell me, what's the matter?'

I didn't want to talk to her about the nudist camp – I knew she had no say in what we did, that Dad was the one in total change.

Mum came and sat down on the edge of my bed.

'Has something happened at school?'

I stayed quiet.

'Come on, tell me, darling, has someone been mean to you?'

I shook my head – I just wanted her to go away. She must have known why I was upset, so why was she going on about school?

'You know, God says you must turn the other cheek . . .' And she looked up to that place just above her head.

Why couldn't she just shut up about God? This was nothing to do with God. I could feel it all bubbling up inside me: the people with no clothes, the swimming pool and the grate of Terry's hair between my legs . . .

Mum put her hand on my hair: 'There now, Jo . . . there, there . . .'

I pushed her hand away. 'How could you?'

'I'm sorry . . . I . . . What is it?'

'How could you make out that you're just not bothered?'

'I am bothered . . . if you're upset of course I'm bothered. You mean everything to me, Jo, you know that, you're my whole life.'

'How come you don't know what I'm talking about then?'

'Oh I do, I do . . . you're growing up, that's all, it's a difficult time.'

'It's a difficult time at that place with no clothes on!'

'Oh you mean . . . ?'

'You know what I mean!'

'Yes . . . try to understand . . . ?'

'I don't want to understand! I hate that place! I never want to go there again!'

Mum closed her eyes briefly. 'You must never, ever tell anyone about where we have been. Where we go.' That made it sound permanent – like this was the way life would be. 'Promise me now? No one must ever know, there're the neighbours to think about, they'd never understand.'

I held back tears. All she cared about was the neighbours gossiping. I was so angry that I thought I was going to burst. I wondered if that's why she smelled of drink, if that was secret, too.

Mum looked heavenward again, as though for encouragement. 'The name "Edendale", and what we did there, must never be mentioned. And your father has a position to uphold at work. The men there look up to him. Promise me now, Jo?'

'Oh yes, I promise, of course I promise!' I blurted. 'D'you think I want to tell my friends about being in a field with a load of naked people?'

And then I was crying like I couldn't stop. I dreaded going back to the nudist camp, but I knew that's what we would be doing at weekends from now on. It was hard to believe, but Mum's words had confirmed it for me, that was her way of telling me that was just the way it would be now. Tough though it was, we'd both have to get on with it.

'Mum . . . Mummy . . . In the pool . . . that man . . .'

Mum closed her eyes and clasped her hands together, 'Hail-Mary-mother-of-God.'

I didn't want to say prayers with her as though we were in a confession box. The only thing I wanted to confess to her about was the way Terry had run his slippery hands all over my bare body. But she didn't want to listen. And now I had no choice but to be part of this club, this secret club that I must never tell any of my friends about.

Chapter 13

When I walked into the classroom on Monday morning, my gang of friends were sitting on desks in the corner, waiting for Miss Masters to arrive. Normally, we'd be really pleased to see each other – as if we'd been apart for much longer than just a weekend – but I didn't feel like that today. I was terrified in case anything I might say would give away our family secret.

'Hello, Jo,' started Sue.

I didn't want to talk to them.

Then they all joined in . . .

'Helen's not speaking to her mum . . .'

'. . . she's been dead snide . . .'

'. . . said she couldn't get her hair cut and . . .'

I wished all I had to worry about was a haircut.

'Guess what?' said Helen.

'No, you tell her . . .'

'Jill's havin' a party this weekend,' interrupted Sue – she liked to be the first to tell me any news.

'Yippee!' they all yelled.

But I couldn't feel excited. 'When is it?' I asked.

'Sunday.'

My stomach squeezed.

'. . . she's got to go to her nan's on Saturday. Anyway, Sunday's the tenth, her real birthday.'

I didn't want to tell them where I'd be on Sunday.

'It's going to be fancy dress!' squealed Sue and she shook her hands with excitement.

'Oh . . . fancy dress . . . right . . .'

'We're all goin' as Barbies, who do you want to be?'

Anyone other than myself, I thought. They'd all be at the party but I'd have to go to that awful nudist camp with my parents.

Sue carried on, 'Jill'll be Birthday Barbie of course.'

Their voices were growing louder and louder and I felt left out.

'Bagsy me Beach Barbie,' shouted Sue. 'Or d'you think it'll look a bit, you know . . . revealing?'

I could feel something winding deep in my stomach, then I came out with it. 'I don't want to go to her stupid party.'

Sue's forehead puckered. 'What's up with you then?'

'Nothing. I'm not going, that's all.'

'Don't bother then.'

'I won't.'

'Don't then. Sorry I spoke . . . get you!'

All week in class they talked about what they'd be

wearing to Jill's party while I continued to pretend that I didn't want to go. How weird, I thought, they'll all be dressing up while I'll have to strip off. I could hear them whispering about me but all I worried about was that the days were ticking away towards Sunday and the nudist camp.

I kept myself to myself and started to turn up later for school so I wouldn't have to talk to them in the mornings. By the end of the week, it was as if I wasn't part of the gang at all. I tried to pretend that I wasn't bothered, but when I got home I'd shut myself in my room and lie on my bed with my llama, crying my eyes out.

As Sunday drew nearer, I became increasingly tense and nervous. I felt sick all the time. Would Terry be there? Would we have to swim again? Maybe I'd been mistaken and, this time, he'd behave like my dad's friends who'd ruffle my hair and give me sweets. Sunday came all too soon and we were packing up for a second 'little trip'. When I put my head around the kitchen door mum was acting weird again, like she was hiding something. I felt sick in the pit of my stomach. The night before, Mum had drunk even more than usual and this morning she was in a bad mood, banging and crashing around the cupboards.

I snuck back quietly to my room. I was so desperate

not to go to Edendale I decided I would try asking God to help me. One of Mum's friends had given me a china angel with a golden halo and white wings stretched to the heavens; it, along with a collection of china rabbits and my beloved llama, was the kind of thing that adorned my bedroom. That Sunday morning, I cleared my dressing table, placed a white doily on it and, reverently, stood the angel on top. Then I knelt down before my makeshift altar – I was willing to try anything. I used to whisper my prayers – normally under the bedspread, late at night with my mum – because Dad didn't approve. Now, I looked hard into the angel's serene face and started:

'Hail Mary, mother of God, hallowed be thy name . . .'

If I prayed to my special angel she would, I hoped, stop my parents taking me to the nudist camp.

'Please angel, please, I know I'm only praying to ask you for something, but if I promise to be good, will you please, please stop them from taking me to the camp?' I looked deep into the angel's face. 'I don't want to go to the nudist camp. I don't want to take off my clothes . . .'

I opened my eyes. I thought the angel might have looked at me but I wasn't sure, she was a bit cross-eyed. I closed my eyes again. If I said the Lord's Prayer all the way through, then she might listen. I'd spoken only a few words when the door burst open and Mum was there, looking from me to my makeshift shrine.

'Jo, what on earth are you doing?'

'Praying to my angel'

'Holy-Mary-mother-of-God . . .'

'No, I don't think it's her, she wears blue doesn't she?'

'I know it's not Our Lady. Mother-of-God, Lord help me . . . What in hell and damnation are you doing?'

'I was praying . . . that's all.'

'To that . . . that idol? No, no, no . . .' And she ran at me and slapped and slapped hard at my legs. She snatched the angel away and held her at arm's length, as though she was something unclean.

'Sorry, Mum. I didn't mean . . .'

'You evil, evil child!'

She lifted the angel above her head. 'Thou shalt have no other gods before me! Say it!'

'I shall have no other gods before you . . . him! No other gods than me . . .'

She threw the angel down on the floor. Its head shattered, its serene face was gone. I rushed to pick it up and saw, poking from its neck, a roll of newspaper with Chinese writing.

'It's just a cheap ornament,' Mum hissed. 'Not a god.'

My stomach was churning. There was an upside to the fear I felt though: I thought if I was ill enough, then perhaps I wouldn't have to go. I stayed in my bedroom while Mum and Dad finished packing up, thinking of my broken angel. I tried to add to the ill feeling by trying to make myself sick – the best way I could think of was to eat lots of liquorice, sucking it hard until the inside of my mouth went black, and then I groaned loudly until Mum came in.

'What's the matter now?'

'Don't feel well.'

'Funny, you seemed fine just a minute ago when you were saying your prayers.'

'I've got a stinging pain, right here.'

'What's that all round your mouth?'

'Don't know.'

'Perhaps if you didn't stuff yourself with so many sweets, you wouldn't feel so sick. Come on! Get in the car. Now. Your father's leaving in five minutes,' Mum screamed. 'He's going without you if you don't hurry up.'

I wished he would go without me, but I knew he never would. I pleaded with my mum to be left at Sue's house.

'Your father says "no".'

'Can I go with her to the party at Jill's house? It's Jill's birthday, will you ask him? It's a Barbie party and . . .'

'You know what his answer will be.'

'But maybe . . . could you just . . . ? Please?'

The truth was that we were both too scared to ask him.

*

On the long drive to Edendale I thought about my angel. She'd been swept away and thrown in with the rubbish; she couldn't help me now, no one could. Our new weekend ritual meant, of course, that Mum would no longer be able to go to church on Sundays, and now she'd have to go to confession during the week: I wondered if she'd tell the priest why she wouldn't be at church on Sundays; because she'd be lying naked on a sunlounger.

While we drove along the winding roads that led to the camp I sat in the back, the smell of the car's plastic seats in my nose, and thought about those naked bodies and I felt so sick I had to wind down the window. We drove into the camp, parked and unloaded – just as we had done one week before. I looked around anxiously to see if Terry was lurking and smiled when I realised I couldn't see him. Dad caught my smile in the mirror and got the wrong idea. 'Happy, Jo?' He clapped his hands on the wheel.

I couldn't believe he'd said that but decided to keep quiet. Mum was still ignoring me; perhaps, if I made Dad happy she'd forget about the angel.

On this second visit, my parents had started to meet new people. All the adults were married – that was one of the rules of joining this club, as was using only first names. I was introduced to various couples: Brian and June, Bob and Jane, Barry and Anne, Terry and Margaret

– ordinary names like people you met in ordinary life – but they all blurred into one. I didn't see any children around this time, just lots of naked adults. Terry didn't behave like a married person – in fact, that day, I hardly saw him together with Margaret. His wife was joining in lots of the club's activities and bustling around and sorting things out. I hadn't seen Terry yet, but one of the other couples mentioned he was somewhere around, busy doing his photographs.

I, too, tried to keep busy, and to stay close to my parents – I didn't want to be alone. Dad went off to help out at the plant nursery and left me with Mum. Some of the women asked Mum if she'd join them in the pavilion.

'We're going to give it a nice spring clean,' one of them said (even though it was autumn). 'You can give us a hand too, dear.' Mum and I followed them.

They looked odd cleaning the pavilion wearing nothing but pink Marigolds. Some also wore aprons which made them look quite ridiculous – and there was always the horror when one of the women would turn around and I'd see her bottom. Why bother wearing an apron? It wasn't as if they were going to spoil their clothes if they spilled anything. And why did some people wear a tracksuit top but not the tracksuit bottoms?

As I helped Mum butter some bread for sandwiches, I tried to think positively about the nudity issue. There were some practical advantages to being a nudist: you never had to wait for your swimsuit to dry; packing your suitcase was easy; you didn't have to worry about messing up your clothes. I worried, however, what might happen if a nudist spilled a tray of steaming cups of tea. And I didn't want a jam butty made by someone in the nude – naked flesh close to freshly cut bread made me shiver. I also didn't want to eat a sausage barbecued by a man who'd braved the whole operation undressed.

While we cut up cheese and sliced tomatoes, I tried again to accept seeing my mum without clothes on; but I just couldn't. Mum belonged in a flowery dress with a pinny on top or, when she was smart, in a pencil skirt and a jacket, nylons – straight seam down the back – and stilettos. She was used to wearing stiff underwear, big knickers, and a girdle to hold everything in. That was the way things should be. When she was dressed up, she was beautiful, elegant and she seemed confident. Naked, she became someone I didn't recognise as my mum.

'You all right there, Jo?' Mum asked. I was concentrating hard on the sandwich making, ensuring that I spread the margarine all the way to the corners on each slice of bread.

'You don't have to be so exact, you know. You'll be there for ever if that's the way you go about it.'

But I wanted to stay in the pavilion for ever,

surrounded by women making sandwiches. It was much safer than walking around outside where I might bump into Terry. Mum handed me a glass of what looked like fruit juice. 'Go on, have a sip' she said as she tipped her glass back and and quickly reached for her pills. I tried it and it tasted bitter. I didn't like it.

'It's punch,' said Mum. 'It's just like fruit juice except it's got a bit of a kick to it. Me and the girls, we made some up to help jolly ourselves along. Don't tell your dad – it's just something for us mums.'

We carried on making up sandwiches and I noticed her topping up her glass. After a while, she seemed to get all happy.

'I do love you, Jo, d'you know that?' Her voice was slurred. 'Do you love me?'

Love wasn't a word we used in our family. It felt awkward to tell her I loved her as she stood there in the kitchen, naked. And I didn't want her to hug me so I turned away.

'Jo, love?'

I looked up and saw her red face as she moved towards me, staggering a little, then throwing her arms around me for support. She held me close – her skin was sticky and I could smell the drink, sweet on her breath. And I couldn't answer her question – I couldn't bring myself to tell her I loved her.

Chapter 14

Late that Sunday afternoon, I was walking down the path when I felt a prod on my bare shoulder. I hadn't heard anyone come up behind me.

'Oh!'

It was Terry. He was the last person I wanted to see.

'Here, I've got something to show you.'

'I'm just going back to my mum.'

'Do you like animals?'

I nodded.

'We're all animals, see, Jo.'

I noticed the dark outline of hair on his shoulders and felt my neck prickle.

Terry smiled. 'Animals don't wear clothes now, do they?'

I wanted to tell him that animals had fur so it was OK. I wanted to tell him that I was cold, that I didn't want to be standing in front of him with nothing on but a pair of plimsolls.

'There's no shame in being naked,' Terry said with his

hands outstretched as though I was supposed to admire him. He drew in a deep breath. 'We're not nudists, we're naturists. Do you know the difference? Naturism,' Terry gestured around us, 'is about being close to nature, being at one with nature,' then he stopped, laid his hand on my back and then rubbed his hand down a tree.

I began to shake. I wanted to tell him that I didn't want him to touch me; that I didn't believe what he said, that I thought there was another reason for going to nudist camps that no one ever talked about – a reason I was too young to really understand but I knew it made me feel uncomfortable. Terry smiled.

'I said I'd show these old photographs and animal postcards to your parents. It'll only take a minute; I'll come with you. Bob mentioned them to your mum when they met last time and she was keen to see them.'

I didn't want to spend a second, never mind a minute with this man but he was my mum and dad's new friend so I had to be nice to him.

'Well, I . . .' I saw him looking at me in that sideways way – maybe I was imagining it?

'Come on, lead the way, Jo. I'm sure I saw your mum by the clubhouse.'

He pushed me gently in the direction of the pavilion and, despite the cold, I felt his hand hot and clammy on my back. Mum was sitting outside at an old wooden picnic table, Dad was nearby, dousing the flames from a barbecue that had got out of control.

'Hello there, Terry,' Dad shouted. 'I told her to leave it to me and steady on with the meths, but she wouldn't listen. Women . . . typical. Come and join us for a burnt offering.'

'Well, I was just about to show you that collection we were talking about last time.'

'Great . . . great . . . let's have a look then . . .'

Terry took out a box full of postcards and some photos and laid it carefully on the table. I didn't want to look at his stupid stuff – I didn't want to make friends with this man and I didn't understand why he wanted to be friends with me, a little girl.

Mum started to get dinner ready and Dad battled with the barbecue, leaving me with Terry. He snuggled up right next to me on the bench and started flicking through the box, with every other card he picked up and examined, his fingers seemed to brush my arm – but he carried on shouting across to my mum and dad as normal and I began to wonder if I was imagining it. Terry turned the cards over slowly, watching my face intently as he explained at length about each animal.

'Isn't it cute?' he said, and squeezed my cheek between his fat fingers. 'Just like you. I love nature, don't you?'

'Suppose so . . .' I wished he wouldn't stare at me.

'You know,' he called over to Mum and Dad, 'Jo here is so photogenic.' Then he whispered to me. 'Pretty as a picture, that's what you are,' and he ran his hand around my face.

'What are you looking at?' I asked quietly.

'Nothing really – I'm just thinking how mature you are for your age, how much more mature you are than some of the other young people who come here.'

As his eyes went up and down my body, he leaned in and added: 'Some of them just don't get it. They don't do the right thing like you. Admittedly, they aren't as pretty as you, but when people don't join in – well it ruins things for others, doesn't it? I can see you aren't like that – not one of those to ruin things for others.'

I couldn't wait to get away from him, and everyone else in that nudist camp, too. I just wanted to go home.

At ten years old my options were limited. I couldn't stay at home on my own and I wasn't allowed to go and stay with Sue. Sometimes I thought about running away from home, but where would I go?

The only other thing I could think of doing was to tell someone about my big secret, someone who might make it stop. But who? My first thought was Sue, but she was just like me, too young to do anything about it. That only left my teacher. There really wasn't anyone else – and I just couldn't imagine sharing a secret like that with Miss

Masters. Anyway, she'd probably think I was making it all up and put me in that seat in front of her desk.

And so I just kept quiet. Only sometimes, I'd look down and notice my hands were screwed into tight fists, so tight that my nails dug into my palms, clenched as if I was ready for a fight. Something was happening inside me. I was slowly cranking up – as though someone had thrust a huge, sharp key inside me and started to turn it.

Chapter 15

'I'm gonna ask you something and you've got to tell me if it's true,' Sue began.

My heart started to thud.

'Promise?'

I nodded.

We were curled up under her flowery bedcover eating hot buttered toast. I kept quiet. Had I let something slip?

'I know it's a big secret, and you don't have to talk to me about it if you don't want to.'

I watched the way the butter was melting on the toast, wishing I could just disappear.

'Well, Jo, can I ask you, or what?'

'Dunno . . .'

'OK, I think I should, 'cos someone told me about it at school and I think you need to know what they know.'

I wondered how they'd found out – I thought I'd been so careful.

'I'm going to say it quickly, 'cos I was upset when I found out, so here goes . . .'

I held my breath.

'I heard there's no such thing as Father Christmas. Do you think it can be true?'

A huge sigh of relief burst from me.

'Helen told me . . . she said it was really our mums and dads, and if you let on you might not get any presents, so you have to just keep quiet about it. What do you think? I need to know what you think.'

I'd known for ages that there was no Father Christmas but hadn't wanted to spoil it for Sue. Helen had told me, spitefully, in the playground one day and then laughed when I cried. Sue loved all that Santa-down-the-chimney stuff, and always made sure her mum didn't light a fire on Christmas Eve so he could get down, no trouble. I'd never quite believed my mum when I'd asked her how he'd get into our house – because there wasn't a chimney – and she'd told me he had a magic key to the front door.

Sue looked at me with her head on one side. 'I reckon Helen's right. You don't mind too much do you, Jo?'

I shook my head. I knew we were supposed to tell each other everything. Then, in the next breath Sue was going on about what she was getting for Christmas. 'Oh please get a Tiny Tears for Christmas, Jo. Then we can play with them together.'

I didn't tell her that I'd rather have a Scalextric set. 'OK, I'll ask,' I said instead, and I made a mental note to put it in my letter to Father Christmas.

*

It was a week before Christmas and I was counting down the days, feeling more and more excited as each day's little door on the Advent calendar revealed a new picture – wrapped parcels, red-breasted robins, spinning tops. Mum got out the same old Advent calendar every year; the big door on the 25th had been ripped off long ago, so it was no surprise to see baby Jesus in his manger. Anyway, I was always too excited on Christmas morning to bother with the Advent calendar.

Mum hauled down the leather-bound trunk from the attic, and the two of us crouched together to open it, like it was a long-lost treasure chest. Mum let me unwrap each tissue-clad decoration, feeling first and guessing the contents – a kind of rehearsal for the real thing on Christmas Day.

With gentle fingers, I unravelled golden baubles frosted with glitter, remembering each one with 'oohs' and 'ahs'. Here was the fairy with the battered wand and the pointed hat – she had short legs and wore no pants under her silver dress. And here was the tiny angel which glowed like magic when you held it under a bright light; the golden cherub with chubby thighs, playing the flute; Santa with his sack of presents forever glued down and the wooden dolls, one with no hair, that sat under the tree. The nativity scene was missing its baby Jesus, who'd crawled off somewhere long ago, and had been replaced by a wooden piglet – I'd often thought about wrapping the piglet in swaddling clothes to at least cover its trotters, but felt Mum might object.

Mum let me take charge of decorating the tree while she sat down and poured a glass of Dad's homemade wine. Dad had taken up winemaking only recently with a group from work and with varying degrees of success. I'd help him gather elderberries from hedgerows and we'd heap them into large containers. Whether the containers hadn't been rinsed out properly, or if his skills required further fine tuning, the concoctions he produced were rarely drinkable except, it seemed, by Mum. Recently, Dad had been trying to perfect a wine called Tokay but he hadn't had much luck. He'd said Mum could help herself to all the stuff that had gone wrong for her recipes and sauces and it seemed like whenever he wasn't around, she'd been doing just that, but not much of it was reaching the food she cooked.

Mum drank glass after glass while I hung the decorations as carefully as I could – even though I knew that she'd redo them later, when I'd gone to bed. It was snowing outside, and it felt like we were in our very own Christmas card. Because of the bad weather, it had been a couple of months since we'd been to the nudist camp and, if I tried really hard, I could almost forget about it.

Lit up with fairy lights of Santas, snowmen and angels, the Christmas tree stood in the corner of the room – and even though it was something else my mum got down year after year and its branches sagged downward, rather than upward, it didn't matter; it was Christmas and the house smelled of mince pies. Mum handed me one.

'We can start on these now, but we must be sure to save one for Father Christmas.'

I was glad she still thought I believed in Father Christmas so I went along with it, just as I nodded along when she got Dad to pour Santa a glass of whisky. Mum raised her glass to me then put it down on the coffee table, not noticing how it spilled over the side as she did so. She lay back against the chair: 'Just having forty winks,' and she closed her eyes. She started to snore almost immediately. I looked around. The house was all neat and tidy, the old battered snowman had taken up his place on the television, like he did every year, a tiny angel was next to him and cards were pegged up on strings like colourful washing lines.

Suddenly Mum jerked and opened her eyes, blinking and trying to focus them on mine. 'So, Jo, love, what do you want for Christmas?' Her voice was slurred. 'Come and sit on my knee.' As I drew close, I smelled the wine on her breath and she saw me look at the almost empty bottle. 'It is Christmas, you know,' she said.

Without a word, I handed Mum the letter I'd written to Father Christmas. It had in it all the usual stuff I wanted for Christmas, including the Tiny Tears doll. But there were other things I wanted, much more than presents. I wished I could tell her that I wanted parents who didn't scream at each other, a dad who didn't mind saying he loved me, and a mum who didn't drink and take funny coloured pills. But most of all, I wanted parents who would never take me to a nudist camp.

Dad came in with a sledgehammer balanced on his shoulder. Mum put her hands on her hips.

'What's that for? I hope you're not doing any of your DIY in here just when I've got the place right for Christmas?'

'Don't tell me what to do, woman.'

And with that he lifted the hammer high and marched across the sitting room. We watched, dumbstruck, as he took a mighty slug at the wall.

Mum screamed at him: 'What are you doing?'

'None of your business.'

I put my hands over my ears as he hammered and hammered at the wall. There was dust everywhere. Soon he was through to the adjoining garage and the cold air gusted through.

Over the next few days Mum and Dad didn't speak. He kept hitting away at the wall, Mum kept drinking, and reminding me that because it was Christmas she needed her forty winks more and more. I tried to keep out of their way. Dad worked hard on it all the time he was off work.

On Christmas morning Dad shook me awake. 'Happy Christmas, Jo. Come and see.' There, set in the wall, was an aquarium. Inside, brightly coloured fish with long trailing tails fluttered past. 'They're guppies,' Dad said, then he pointed to a long pink and white creature that snaked along the bottom, 'that one's a coolie eel.'

In the corner of the tank was a seashell and, as I watched, suddenly it opened up with a bubble of air to reveal a glistening pearl. It was a magical underwater world. I looked at him, not knowing what to say.

It was my job to go around to the back of the tank in the adjoining garage and put in flakes of food. Then I'd rush back into the sitting room to see the angel fish hunt them like prey. Dad showed me how to hold up a mirror to the Siamese fighting fish and watch its bright frill open like an umbrella.

'It thinks there's another one there,' he said. 'Stupid thing, fighting with himself.' And I looked at my dad intently.

I'd really wanted a Tiny Tears so that I could be like Sue. So much so, that I nearly cried when I didn't get one. I knew as soon as I'd spilled the pillowcase containing my presents on to my bed, that nothing there was the same size as the Tiny Tears box, so when Mum and Dad came into my bedroom to watch me open my presents I was prepared.

'Do you like your doll?' asked Mum.

I held up the Pouting Pretty doll and showed them how with her right arm up she smiled and when you put it down her mouth curled into a pout.

'Just what I wanted,' I smiled. And I realised it was the same 'just what I wanted' face I put on when I went to the nudist camp. It was easier that way.

When Dad wasn't around, I took one of his screwdrivers and made a hole in her mouth and another one between her legs. I couldn't make her shed tears but if I fed her with water, though she leaked through the joints in her arms and legs, it sort of worked to wet her nappy. It wasn't as good as a real Tiny Tears but it would do. And it had the added feature that when I put her arm down she'd keep the bottle in her mouth all by herself. Sue said it was even better than her Tiny Tears, and I loved her for that.

All through the Christmas holidays, we played with our new dolls, pushing them in Sue's pram. I felt normal, I could relax and pretend I was just like all my friends. I didn't have to worry about taking my clothes off, or seeing anyone else naked.

*

One Saturday in early January, I woke to the sound of my parents arguing. Dad was going on about Mum drinking again – 'God damn it, get a grip' – and she was screaming at him to leave her alone because she had a headache.

Dad burst into my room and told me the fish didn't need feeding because he'd given them a special block that would last a couple of days. I wondered why he'd done that when feeding the fish was one of my favourite jobs.

I went to find Mum who was in her nightdress putting sandwiches in Tupperware containers like we were going somewhere. She looked as if she'd been crying.

'What is it?'

'Nothing.'

'Are we going somewhere?'

And she nodded slowly.

'Come on, Jo,' Dad shouted from outside, 'we're off.'

'Where are we going, Mum?' I asked. But deep inside I knew. She took the containers to the car and I opened the kitchen drawer quietly. There was the Voodoo doll again with pins in its head, but Mum's bottle of pills had gone.

I didn't want to go to the nudist club on a Saturday. Saturday, along with the Sundays we hadn't been to the club, were my special days with Sue. My normal time. As we drove off, I kept quiet in the back of the car with my

Pouting Pretty doll on my knee, her face curled up all miserable.

'We've got a special surprise for you, Jo,' Mum began.

Dad gave her a warning look. 'Not now.'

'Never mind. You'll see when we get there.'

I didn't want to get there. It was still winter, even though the snow had melted. Why did they want to go to a place where you took off all your clothes when it was freezing cold? I hoped, just a tiny hope, that we weren't going to Edendale, but then I recognised the motorway bridge that we always drove under on the way and I knew. By the time we reached the gate to the field I'd worked myself up into a state. When Dad got out of the car to unlock the padlock on the gate I started to plead.

'But it's cold . . . Mum . . . it's winter.'

'I know, Jo, but we've got a big surprise waiting for you, you'll see . . .'

We drove through the gate and down the bumpy road to the car park and got out. Mum put her hands over my eyes as she walked me down the little path. When she said I could open them, I was staring at a cream and blue caravan, and white dots danced before my eyes. I felt dazed and disorientated.

'Now we can come here for the whole weekend!'

I couldn't speak. Proudly, Dad opened the door and Mum led me in and showed me round.

'At last we can have some privacy when we get changed.'

That didn't make any sense to me at all. Why did that matter in a nudist camp? Mum showed me the sofa which turned into a bed, just for me, and I sat on it trying not to cry.

Sundays had turned into whole weekends. Often, now, we'd pack up on a Friday night and not come back till late on Sunday. It was the end of everything.

Chapter 16

The weekend after I'd been presented with the caravan, Sue wanted to know why I couldn't go down to the local baths that Saturday.

'Because I'm going away with my mum and dad.'

'Thought you did that on Sundays?'

'I do, it's just that I do it on Saturdays now as well.'

'Where you going then?'

'Oh, just away.' My heart started to thud.

'You're never around no more. Why can't you tell me where you go? We used to tell each other everything; now you're just weird all the time.'

'Sorry.'

She didn't know how sorry I was. I missed my Saturdays at the baths with Sue, swimming until we were shivering, then going for hot chocolate and cake to warm up. We'd spend ages over that hot chocolate, stirring and stirring it, discussing whether I should get my hair feathered like hers or just go for a pageboy. I missed going down to the market together, too, and spending our pocket money on stale sweets.

Sue looked at me with that face of hers she pulled when she hadn't got any money.

'Can I come with you on the weekend?'

'N . . . no.'

'Oh go on, ask your mum.'

I shook my head.

'What about if I ask her?'

'No, it's not a good idea.'

'Please ask her.'

'OK, I'll try, but you know what my dad's like when he's in a mood. He'll just say "no".'

But, of course, I never did ask.

Our visits to the nudist club went on and on like some recurring nightmare. They all blended into one until one weekend in spring. It was early on a Saturday morning and I was in bed waiting to leave for the club, listening to Mum and Dad packing with the usual sick feeling deep in my stomach. I noticed that the buds on the young tree in our garden had just started to appear and, as I looked at the pale bark, I shuddered, thinking about what Terry had said about naturists being closer to nature. I felt like that tree, cold and bare, missing its leaves.

Mum came in with a mug of tea and a piece of toast and put them carefully down by my bed.

'Time to get up now, Jo, chop, chop!'

I hated the way she pretended to be cheerful when she was trying to make me do something.

'Won't it be too cold to go?' I asked.

'Your father has agreed to sort out the swimming pool – he wants to help.'

'Can't we stay here while he goes and does that on his own?'

She shook her head.

I put my head under the bedspread and clung to my llama, rocking him, staying under the covers – in the warmth – for as long as I possibly could.

I followed my dad around the house while he did a few last-minute things, hoping he might have changed his mind about going. Dad had a ritual on the Saturdays we were at home. Saturday had always been clock day; he'd always wound the clocks on a Saturday. It usually took him most of the morning, but today he was hurrying.

'Dad, can I help?'

'No, you'd only mess things up.'

But I wanted to hold the heavy keys with intricate patterns on their heads, to match the labels with fine silk tassels, each to their allotted clock. I wanted to put the keys in the keyholes and listen to the click-click-clicking as they were turned. Maybe, if I showed him how well I could do it, we wouldn't have to go to the club?

'Please?'

'You'll over wind the mechanism. Just leave it, Jo.'

My favourite was the cuckoo clock on the wall by the front door. It was carved with secret forests in dark wood and hung with weights like pinecones. I knew I mustn't touch the clock. It was special. Special because of what lived there.

It was almost ten o'clock. I watched for the bird – bright blue with an open beak. I felt sorry for it only coming out on the hour and wished it was free. I waited for the arched door to open. Dad was in the other room – still on winding duty. It was one minute to ten. I heard the mechanism cranking up. The bird would come out soon and chirp ten times.

I locked my eyes on the door. Suddenly, the clock whirred into action. The door opened and the bird came out, beak open, singing to the wide sky through the window – its feathers were as blue as that sky. I wanted to see the rich plumes of its tail, hidden in darkness. I wanted to hold the bird, just for a moment, clasp it fast in my hand, then set it free. On the last trill I caught it. The clock made a screeching noise as the bird snapped off its perch and the door closed behind. Dad rushed into the room.

'What the hell are you doing?'

The bird was dead in my hand. I tried to hold it so Dad couldn't see. I smiled wide and bright. 'Nothing.'

'What have you done?' He opened the clock's door. 'You've got it there, haven't you?'

Slowly, he took off his glasses, then gripped my wrist until my fingers went numb and the bird dropped from my hand. I noticed it had no real tail at all, only a stubble of broken feathers. All around the house the clocks struck ten as I closed my eyes.

Dad hadn't put his glasses back on, so I knew I was in for it. He lurched in my direction – going red as he tried to grab me. I got up and ran, slamming the door behind me. I heard him shouting my name, banging around as he cursed me and my stupidity.

Even without me breaking the clock, the atmosphere in the house was always really tense before we set off for the club – I'm sure Dad reacted because he knew that Mum and I would rather be going anywhere but there. The best thing to do now would be to get right out of his way, so I snuck out to the garden. I was trying to hide among the bushes where the fence was broken when I noticed something glinting in the light – like glass. There, among the weeds in the scrubland at the very foot of our garden lay bottle upon bottle. I crouched and picked one up, recognising the handwritten label immediately: Tokay.

'Mum? Oh no, please . . .' I murmured.

I knelt, hugging the empty bottle, rocking to and fro –

and surrounded by too many other empty bottles to count. There, on my knees in that rubbish tip of my mum's drinking problem, I felt I could sink no lower. How had it come to this? Then I heard Dad shout.

'Just get in the car!'

Throughout the long journey to the club I didn't speak a word to either Mum or Dad. I felt sick. I knew Mum had a drink problem, I'd heard her and Dad rowing about it time after time, but I hadn't known how bad it was – not until I'd seen those empty bottles in a big heap like that.

Although it was brightening up outside, it was cold and damp inside the caravan as we took off our clothes. When we got to the swimming pool the wind was blowing its cover off. I stood with Dad, shivering, holding one corner of the huge cover, while he mixed chemicals in a bucket.

'Watch this stuff on your bare skin now, Jo.'

I wanted to ask him why we had to do risky things like this with no clothes on, but I knew it would set him off. And I wanted to talk to him about my mum, but I knew that, too, would make him angry.

'Look, hold the bloody cover further up – you're making a right pig's ear of it. Want a job doing properly . . .'

'Do it yourself!' I said louder than I'd intended. I

thought I might have got away with being cheeky because, after all, I was just finishing off his sentence, but he didn't see it like that.

'Get back to the caravan, just clear off!'

It was cold, even though the sky was blue, and although their numbers had dropped with the temperature, a stoic band of nudists were braving the day. I could hear Dad's booming voice calling 'hello' to someone as he walked off in the direction of the nursery. He really loved it at the club, there was a great camaraderie among the members as trenches were dug and saplings planted, roofs fixed and drains unblocked. Outside work and family, Dad made friends easily and I could hear his laughter as I walked back to the caravan. Here, Dad was in his element; he felt free.

Freedom, however, was the last thing that I felt here. I felt trapped, as if I were some strange creature that had been put in a cage to be observed. I thought about the way Terry looked at my naked body and I stamped down the path, trying to understand why Dad and I felt so differently.

Dad rarely talked about himself. It was as though no words could pass easily under that stiff upper lip, but sometimes, when he was in the mood to tell a story, he would talk – usually about the war. I'd heard about how he landed on a beach in Normandy; sick from the swelling sea, he'd run up the beach while his friends were blown to bits around him. And I knew about the execution squad when each man – including Dad – was handed a bullet and, to ease their consciences, they were told that only one or two were real, the rest were blanks.

As I listened to the banter between him and the other men in the nursery, I wondered if that easy talk reminded him of the fellowship in the trenches. It was as if when he dug, planted and worked as part of a team, that was Dad's way of recreating a little bit of his past.

It was no surprise when I got back to the caravan to find Mum fast asleep – I'd noticed more and more that she seemed to isolate herself, lost in her daydream world. And she'd wrap herself in a blanket and sleep for hours. In the confines of the caravan I smelled something familiar, something I'd first smelled way back – in Sussex. I leaned close to her and sniffed the smell of alcohol. I searched around for bottles, evidence, but I couldn't find anything. I wondered what hiding place she must have found.

Why was she drinking so early in the day? But then, drinking made her go to sleep, and if she was asleep she wouldn't have to think about why she was here. I wished I could go to sleep right then and forget about this place and everything in it.

*

That weekend, I did what I could to keep myself to myself. I wanted to be alone. In the months following my initiation to Edendale my hormones had cranked up a little. Everything about me felt awkward. My breasts had started to sprout – earlier than most of the other girls in my class.

'How do they feel?' Sue had asked.

'Hmm . . . dunno really. A bit strange.'

'Let me have a feel.'

'No.'

'Go on . . .'

'Watch out, they're sore.'

I didn't want to be the first in my class to wear a bra. I wanted to stay like my friends, in vests. Mum had given me my first bra, which was white and stiff, constructed from hoops like something you'd make in pottery and just as hard. It was so stiff that it creaked under my jumper. You could hear me coming from the far end of the school playground.

But I wasn't just sprouting breasts, I had also developed a fine down on my underarms and down below.

That early spring weekend at the club, wanting to be alone, I took a walk down the long path, following the tracks of animals through the woods. I walked and walked until I reached the edge of the camp where the hedges were high and double and there were wood and barbed wire fences, then I walked along the whole perimeter, looking for gaps. I knew how a caged wild animal must feel – I felt wild and angry that I had to be here.

I sat down on the cold ground and laid my head on my knees and let the tears come out. Then I began to howl, long and loud like an animal. I cried that my mum might come back to me. And most of all I cried that my dad would just stop bringing us to this place.

I was stiff from being on the ground by the time I got up. There were trees everywhere in this place, their branches joining over my head as if I was still in that cage. It was dark in the wood even though it was bright outside. I'd started to shiver, rubbing my bare body for warmth. Then there was a sharp crack from behind.

'Hello, Jo.'

I turned and saw Terry's teeth, yellow behind his smile.

'What're you doing here all on your own?'

I hadn't ever got used to the way that he always seemed to appear out of nowhere. I stepped back, heard a twig snap under my foot in the empty forest, and shuddered.

'Don't be frightened, I've got something to show you.'

I wondered what he meant. I was naked. I was alone,

far away from the clubhouse and our caravan. I kept still but I could feel my heart thumping. He was carrying something in a bag and reached down, pulling out a shiny camera and holding it up. He handed the camera to me. It glimmered slightly in the dusk.

'Shall I show you how to switch it on?' Terry pressed a button and the camera buzzed and came to life. He showed me how if you touched the zoom button, the lens would extend.

'I wondered if you could help me?'

I looked from the camera to his face.

'I'm making a photo album, sort of a record of life in the camp, and I'd like you to be in it. It's got to be our secret though, as it's a surprise for someone.'

I wasn't sure what to think about that.

'You're not like some of the youngsters here – you're grown up enough not to mind being naked. You've got it right.'

Terry smiled. 'What I want you to do, is to walk through the trees over there, that's all, and I'll take some good shots of you. That's what this place is all about – getting back to nature, so they should look good in the album.'

I noticed that Terry's eyes started to twitch and his face got red. I kept my eyes away from the part down there.

'Shall we give it a try?'

I walked over slowly to where he'd pointed.

'Go on, deeper into the trees, like you're hiding.'

I went right in to where the trees grew close together. The bracken was curled and crispy, the brambles scratched at my legs.

'That's right. Now come towards me, slowly. I want you to look really scared, like a little frightened foal, lost in the woods.'

It wasn't a hard part to act because that's exactly how I felt. Terry was holding the camera to his eye, focussing the lens.

'Come on now, look at the camera, I want to see your face. That's it, your frightened little face.'

The camera clicked and Terry began to zoom in on me. I froze. He started to get cross.

'Stop covering yourself up! You're a little foal, remember? Animals don't cover themselves up.'

I started to feel sick. I didn't want to be here in the woods with this man. I didn't want to be in his pictures. Why was he getting cross with me? I didn't understand.

'Come on, Jo . . . and again. You're walking through the forest, and you look up and see me – that's right, just like that. Now when you see me, you're scared. That's it, that's it. You've got it. Now in a minute you're going to turn and run, you're frightened, you're going to run, run for your life . . .'

All the time he was saying this he kept taking photo after photo. I didn't think you could get so many photographs on one spool. But I guess he must have changed the film and I hadn't noticed.

I saw him look down, all over me. I saw something stirring in the nest of his hair down there. I thought to myself that maybe that was just the way it was lying. I moved back into the dark wood.

'Come back here, where're you going?'

I didn't know – anywhere, away from him. I turned and started to run.

'Hey!'

I ran and ran through those scratching brambles. He shouted after me but I kept running. He was shouting something about it being our secret, how I wasn't to tell anyone, not anyone, not even my mum and dad. I heard him behind me, panting. 'Come back!' he was shouting, but I kept on. He was catching up. I could hear the young trees behind me snapping, and Terry's breath coming in short, rasping gasps. 'Stop!'

I ran until I reached a clearing. I realised my feet were bleeding as I found the path that led down to where I knew my Dad would be digging in the nursery. Then I saw him knee deep in a trench.

'Dad . . .'

'What is it? What're you shouting about?'

The other men looked up from their work. I glanced behind me, but Terry was nowhere to be seen. How could I tell him what had happened? Terry was his friend – he'd never believe me.

Dad thrust his spade down and left it to stand.

'What've you done to your legs?'

'Just brambles . . . I was running . . . playing in the woods.'

'Better get your Mother to see you Jo, don't bother me know, run along to the caravan.'

'I'll just wait here a bit and come back to you when you're ready if that's ok?' I said, hoping he wouldn't ask why.

Dad shrugged and turned his back to his work, heaving great clods of earth and joking with his friends.

I licked my hands and wiped at the scratches on my legs, trying to get my breath back properly, wondering what had just gone on. Terry had told me not to say anything, and I was scared.

It was our secret, Terry's and mine. And I was good at keeping secrets. In my head, sometimes, I imagined it happened a different way – as I did in more recent years when each time I watched *Titanic* I hoped the ship wouldn't go down.

So, in my imagination, I don't go to the woods that day. Or if I do, I tell my dad and he gives Terry a piece of his mind. But I know that it didn't happen that way: I didn't tell my dad. If I had, there might have been a happy ending.

Chapter 17

The young people at the club were referred to as the Rebels and tended to keep themselves to themselves, but it would not be long before I would encounter them properly. Recently, the Rebels, who were a little older than me, had taken to wearing clothes – they were taking a stand which was frowned upon by the adults, especially Terry. I bumped into him in the morning on my way to the toilet block, swinging a towel by his side.

'Hello there, Jo, haven't seen you in a while.'

I was wrapped in a towel, my sponge bag in my hand. He noted my towel and shook his head. I hurried past him with a quick nod, shivering as I passed, and joined the queue inside. It was one of the things I most dreaded, that morning ritual, whatever the weather. There, staring at the damp, tiled floor, people would make small talk:

'Think it's going to brighten up later?'

'Yes, might even be nice enough for a dip.'

'See you around the pool then.'

I stepped into the shower and, standing in someone

else's scum, turned the dial on full in an effort to warm up.

'Don't hog all the water,' someone called through the door. 'Rebels . . .' she added, as though I was one of them.

Then I wrapped my towel tightly round myself and made my way back to our caravan, the water chilling my skin until it was pimpled.

The Rebels' behaviour was to be discussed at the club's AGM, my dad told me.

'What's an AGM?'

'An Annual General Meeting. You ought to come along, it will be good for your education.'

'But I . . .'

'I don't want you getting into any of that silly behaviour,' he said. 'You stay away from that bunch – they need to understand what this place is all about. They don't make the rules and what we do here is nothing to be ashamed of. I don't understand their problem at all.'

I stayed in the caravan whenever possible, playing clock patience and whiling away the hours trying to think of a solution to this horrific weekend ritual but, in all those hours, I never did. I saw Terry walk past and shuddered at the memory of meeting him in the woods. Perhaps it would have made more sense if I'd talked it through with my parents but they were rarely around.

Other than mealtimes, they would be out and about somewhere around the club. And at home, the subject of the nudist camp was just as taboo.

On the day of the AGM, Dad insisted I walk with him to the pavilion clubhouse. When we opened the door, all the chairs had been laid out in rows and people were fussing about where to sit. I sat near the back next to the high desk where you signed in, on which were arranged a collection of *Health & Efficiency* magazines. Waiting for the meeting to start, I leafed through one, looking at pictures of nudists at play with their private parts blocked out by black triangles that, somehow, drew attention to them even more. There were advertisements for naturist holidays and, thinking about that first holiday at the camp in Sussex, I shuddered. I never wanted to go on one of those holidays again.

The magazine was full of all the small issues that filled the naturists' little world, like which beaches they'd been banned from. An article caught my eye about introducing your children to naturism, advising that the best way of getting them to lose their inhibitions was by letting them splash around naked in the pool. I remembered when I was splashing in the pool and how Terry had hoisted me up on his shoulders. Some introduction that was . . . I could see Terry sitting a few rows in front of me and, as though he could sense me looking at him, he turned around and gave me his creepy, yellow-toothed smile. I folded my arms tightly and looked down.

Sid was standing at the front, I knew he was the chairman from that very first day we'd come here when he pushed that wheelbarrow in nothing but his Wellington boots. He was banging a small hammer on an old table. 'Quiet now, can everyone take their seats?'

It felt as if I was back at school except that, rather than just one teacher, a whole row of people were sitting at the front, facing us. Dad told me they were the committee and I had to be quiet now and listen. It was just as boring as school, with people droning on about things like remembering to take their rubbish back home with them. I couldn't get over the way it was all so serious as the committee talked gravely about matters such as not putting too much toilet paper down the loo. They treated every small issue like it was so important; writing notes, asking people to second the motion and then Sid banging his little hammer – it was almost as though they should have been wearing business suits.

When we got to the part about the Rebels, everyone seemed to be talking at once:

'They need to embrace the concept of naturism . . .'

'It's just a phase . . .'

'They shouldn't be ashamed about themselves . . .'

I looked around, noticing that the only one anywhere

near the age of a Rebel was me, and I was only there because Dad had made me go. I wished I had the guts to say that they didn't understand, that it was bad enough coping with growing up even when you had all your clothes on. But I had a sneaking suspicion that even if I had said something, no one would have listened to me.

On the way back to the caravan, Dad and I walked in silence. I glanced up and saw his jaw tighten in his cheek but I knew he would never say anything directly to me about why I wasn't joining in properly at the club. Perhaps he thought that in the end I would just come around to his way of thinking, I wasn't sure.

Mum was asleep when we got back to the caravan.

'What's there to eat?' Dad asked.

Flustered, Mum tried to rouse herself but she fell back on to the bed.

'It's dinner time, why're you still asleep?'

'I was just having a little doze.' Her speech was slurred.

I watched her staggering out of bed and suddenly it all boiled up inside me – being shut away in this place, Mum drinking, Dad shouting, the AGM and their stupid ideas. No one seemed to understand, least of all my parents.

'I'm not hungry.' I hadn't realised my voice would come out as loud as it did.

Dad turned to me. 'You will sit down and have a proper meal, just as soon as your mother here gets around to it.'

'I said I wasn't hungry, and I'm not.'

'Just do as you're told.'

Mum steadied herself on the bed. 'I was just about to boil some eggs, Jo, your favourite . . .'

'I'm not a little girl anymore.'

'Jo?'

'Just apologise to your mother.'

'Why, what have I said?'

'Causing ructions, that's all you do. Now sit down and we'll have a nice meal together.'

I looked from the naked form of my father to that of my mother. 'I don't want to be together. Not stuck here like this in this caravan, in this field . . . I want to go home . . . I want to be with my friends . . . I want to see Sue . . . I . . .'

'JO!'

And my mum was running at me with her hand up. I twisted on the step and was off, running away as fast as I could, the tears hot on my face. I didn't know where I was going, except away, away from everything.

'Let her go,' Dad shouted after me, and slammed the caravan door.

*

Sometimes you reach a point when you stop caring. During the week I was isolated and ignored at school. At the weekend, I was stuck in the club. I was in limbo, between two worlds, not quite sure which way to go. It was a fitting time for me to meet the Rebels. One day, one of them came over to our caravan and knocked on the door. I was too embarrassed to answer it with no clothes on when he was dressed, so I opened a window.

'Yeah?'

'You're Jo aren't you?'

I nodded.

'I'm Peter.' I'd seen him around with the rest of the gang.

'Oh.' I pulled at my hair.

'What're you doing?'

'Nothing much.' I stayed close to the window so he couldn't see down below.

'Why don't you come over to our caravan sometime?'

'No, I . . .'

'Oh come on. There're no adults allowed. We can do what we like.'

I looked at his clothes, understanding.

'OK, maybe I'll pop over. See you . . .' and I shut the window. His clothes were beginning to make me feel uncomfortable.

I decided to take him up on it. I grabbed some trousers

and a jumper and hastily put them on. If I bumped into Mum or Dad I could always say I was cold, or something. I knew the Rebels' caravan was over by the volleyball court, so that's where I headed. I was glad of my clothes because the early spring air was damp and cool in the wood.

As usual, I kept on the lookout for Terry. He was always appearing like a shadow from out of nowhere but on this day he was nowhere to be seen. I passed various people along the way – all of them looked odd to me: an elderly lady, otherwise naked despite the cold, had slung a jumper over her top half – It looked even more indecent somehow, drawing the eye to places it would rather not go; a woman carrying a handbag, like she was going shopping; a man wearing nothing but a cigarette behind one ear, and I realised he had no pocket to put it in. A middle-aged woman sauntered past wearing a cardigan. Another woman, wearing a large pair of pants, her sanitary towel belt clearly visible, said 'hello'.

The Rebels' meeting place was an abandoned, faded-green caravan, propped up on one end by bricks. I knocked softly on the door and Peter opened it. He had a fat, welcoming smile with large lips that shone with spit.

'So you finally plucked up the courage to come?'

Even though he must have only been around fourteen, he had the beginnings of a belly.

'Come in and meet the gang.'

There were four of them. I looked at the boys who I recognised vaguely from seeing them around the club and felt my stomach tighten.

'I . . . I'll come back later.' Ideally when there were some other girls, I thought.

'Oh come on in, don't be daft. We were just going to play a game.'

Thankfully all the boys were dressed. Other than Peter, there was Simon, Roger and Edward. Simon had straight greasy hair and angry red spots. Roger and Edward were even more difficult to warm to: Roger was freckled all over and wore thick glasses that made his eyes boggle. And then there was Edward, who just had a weird look in his eyes that I couldn't quite make out.

The caravan was all at an angle like a crazy house and my steps were unsteady as I made my way to sit down; I tried to smile. It was better in here, with this odd-looking bunch than out there with the hard-core nudists. We all thought the same. We didn't like Edendale. We didn't want to take off our clothes. We were united.

I felt as if I'd come to the right place. We played cards, sang songs and, gradually, I began to feel something that I hadn't felt in a while – a sense of belonging. Things weren't so bad after all. I'd taken a big step forward. I'd started to make new friends. Perhaps not the sort of friends I'd have made if there had been any choice, but friends nevertheless. For the first time since I came to Edendale, I started to relax.

'Let's play something different,' said Peter, and he got out an empty Coke bottle. 'Ever played Spin the Bottle?'

I shook my head. Edward sat and grinned while the others talked all at once, trying to explain how to play. Apparently, whenever the bottle stopped, you had to do a dare or be given a forfeit. I wasn't quite sure what a forfeit was but didn't like to ask.

All eyes moved to Peter and the bottle. He laid it in the centre and began to spin it. Round and round it went in a blur and then started to slow and stopped – at me.

'Ah, unlucky for some.' Peter laughed.

'But not for others, eh?' Simon replied.

I felt my body stiffen.

Simon looked at me and smiled. 'Take off your top.'

I didn't want to. I couldn't do that. I didn't want to take my top off in front of a gang of boys. I shook my head, felt the tears sting at the back of my nose. I wanted to go, except I'd joined in the game so I couldn't back out.

'What the hell are you worried about?' said Simon. 'We've all seen you before. This is a nuddy camp, in case you haven't noticed!' They all laughed. 'If you don't want to do that, then you've got to do a forfeit. What's it going to be?'

'What's the forfeit?' I asked, uncertain.

'Ah, that would be telling now. You've gotta choose. The dare, or the forfeit?'

'Top! Top! Top!' Edward was chanting from the corner, his grin wide.

My heart was pumping. 'I'll do the forfeit.'

'OK then, this is what it is. You've got to kiss one of us. Got that? So pick someone.'

Edward grinned at me. Roger's eyes went round. Peter was the only one who seemed to look away. I didn't like Simon. I pointed at Peter and his fat lips curled into a slow smile.

They were all watching as Peter came over to where I sat and hitched his thumb away at Edward, clearing a space. He sat next to me while I took a deep breath and clenched my teeth closed tightly behind my lips. As he came towards me I tensed, held my breath and closed my eyes. If I could just think of something else, something pleasant . . . This would soon be over, I told myself.

The others watched as Peter clamped me between his arms, fastened his mouth to mine, limpet style, and began. His tongue was pushing at my teeth and his mouth – soft and wet, like glue – was open, sliding all over my face. I struggled for breath as Peter sealed his slimy mouth over mine. Surely he would have to come up for air soon?

But then he pushed me down, using all his weight so I had to lie flat on the settee and then he got on top of me. It was far more than a kiss. His mouth and groin moved together in a slow grinding motion and he grunted as he went faster and faster. I could hear the others laughing. It seemed to go on for ever, as I lay squashed beneath him, taking the full weight of him as he ground away, his hands working their way up my jumper. Suddenly he jerked and his whole body went into spasm. His eyes were dazed as he got up, wiped his mouth and adjusted his trousers.

I sat up, trying to catch my breath. I felt as though I'd been mauled. I wiped my mouth, feeling sick – I couldn't believe what he'd done to me.

Still grinning, Edward reached for the bottle. 'Me next, me next . . .' But I'd had enough. I clenched my fists tight, suddenly I felt so angry – angrier than I could ever remember. As I stood up, I was shaking. Simon tried to block my way as I made for the door.

'Get out of my way!' I pushed him so he went skidding into the wall of the caravan. I burst out of the door with a rage so strong that I could have torn that caravan apart and I ran. People stared at me – stared because in this topsy-turvy mad world I was wearing clothes.

Then there was Terry, appearing as he always did out of nowhere, shaking his head.

'What do you think you're doing? You know all the fuss there's been with you youngsters. Take your clothes off right now.'

'Leave me alone!' I screamed.

I'd found my voice.

Chapter 18

I'd always hoped that my first kiss would be special, not something that would make me feel so bad. I felt something important had been taken away from me but, then, I was to find out that many things would be stripped away from me, along with my clothes, that I wasn't ready to give.

All through the spring, we carried on going to the club. Dad decided that as we had a lovely caravan of our own, we would spend our summer holiday there, as well. I tried to get on with it as best as I could, hanging out in the caravan whenever possible. I didn't want to risk being in the swimming pool or the woods in case Terry turned up, though he seemed to be keeping clear of me since I'd screamed at him. And if I stayed well away from the Rebels, then I wouldn't have to risk playing their disgusting games with that boy kissing me again.

Summer at the club brought with it some new recruits and, for the first time, I spotted a girl about my age. She didn't seem like me at all. She walked around naked like she had nothing to be ashamed of – not clutching a towel trying to hide herself. When she passed by our caravan, she held her head up and her shoulders back. I was amazed by her boldness – the way she strode out wearing nothing but her gleaming white pumps and socks.

I thought I might bump into her at the children's party that was being held the next day. There was no way I was going to be allowed to get out of that one; Mum had already told me that I was expected to go and she and the other women had been busy helping to decorate the pavilion.

On the day of the party, I reluctantly went along. Because it was being held in the evening, we were allowed to wear our clothes. It was mostly just little kids chasing around the centre of the room with balloons – the Rebels sat in a corner, smirking. Then I spotted the new girl and she came over to me straight away.

'Hello, I'm Katherine. You're Jo aren't you?'

'How d'you know my name?'

'I asked your mum.'

Mum was standing in the kitchen doorway with a glass in her hand. It wasn't even seven o'clock. I hoped Katherine hadn't noticed she'd been drinking.

'Can you jive?' she asked, smiling.

I shook my head.

'Come on, I'll teach you.'

And before I could protest, she'd grabbed my hand. It

didn't matter that the music playing wasn't rock 'n' roll, Katherine was swinging me around, showing me how to follow the steps, twirling me under her arm. We spun around and around and I began to forget where I was – it was easier, almost normal, because we had our clothes on. Katherine showed me how I could roll in against her straightened arm, then she'd swing me out quickly until my head went dizzy and I couldn't stop laughing.

At last, I'd made a friend and we agreed to meet up the very next day. I put on the whitest socks I could find and spent ages putting whitener on my pumps.

'Where are you off to?' Mum asked from her bed, her voice thick from a heavy night.

'Oh, just to meet a friend.'

I felt almost happy as I jumped off the top step of the caravan. Now I wouldn't have to be alone anymore – and I was pleased to have met a girl rather than those awful boys. The air was warm and sticky, it was going to be a hot day. Katherine had said she wanted to show me something. She was smiling, leaning by the door of the pavilion as I arrived and immediately grasped my hand.

'Come on, I've been waiting ages.'

I ran by her side, down a path I knew well, deep into the woods. Finally, we reached the end of a tiny covered path and Katherine pulled me towards a green tool shed, abandoned and crumbling.

'Is it safe?' I asked.

'Course it is, silly.'

Katherine climbed the three big steps up to a little veranda and held out her hand to me. Inside was a rowing boat. We climbed in and sat opposite each other. It was a hot morning and the flies buzzed around us as Katherine jotted notes in her diary.

'D'you think anyone could ever find us here?' she whispered.

Suddenly, a bird came swooping past the open door and I flinched.

Katherine leaned toward me. 'Don't be scared . . .' I thought she was going to touch me, she came so close, and then she shot forward, her lips on mine, dry as a leaf. I pulled back.

'I . . .'

'Sorry, I didn't mean . . .'

'I . . . it doesn't matter,' I mumbled awkwardly.

'Do you like girls?'

'Yes . . . Well, no. My best friend is Sue and . . .'

'Oh . . . I see . . .'

The silence hung around us like the flies.

'You don't mind, do you?' Katherine asked.

I looked away, not knowing what to say. Years ago Sue and I would play house, I'd play the wife and she the husband and she'd kiss me on the cheek when she came home from work. But that was when we were very young, I was eleven now and Katherine must have been even older. But we'd never kissed as Katherine had kissed me, not on the lips, not like that. She was just staring at me. I felt I could hardly breathe and I kept my eyes on her socks, so pure and white. We heard a noise:

'Lezzies!' Peter shouted, appearing from the bushes and standing in front of the open shed door. 'We saw you,' and he threw a stick at the roof. The other Rebels soon followed his lead and sticks and stones started flying towards us. Sticks and stones may break my bones but names will never hurt me, I thought as they jeered. Pair of lezzies – that's why you don't like boys!

Katherine held her head high as she got up and made her way down the stairs. The boys looked on and I tried to pretend I wasn't bothered being naked while they were dressed and that they hadn't just seen Katherine and I kissing. And I tried to block out the fact that I'd just been kissed by a girl.

We walked, one behind the other, up the path, the boys calling after us.

'See you,' Katherine said simply. But I never did see her again.

When we were at home, I tried to get on with life as normally as possible. I tried not to think about Katherine, or Peter's horrible kiss, or Terry. I tried, instead, to catch up with Sue but it was hard – my family's weekends at the club meant I'd missed much of what was going on in her life, and I certainly didn't want to tell her what was going on with my life. Added to that, Katherine's kiss was yet another secret I must hide away.

I was going into my final year at primary school and hoped to get a place at the grammar school – that was the one thing dad and I agreed upon. 'You'd better pass your eleven plus, or else . . .' he'd tell me.

Going to the grammar school would be the reward for all the times I'd spent on the stairs, doing those sums he'd set me. I worried a bit that I'd cheated – turning division symbols into plus signs – and wished I'd worked a bit harder. I wanted to wear the navy blazer with its fancy badge, the school motto inscribed in Latin on it and I tried to focus on that ambition. I wondered if going to the grammar school would mean fewer camp visits as I'd have too much homework.

Sue and I hoped we wouldn't end up at separate schools after the eleven plus. Sucking sherbet lemons on our way to school, we'd talk about what we were going to be when we grew up.

'I'm going to have a sweet shop,' I told her, 'with sherbets and toffees and chocolate éclairs in lots of those big glass bottles . . . then we can eat sweets all day, and night if we want to . . . but I'd let people taste them first, so they wouldn't buy those nasty ginger sweets that burned our mouths like last week.'

'Can I run it with you?'

'Course you can.'

Sue kept her eyes on the pavement. 'I know you'll be going off to the grammar. You're really clever and will pass your exams with flying colours. It won't be the same.'

Miss Masters was trying to teach us etiquette.

'Right now, girls, in preparation for your move up to your next schools, we'll be teaching you how to become young ladies.' She frowned as she looked around the room and settled her gaze on me. 'If that's at all possible . . . This is a lesson on deportment.'

'Isn't that when you get sent to Australia, miss?'

'Jo. Now there's a stupid girl. That's being deported. Just pay attention.'

Miss Masters balanced a book upon her head and began to walk around the room. 'This, Jo, is what I mean by deportment. This will make a young lady even out of you.'

I didn't think balancing a book on your head was a very likely thing for a young lady to do, but that's what we all got up from our desks to practise. We were teetering around the classroom, trying to walk like Miss Masters, when Sue whispered, 'Have you ever kissed a boy?' The book on my head wobbled. I didn't want to lie, but neither did I want to tell her about Peter kissing me, and I definitely didn't want to tell her about Katherine.

Sue moved closer so that only I could hear her.

'I met a boy in the Isle of Man, he was lovely.'

I steadied the book on my head. 'Did you kiss him then?'

'Yeah. Why not? What about you?'

I shook my head and the book fell on the floor.

Sue crouched down. 'Go on, Jo, tell me. I bet you did meet someone over the holidays?'

I could feel Peter's slimy mouth stuck to mine. I shivered at the memory. Then I thought of Katherine's kiss, her dry lips hardly touching mine at all.

Sue bit her lip. 'Tell you what, if you want to know what it's like, give your arm over here.'

I stretched out my arm and she puckered her lips and fastened them onto it, sucking and moving her head around.

'You soon get the hang of it, Jo. It feels dead nice, honest.'

I wanted to tell her that I had been kissed and that it hadn't felt nice at all.

Helen looked down at us. 'What are you doing?'

'Nothing,' said Sue, quickly lifting her head.

'Were you kissing her arm?'

'Well, I was just showing her . . . I met this lad on holiday and well, Jo's never kissed anyone.' I looked away. Helen tossed back her hair.

'Oh is that all? I did that ages ago. Did you do tongues?'

Sue looked from me to Helen. 'Eeh . . . don't like the sound of that.'

Neither did I. I'd heard Helen talking about this sort of thing by giving numbers to the various stages of sex: one was kissing, two was with tongues, three was a quick feel, and so on. She said it took weeks to get anywhere with a boy and by that time he'd normally got fed up with the wait and finished with you.

Miss Masters clapped her hands, called us to attention and, standing up straight behind our desks, to repeat after her:

'Perfect posture.'

'Perfect posture,' we repeated.

'Do not slump,' and she slouched forward.

'Do not slump.'

'We must grow up handsome,' and she straightened up.

'We must grow up handsome,' we repeated.

'Hide that hump!' And she pushed her shoulders back.

'Hide that hump!'

Sue and I were giggling by the time we'd finished.

Miss Masters shook her head at me. 'You know, Jo, I don't think we'll ever make a young lady out of you. I wish you would just grow up.'

I didn't want to grow up, not if growing up meant you had to kiss boys and 'do tongues'. I wanted to remain a little girl for ever.

The day of our eleven plus duly arrived. We came into class to find three sharpened pencils placed neatly on each desk and Miss Masters told us there was to be no talking. My stomach did a little flip – I was terrified of doing the exam – if I failed I'd be in so much trouble with my dad. I sneaked a quick look at Sue; she'd gone white. Earlier, I'd said she could copy my answers but now, for the exam, our desks had been put miles apart and, anyway, I was scared of getting the answers wrong.

When Miss Masters said the words 'You may start', I froze completely. I simply couldn't get going. I was terrified of what my dad would do to me if I didn't pass. My chest felt tight and then it was as if everything I'd been bottling up welled up inside me: Dad screaming at me, Mum's empty bottles in the garden and the sickly sweet smell of alcohol on her breath, Terry's yellow teeth and the time he tried to photograph me, Peter's wet lips smothering mine and Katherine's dry lips which barely touched me.

It all poured out and I was sobbing and sobbing all over the exam paper. Sue looked over but she couldn't help me, no one could. I stared at the questions but couldn't focus on the words. Then Miss Masters was looking down at me and I saw her smile. It was just a tiny smile but its warmth flooded through me. She nodded, too, ever so faintly. I'd never thought until that moment that she had any kindness in her, but here it was when I needed it most. Even then, I don't know how I got through that exam but I did, just managing to finish the final question in time.

'You all right?' Sue had asked after the exam. I'd nodded.

'I thought it was scary too,' she'd said, 'but my dad said it didn't matter which school I went to as long as I was happy.'

I wished I had a dad like that. I knew my dad wanted me to be happy; it was just that he found it difficult to show.

'Cheer up,' said Sue, 'it's almost your birthday, remember?'

She was right, there were better things to think about. I didn't want to dwell on the exam with my birthday coming up.

'Please can I have a party, please Mum?' I'd asked.

'I'll have a word with your father, now run along.'

I don't know how she got round him, but she did. All my friends were coming and it seemed the party was all we talked about at school. It wouldn't be on my actual birthday because that was a Friday, and Mum said the party had to be at the weekend. I was glad about that because it also meant there was no danger that we would be going to the club.

On the day of my birthday, Mum woke me really early.

'Jo. How old are you?'

'Eleven . . . er . . . I mean twelve.' And we both laughed. She always did this on the morning of my birthday.

'Happy birthday, my love. Oh, you're so grown up.' And she stroked my hair. I felt a warm tingle inside me.

'Thanks, Mum.'

'Daddy wants to see you before he goes to work,' she said. And the flutter of excitement died.

I was worried that he might have changed his mind about the party – he was always changing his mind about stuff like that – or worse, that he had decided we should go to the nudist camp. I looked out of the window and was pleased to see the rain slanting down. There was a chance . . .

When I went downstairs I was surprised to see Dad smiling.

'Have you been a good girl?'

I nodded.

'Then I've got something special for the birthday girl.'

From behind his back he pulled out a package wrapped in old newspaper.

'Don't believe in wrapping paper, waste of money. But here you are . . . Happy birthday.'

He fumbled with the package. I thought, just this once, that he might kiss me, or give me a little hug, but he didn't. I looked at Mum and she nodded.

'Better open it up on the table, Jo.'

Inside the worn newspaper was the most beautiful wooden box, set on tiny feet with ringed handles on each side. On the front, carved in different coloured woods, were dancing ballerinas.

'Well, open the lid . . .' Dad was smiling now, watching me closely.

When I lifted the lid, music started to play.

'It's *Swan Lake*,' Dad told me, and came to kneel by my side.

As I looked inside the box I gasped, I couldn't believe it, it was like looking into a fairytale world. There, centre stage, was a princess twirling around and around. She wore a white dress, made of real material, with shining gold stars and she stood in golden shoes, balanced on tiptoe, holding one hand above her head and the other on her hip. Behind her, set into the mirrored backdrop of her palace, were six dancing girls, three on each side. I watched her, transfixed, as she danced, her tiny form reflected in the mirror. I had never seen anything so beautiful.

'Well, say thank you!' And Dad laughed.

But I couldn't speak.

'She's overwhelmed,' Mum said. 'Your father there, he made that for you, carved every single bit, even those round handles. Took him forever, working out there in the garage night after night.'

'Yeah, it was one hell of a job. D'you like it?'

I looked at Dad, trying to say the words that stuck somewhere in the back of my throat.

'Thank you,' I managed, eventually. 'It's the best birthday present I've ever had.'

And I meant it.

I wanted to take the music box to school and show it off to my friends but Mum said it was very precious and I must wait and show them all at the party instead. I longed for the day to come quickly.

Next morning, the day of my party, Dad came into my room laughing.

'Come on you, I'm going to take you out for a big surprise – give your Mum a chance to get on with the party.'

We drove into the city and sat in a posh café in a

department store. I sat opposite Dad, with a straight back like he'd taught me, and watched the ladies with tight curls and bright lipstick eating cakes with silver forks.

'Choose anything you want, Jo.'

'Can I have chicken and chips?' It was always chicken and chips.

'Of course you can.' And he reached over and tousled my hair. 'Happy birthday.'

He didn't order anything for himself – he just sat with a glass of water, watching me eat. He'd said he wasn't hungry, and I didn't know, then, that he just didn't have enough money for both of us. He smiled as I ate and I did my best with the large cutlery.

When we got home, Mum helped me into my white chiffon party dress and tied a big pink bow at the back, showing me in her dressing table mirror how pretty it looked. I followed her downstairs to the kitchen and watched her add the finishing touches to a tray of fairy cakes, slicing off the tops, cutting them in half and sticking them, like wings, with butter icing. I touched one with my finger. 'They look like fairy wings, is that why they're called fairy cakes?' And she laughed.

Dad had put the precious music box high up on the pelmet where it would be safe. When my friends arrived, he brought it down and showed it to them. I was so proud that I had a dad who'd made me something like that. Then he put it back while we played pass-the-parcel and sat on balloons until they popped. Dad blew up some long thin balloons – his face going red – and made a sausage dog and a swan, handing them out to my friends who were all screaming for more.

'Who's for musical chairs?' Dad shouted and everyone squealed.

Around and around we went until Mum stopped the music and we scrambled for a seat. There were only three chairs left and I was still in the game, going carefully, watching for when Mum's hand would stop the music. I saw it twitch and we all made a dash for a seat but one of us – I don't know who – caught the curtain. There was a crack, and I saw my music box falling. I rushed to catch it, but too late. There it lay, in pieces, on the floor.

'Bloody hell,' Dad shouted. He looked really upset and left the room as we all did our best to struggle on with the game.

After everyone went home, I gathered up the pieces in the skirt of my party dress and carried them carefully up to my room. The beautiful princess was broken at the feet and I knew she'd never dance again. But when I wound up the box, the music still played. I kept all the pieces in the drawer under my bed but dad never fixed the beautiful box. Something that had been there between us, albeit briefly, had gone forever.

The day after my party we went to the nudist camp and, with that, a new silence that I just couldn't shake spread over me.

Chapter 19

In Warrington, the town we lived in, it was unusual for people to go abroad for holidays. My friends went to places like the Isle of Man, Rhyll or Blackpool, and if you were posh you went to Southport. When I heard we were going to the South of France I was really excited – but I was also anxious that this might be another 'bare it all' kind of holiday.

There was a terrible noise coming from the kitchen and I rushed in to find Dad dropping china plates on the floor.

'What're you doing?' I asked.

'Bouncing plates.'

'But that's one of Mum's favourites, with the pink roses.'

'It's got a chip in it, can't stand chips.'

Mum came in as Dad was just about to drop a cup on the floor. She put her hands to her mouth and I looked from one to the other and shook my head. Now certainly wasn't the right time to ask them what sort of a holiday we'd be going on.

I never actually plucked up the nerve to ask my parents the big holiday question, I wished I was brave enough but the new, silent me couldn't do it. I kept quiet, worried that it might spark off one of Dad's tempers. Mum and Dad kept reminding me how lucky I was to be going to the South of France – other people didn't go abroad for their holidays. Perhaps, I hoped, they didn't have nudist camps abroad? Perhaps it was just a weird English thing?

When we arrived, I saw the houses painted in pastel colours and hung with washing, and I began to relax. This didn't look like the kind of place where you'd find the tall fences of a nudist camp; it looked like an ordinary, bustling town.

It wasn't until we started driving out of town that I began to get that familiar sick feeling. Even though I had no idea where we were going I knew, somehow, what we'd be going to and, when I saw the tall fences and barbed wire around the campsite, my fears were confirmed.

This time, instead of a tent or a caravan we had a chalet. I didn't like the confined space of the chalet – like the caravan, there wasn't enough room to be naked and I needed a wider berth. It wasn't only about claustrophobia, but also about coming into frequent and unwelcome contact with my parents' nakedness. I didn't want to watch Mum, naked, boiling vegetables, I wanted her in clothes with her pinny on top. I didn't want to see Dad, naked, bending to haul gas canisters. It made me feel sick.

I'd pull my hair down over my eyes to screen out what I could. When I had to look at them, I'd maintain steady eye contact. I kept a towel with me whenever I could, though they were miserable little towels that Mum had brought from home but if I held my stomach in they covered my bottom half.

The chalet had a bathroom – so, thankfully, no naked parade at the toilet block. There was a mirror over the hand basin so, however I tried to deal with it, there was no way to avoid the horror of being naked and I was particularly self-conscious about my top half. I remembered how when I was little, Mum used to rub my chest with Vicks before I went to bed – the smell made my head spin – and how it didn't seem rude or odd because my chest was bare and flat. But now, aged twelve, my breasts were developing. They felt so delicate, hurting even to my own touch. I didn't want them on display like produce in a greengrocer's shop. In fact, I didn't want them at all, I wanted it the way it used to be with my mum rubbing Vicks on my flat, little girl's chest.

The good thing about the chalet was that I had my own room with bunk beds. I could hang a towel down from the top one and shut everything else out and just lie with my beloved llama. And I wrote mournful poetry about how I wished I were dead, mouldering in a coffin – probably not the best pastime for a young girl on holiday but I seemed to get some relief from it. I wrote, in code, how I hated my f . . . ing parents for bringing me here, how I wished they were dead too.

After we'd unpacked I looked out of my bedroom window and noticed lots of teenagers and, interestingly, they were wearing their towels. I wanted to join them so I could blend in with my towel on, too. Whenever they walked past our chalet they always seemed to be laughing and they were not at all scary like the Rebels. They actually seemed almost normal.

Perhaps they, too, felt like me? Just dragged here by their parents and forced to get on with it? When it was time to go to the beach, I fixed a towel around my hips hula-hula-style and, with my long hair, I thought I looked a bit like one of those Hawaiian girls. Baring my breasts wasn't too bad as long as I could cover up everything else.

My parents didn't seem to mind that I'd started hanging around the little beach hut where they sold lemonade and, there, it didn't take me long to meet Jan. He was from Belgium and he wasn't the best-looking of boys, but perhaps his saving grace was that he wore a towel all the time and, also, he was older than me.

Jan would sing Beatles songs to me – in one of those transatlantic accents. I didn't exactly fall for him, but he was a distraction from my surroundings here at this dreadful camp.

'Blackbird singing in the dead of night,' he sang with his eyes closed, 'take dees broken vings and learn to fly . . .'

I hoped he'd keep his eyes closed so he wouldn't see me laughing.

One hot afternoon, Jan was walking me back to our chalet through the pine forest and singing softly, out of tune, 'She loves you yeah, yeah, yeah . . .' I hoped he wasn't actually singing that about me. I was warming to him, but only slightly. I suppose it could have been quite romantic, with the sun setting behind the trees and the crickets chirping – except I was with Jan.

He stopped and parted his greasy hair. Then, without warning, he puckered his lips and began to zoom in slowly towards my face. There was no getting away as his lips, the mouth, everything, came nearer and nearer. His lips were slobbery when they came into contact with my dry mouth and I flinched, remembering Peter's kiss in the Rebels' caravan.

'Just try to relax,' Jan coaxed.

My whole body was rigid. I didn't like this kissing thing at all, no matter what Sue had said. It gave me a queasy feeling in my stomach.

After this first attempt he took a step back. 'Open de mouth, like so . . .' and he gaped at me. Having always been a good girl at the dentist, I did as I was told. But I wasn't prepared for what came next. Jan pushed his tongue deep into my mouth. It felt like a wet sausage and the smell of garlic made me want to be sick. I kept trying to tell myself that I should be enjoying this, that this was the way grown-up people kissed and I needed to get used to it.

He stopped and moved his head away again. Using his two index fingers, Jan wound them around each other.

'De tongues go like dis.' He nodded encouragement.

It was a lot to concentrate on, following his tongue as it wound clockwise around and around and trying to hold my breath to minimise the effects of the garlic.

When I pulled away, panting for air, he must have got the wrong impression because he was right back on my face again, stirring away with his tongue. Then, without so much as an introduction, his hand was on my left nipple, grasping it between his finger and thumb. I supposed because my top half was naked he must have thought it was sort of OK. No one had ever touched me like that and I didn't know what to do. His fingers worked with a similar circular motion to his tongue and he twiddled away.

I halted my tongue and froze. I tried to pull away from him, but with just our towels between us, the gear change went from first to fifth in about thirty seconds. I was way behind the others at school on the numbers front but now, without really realising what was happening, I was speeding through them like I was in a Formula One racing car.

Suddenly, it wasn't funny any more. Right next to the path were pine woods. In the twilight it was dark in their midst and all I could think about was what had happened with Terry. Jan led, half pulling me in there. Clouds of flies were feasting on my skin, the smell of pine was like disinfectant and the air in the wood was still, almost clammy. Among the tall pines I felt so very small.

Jan took off his towel and laid it on the ground. My chest felt tight. His penis was pointing upward – I knew it was called a 'hard on', Helen had told us all about that at school, but I hadn't expected it to look so threatening. He pushed me down roughly then he was on top of me – the slobber and the garlic, the 'hard on' penis, the heaving and sweating. His hands were everywhere. I didn't fight but I didn't join in either. He wasn't interested in my mouth anymore. His tongue was elsewhere, all over me like a slithering, searching eel.

I didn't make a sound. In the quiet of those woods, I

just went still, silent. Maybe it was some ancient animal instinct that kicked in – I played dead. I remember the feeling of the life, the energy, leaving my body. I could have been dead, like in the poems I'd been writing, because that's how I felt. Then I started to cry. Not the wailing, angry sobbing that you cry as a child, but a different kind of crying – one with no sound at all.

I lay there feeling dead and lifeless, silent tears running down the side of my face. I was crying for what was about to happen to me, I was crying for my helplessness. I cried because I had no voice. I was just a child, a frightened, helpless child.

I closed my eyes, trying to block out what was happening and, suddenly, all feeling drained from me. I couldn't feel Jan at all. When I opened my eyes he was still there but he'd moved away from me and was staring at my face. He stood and helped me up then handed me my towel. I wrapped it around me tightly. I was starting to shake uncontrollably.

I'll never know why he stopped when he did. I'd like to think that some spark of decency prevented him from raping me but maybe it was just no fun with a limp, lifeless girl.

Jan walked back with me to the chalet where Mum made him a cup of tea and smiled politely when he poured it into the saucer and drank it from the teaspoon.

'What's the matter, Jo?' Mum asked. 'Cat got your tongue?'

I rolled my tongue gently around my mouth, feeling its rawness. I never saw Jan again after that.

Chapter 20

After the experience with Jan, I remained in the darkened chalet as much as possible. I hated sunshine and everything it stood for – beaches and sea, suntan oil and bare skin. I hated people who thought that just because you were naked, it didn't matter how they behaved. And I hated being naked because it felt as if you had nothing at all to protect you. I would never understand why my parents wanted to lie in the sun all day with no clothes on. I wanted to stay in the chalet, in the dark. I didn't want anyone to see me naked, even if that was how God had made us.

I held on tight to my llama, grating its rough fur on my bare skin. I wouldn't go out in the sun; I liked it here in the shadows.

A few days later, Anthony arrived at the camp, his appearance heralded by the sound of high revs from his motorbike. From the first moment he introduced himself to us, I could see that Dad admired him – it was almost as though Anthony was the kind of man Dad had always wanted to be, driving around the Mediterranean on his big shiny bike, picking up a girl here and there – whenever he fancied.

'He's a free spirit,' my dad said. And I was soon to find out exactly what that meant.

Anthony was younger than my parents – but still a proper adult to me. I suspect Mum and Dad were flattered by his friendliness towards them. For Anthony, making friends with a couple who happened to have a young daughter was just fine.

Very quickly he seemed to become great mates with my dad in particular. He'd take Dad off on the back of his bike and they'd come back roaring with laughter. Anthony got into the habit of bringing round a bottle of wine in the evenings, pouring it into plastic cups and laughing, as he joked about me knocking it back in one. I tasted it once, but hated it.

Dad raised his glass to him. 'Cheers!' he said as he went to get some nibbles to go with the drinks.

'Bottoms up,' Anthony said, and gave me a sideways wink.

Anthony told us stories about his travels and his conquests and Dad howled with laughter, now and again, Anthony would break off and compliment me.

'What a beautiful young daughter you have. What wonderful hair.' And whilst Mum and Dad were busy getting plates and cutlery ready, he'd run his fingers through my hair, feeling its weight, putting his nose right in and breathing deep. Flicking it up and bringing it round to the front then stroking it down over my breasts. He smelled of stale wine and cigarette smoke. I didn't want to upset Dad by telling him that I didn't like Anthony's visits as I could see how much they liked each other.

So, Anthony would turn up with his bottle of wine just as the sun was setting and just when Mum was cooking supper. He'd stay, of course, and they'd all end up drinking – Dad's voice would grow louder and Mum's speech would slur as they knocked back glass after glass. After he'd been round three nights running I told Mum that I didn't want to stay up late with them anymore. Despite the fact that eating with the adults was supposed to be a holiday treat, it wasn't one I was enjoying.

'Don't be so miserable,' she said. 'We're on holiday.'

I couldn't tell her about the way he looked at my breasts or that, sometimes, when she and Dad weren't looking, he would lean over me and his hands would linger just a little too long on the inside of my thigh. Anthony knew, and I knew, what he was up to. And I knew that it wasn't right but I didn't know how to broach it with my mum. I wanted to tell her but I'd never talked to her about boys, or anything like that. She'd told me, of course, never to let a boy touch me 'down there'.

But Anthony wasn't a boy, or even a teenager, he was grown man who ought to know better – and he was my parents' friend. My memory went back to Terry and I got the same awful doubt. I wondered if I was just imagining some of the things Anthony was doing. One day in particular, when Dad went off to find a map, Anthony lifted me up under my arms and swung me around – spinning me until my head was dizzy and I didn't know where I was. Then he just dropped me on the floor. It was so much worse because I wasn't wearing anything.

Whenever he came near me my stomach heaved but, I thought, surely it must be OK as Anthony was open about everything – it was as though he had nothing to hide.

'How about if I take Jo out for a ride?' he said to Mum and Dad. 'What d'you think?'

'Just be careful how you drive now . . .' Mum began.

Anthony flashed me his smile. 'Ever been on a motorbike, Jo?'

I shook my head, meaning I didn't want to go, but he got it all wrong.

'Oh, we'll soon sort that one out.'

And I thought, well, at least I'd be able to put my clothes on.

'I'll have her back in no time. Then you're next.' And he pointed to Dad. 'We'll be back in twenty minutes.'

Anthony hurried off to fetch his bike and I was soon bundled on to the back. Giving his big smile, he waved at my mum and dad.

'Back in a jiffy,' he said to Dad and revved up the engine.

Dad slapped the side of the bike. 'Go on, Jo, off you go.'

We followed the wobbly beach road to the camp entrance then turned onto the narrow coast road. 'This'll put the wind in your hair,' said Anthony, then he threw back his head and laughed.

My hair was whipping around my face and he reached behind to pat my thigh.

'I can't see you under there,' he shouted over his shoulder. We took bend after bend and I had no choice but to cling on to Anthony for dear life.

'Hold on to me tighter if you're scared,' he bellowed excitedly.

'Please, slow down, I feel really sick.'

He revved even harder and my stomach lurched as the force almost made me lose my grip and fall off.

'Let's watch this baby really go,' he shouted.

Then, with one hand he reached behind and squeezed my thigh, sliding his hand up and down.

'I want to go back now,' I screamed.

'You're not frightened are you?'

I wished I could find the words to say I was frightened of him, much more than the fast bike.

'I think we'd better go back, my mum and dad will be worried.'

'Oh they know you're safe with me . . .'

When we finally got back to the chalet I felt sick deep inside, but it was from total, crushing fear.

'Think I'll go and have a little lie down,' I said to Mum and Dad.

'She just loved it,' Anthony told them, 'except I think she's had quite enough excitement for one day . . .'

The following day, knowing my parents were on the beach and that I would therefore be alone in the chalet, Anthony popped round.

'Yoo-hoo, anyone in?'

I fixed my hair so it was covering the top of me and checked my towel was wrapped tightly round my waist, 'Coming . . .'

He was leaning back on the veranda rail, smiling. I found it bad enough seeing people with no clothes on but with him it was worse, it was as though he wanted me to look at him naked, with his chest all puffed up like he was showing off.

'How are you today, my lovely?'

I hated it when he called me that: I wasn't his lovely and never wanted to be.

'Saw your mum and dad on the beach,' he added in his phoney posh voice. 'Told them I'd just look in to check you were all right.'

He stroked down his chest hair that grew to a 'V' below his stomach and I tried not to look. Then he smiled and came close to me and I caught a whiff of cigarettes.

He puckered up his lips, 'Where's my hello kiss?'

I didn't want to kiss him, particularly as he seemed so pleased with himself. It made me recoil in horror. I felt so awkward but he was leaning right towards me and I started to feel scared so I went along with it. I didn't want to upset my parents and I didn't want to upset him.

He licked his lips. 'What d'you do in here all day on your own?'

'Nothing much.'

Then he gasped. 'Wow! Stop there, just a moment . . . wow . . . I just love the way the sun catches your hair . . . it's like spun gold.'

He came towards me and started to stroke his hand

down my hair. I moved back: he was doing that trick again and feeling my breasts underneath.

'Please . . . I . . .'

'Sorry, Jo, it's just that, well, you're so lovely, anyone ever tell you that?'

'No . . . I . . . er . . .'

'Oh, look at you going all red, you're so sweet.'

'Look, I've got to get on.'

'Only on one condition . . .' and he puckered up his lips again.

I dreaded him coming round the next day with his stupid chat and his overpowering smell of his cigarettes and his searching hands. I didn't know what was worse: going naked to the beach with my parents, or staying in the chalet hoping that Anthony wouldn't come looking for me. I decided to go to the beach.

Mum and Dad lay stretched out in the sun and I sat a little apart from them, watching a little girl making sandcastles with her dad. It didn't seem so long ago that I used to play on the beach – those were the days when we had normal holidays. I remembered one particular cold holiday in England and how Dad wouldn't let me have the towel to keep warm. 'We have to take a photograph,' he said. 'You can't have a towel around you in a photograph, it isn't right for a holiday snap.' It was ridiculous, but he snatched the towel away from me, even though the wind peppered my legs with sand and the rain poured. My swimming costume was wet and stuck with sand. I could feel it grate on my skin as I crouched by my sandcastle, shivering.

That sandcastle had been my pride and joy, I'd worked on it throughout the wet, windy afternoon, fashioning a moat and a drawbridge, then decorating it with shells I'd found on the beach. I'd made four perfect turrets using my upturned bucket and – the best bit – I'd watched Dad spiral the towers into points, running wet sand through his fist. Inside the window, he'd placed a princess, modelled from a piece of silver paper. She looked out at the empty expanse of beach, waiting. I felt like the princess in that tower. Mum had read me stories about the prince, how he would come one day on a great white horse and carry me far away.

Until lately, I had no idea I would look back on those cold beach holidays with any fondness because I had no idea I'd be taken on holiday to nudist camps which would make anything else seem like paradise.

The following day I couldn't face the beach so I shut myself in the chalet, worrying whether Anthony would turn up. There was nowhere for me to hide. The day passed without any sign of him, and when Mum and Dad came back from the beach I was looking for an excuse to go to bed before his evening visit.

'I feel sick,' I tried in a weak voice.

'That's because you stay in here all day!' Dad shouted. '"Them's that lie abed die abed."' It was one of his favourite phrases. 'There's nothing wrong with you – you're not sick.'

But I was sick, I was sick of Anthony singling me out. That evening, he arrived at the chalet even earlier than normal. My parents were in the kitchen making supper with the door open. He seemed quieter than usual.

'I've got some bad news, Jo.'

'Oh?'

'I've got to go away soon.'

I almost smiled.

'Going to miss me?'

I shrugged my shoulders – I didn't know what to say.

He rubbed his leg. 'Come on here and give me a cuddle.'

He was sitting in that way that some men do, with their legs wide apart and it was awful because he had no trousers on. I tried to look away from where his penis hung down between his legs.

'Come on, beauty.'

'Sorry but I've got to get going.'

'Ah, shunning me again. My poor, poor heart,' and he gave the kitchen a double check, just in case anyone was watching.

'No . . . I . . .'

'Come on then and give me a little kiss.'

He grabbed hold of my hair and pulled, this time his mouth was slightly open. I knew what that meant and I also knew that my parents couldn't see what was going on. I tried to push him away and he laughed. I couldn't wait to excuse myself and shut myself back up in my room. Before I got into bed, I washed round my mouth with soap and a flannel and dried it on a hard towel.

It felt as if we'd been in the South of France for ever. I'd been counting off the days and they were going very slowly. It was late afternoon and I felt almost relaxed there in my little room writing my diary. Then I heard Anthony's deep voice.

'What're you doing cooped up in here all alone again?'

'I'm . . . Oh, never mind.' I'd been writing in my diary about how disgusting he was. Maybe I should just give it to him to read then he might not bother me anymore. There were some things I could write that I could never quite say.

'You'll never get all sunkissed there in the shade, Jo. Come on out here.'

I didn't want to join him outside.

'Come on, don't be shy, I won't bite you . . .'

I wrapped my towel around my whole body and ventured out. The towel was so tight that I was worried about it pinging open so I kept my arms clamped down by my sides to keep it in place. Anthony had his hands around the top beam of the veranda and was doing pull-ups. I couldn't help noticing that his muscles bulged and his penis twitched as he moved up and down. I didn't want to notice things like that – I thought he was disgusting. He looked at my towel.

'Aren't you hot in that?'

'No.'

'You should be splashing around in the ocean. Anyone ever tell you, you look like a mermaid with all that lovely long hair?'

I shook my head. But I thought to myself, my dad used to call me his little mermaid, and even though we hadn't been getting on I wished Dad was here right now so I wasn't on my own.

'You're going to be a real beauty when you grow up.'

I didn't want him saying things like this to me.

'Can you fetch me a nice cool drink, darling?'

The best I could do was from a carboy that had been left in the sun. It was difficult because I was worried about my towel coming off, then, as I bent down, that's exactly what happened. Even though I snatched it back up, he'd seen.

'Don't know what you're so worried about, beautiful little thing like you.'

'I have to get going now,' I told him.

'Come off it, Jo, it's nothing I haven't seen before.'

'I said I'd meet Mum and Dad, they might even be coming back for me.'

'I'll walk with you.'

He stayed close to me as we walked to the beach and I struggled to stay covered by my small towel. The sun shone hot on my head as we trudged through the deep sand and I felt dizzy. Anthony's fingers brushed my arm – it could have been by accident, but it made me feel awkward. As we came close to the beach, he turned: 'Have to bid you adieu, I'm afraid.' And before I knew it, he'd kissed me, and this time I could feel the wetness of his mouth.

After he left, I doubled back and headed for the chalet. I didn't want to spend the day on the beach with my parents. Inside the chalet it was quiet and smelled of warm wood. I lay on the bottom bunk, staring at the wooden slats above me, counting them, filling my head with numbers so I wouldn't think about Anthony. Some people – some men, I thought – seemed to go to these nudist camps for something more than fresh air on their bare skin.

I shuddered and slid under the cool cotton sheet. All I

wanted to do was go home, but even there it wouldn't stop, I'd still have to go to the nudist camp at weekends. If only I could be someone who had conventional problems – like, who wasn't speaking to them that day at school? Or why that boy they liked didn't feel the same way about them?

I stayed in the chalet all afternoon but it didn't feel safe any more. There was no lock on the door – in this wretched place all the nudists trusted each other.

When Mum and Dad came back from the beach I was still in my bedroom.

'Where's your daughter?' I heard Dad shout.

It was always 'your daughter' when I was doing something he didn't approve of, like somehow it was Mum's fault.

'There's nothing I can do with her,' I heard Mum say in that pious way like she was about to break into a Hail Mary.

'Get her out here!' Dad began.

'I can't, she's just at that age . . . You know.'

'No I don't know, but one thing I do know is that she will get out here and enjoy this holiday. Breaking up the family, that's what she's doing. Get her out here right now, or I will!'

Mum came into my room.

'I've got a headache,' I told her.

'Your father wants to see you.'

'I know, I heard what he said.'

'Come on, Jo . . . please?'

I followed her out. Dad had his back to me.

'Now look here, young lady, you will do as you're told and be sociable. Go and help your mother.'

Mum cooked a nice meal and made a real fuss – we had a starter and pudding, too. Plus the table was set with a cloth and the knives and forks were all shiny. This time when Anthony came round I was determined not to stay up while they drank wine. I didn't care what Dad had said. I couldn't stand the way Anthony acted as though there was something special between us. After our meal I shut myself away again in my room. I didn't want to see that slimy man ever again. If I stayed in my room then maybe he'd get the message.

'Going so soon?' he'd asked with a fake sad look on his face.

'I'm tired.' And I was tired, tired of it all, tired of the fact that my parents brought me to places like this and seemed to have no idea what was going on.

'Where's my goodnight kiss?' he joked. I knew he couldn't push his luck as Mum and Dad were there. I lay there in bed listening to the sound of their voices on the veranda.

I was in a half sleep when I was woken with a kiss. I

knew it wasn't my dad because he never kissed me; he never even kissed me goodnight. I didn't realise that's what fathers did until I'd stayed the night with Sue. Her dad came into her room, tousled up her hair and kissed her on the cheek. He joked that if I didn't go straight off to sleep he'd kiss me too. I lay quiet in the dark, thinking about my dad, wondering what I had done wrong, as Dad never seemed to want to kiss me.

Once, I tried to kiss him goodnight. I walked up and leaned against the rough fabric of his armchair and popped a quick kiss on his cheek. He moved back, almost as though he'd been stung. I didn't do it again.

In bed in the chalet I started to wake up. 'That you, Mum?' Then I felt another kiss, this time it was wet. The smell of alcohol and tobacco rose around me as I opened my eyes. I knew it was Anthony.

'I missed my goodnight kiss. Shush. I've come to tuck you in.' He smiled, his teeth shining out in the semi-darkness.

I felt the muscles in my stomach tighten.

'You know you really are a gorgeous little thing. D'you know that?' He stroked my hair. 'Now come on and give me a little night-night kiss.'

I didn't want to kiss him. Not here, on my own, in bed. I could hear my dad talking loudly. Anthony cupped my face firmly between his hands and planted a long wet kiss on my lips. He didn't use his tongue like Jan. I had my mouth and my teeth firmly clamped together so maybe he could feel that I was shutting him out. I knew about men and their tongues. When he stopped I wanted to call my dad, except that I knew I was doing something wrong, that somehow it was my fault. I knew I'd encouraged him. I didn't know how, but I had.

'You little tease. Come on!'

Anthony's hands were under the bedclothes, pulling and pulling at my nightdress. He looked quickly over his shoulder and unzipped his trousers; then grabbed my hand in his and curled it around his penis.

'You like that don't you?'

I was twelve years old. I'd never touched a man's penis before and I didn't like it. Helen had told me that men liked you to hold them like that but I thought she meant you did that through their trousers. Anthony had his head sort of back and was moaning with strange deep sounds that made me shiver. He held my hand tightly over his penis and it started to inflate like a balloon, and then it was out, way out of his trousers. Due to the drop in temperature most people wore normal clothes once the sun went down. He was all hot and sweaty, he had his tongue out and started to lick my neck.

'That feel good?'

I wanted to tell him 'no', but I couldn't form the

words. He was half on top of me and I was trapped in the cage of my little bunk bed. He was panting and grunting and I was shaking so much that I couldn't stop. I felt the tears coming up and I felt sick. I was holding my breath. I wanted my mum and dad, except what would they do? I couldn't shout out for them because somehow all this was my fault. What would my dad do if he found me like this?

Anthony kept his hand gripped firmly over mine as he rubbed faster and faster in a magic lamp kind of way – until, suddenly, I heard a glass smash and Mum rushing round, slurring her words as she shouted at Dad not to worry, that she'd clean it up. That must have scared Anthony, as he stopped suddenly and quickly, stepped back and zipped up his trousers.

He didn't say a word to me as he turned and went back to the little party on the veranda, winking as he closed the door. I ran to the bathroom, switched on the tap and rubbed my hands underneath it, waiting for the water to go scalding hot to burn away where I'd touched him. Then I washed the tap where my hands had been. I scrubbed and scrubbed, trying to rub him all off me. I could hear him laughing out on the veranda. I couldn't understand how he could laugh like that after what he'd just done, like it was all some big joke.

I went back to my room and looked at the twisted

sheets on my bed and felt sick. I couldn't face getting back in, so picked up my llama and climbed the small ladder to the top bunk. I lay awake trying not to think of what had happened. I told myself that Anthony was going away and that I would never have to see him and his stupid smiley face again.

Chapter 21

Anthony was leaving the next day, then there were only a few more days to go before we would leave this horrible camp ourselves. At least I'd be rid of him. Dad had been talking about how he was going to have a little surprise dinner for him, then no more Anthony. I closed my eyes – I'd have the rest of the day to myself before all that stuff began again, with the drinking and Anthony's wandering hands.

I couldn't tell Mum or Dad what Anthony had done to me. I could hardly believe it myself and it wasn't the kind of thing I could just drop into polite conversation.

'Oh by the way, I forgot to tell you something . . .'

Their eyes on me.

'That friend of yours – Anthony – put his penis in my hand and made me rub it.'

I thought about leaving them a note about it but I just couldn't bring myself to tell them. But I wrote it in my diary in code. My diary was getting pretty full now – I flicked back through the pages, thinking about everything that had happened to me since we'd started going to these nudist camps. I wondered what I would have written about if none of that had happened. What would it have been like to be a normal child who didn't have to keep secrets shut away in a book? And then my stomach knotted up and my fists went tight. I felt a heat burn through me and began to shake.

I stood up and threw my diary across the room. Why couldn't I just be someone else? Anybody else but me. I picked up my llama by the neck, it was just a stupid toy, no comfort at all. Slowly, I dug my nails into one of its eyes, pulling and pulling the wire from its socket. I wrenched and twisted it until it snapped. Then I grabbed at the other glass eye and did the same and I threw the eyes on to the floor. I looked at llama's face. 'There,' I said. And something inside me broke. What had I done? I searched the dusty floor for those glass eyes, promising that I'd put them back, saying that I didn't know why I'd done it, that I was sorry. I didn't know I was howling until Mum came in.

'Jo, what on earth's the matter?'

If only I could tell her what their new friend had done then maybe she could make it go away.

'Jo, please . . .' and she came towards me, naked.

'Go away,' I snarled. 'Why don't you just get back to your bottles?'

I felt the slap almost before she'd done it. She'd missed

my cheek and got me just over my eyebrow. My eyes started to water but I wouldn't cry, not now, not ever.

'I hate you.' And at that moment I really believed I did.

I stayed in my room after that. Mum and Dad didn't even ask me if I wanted to join them. The last thing Dad called through the door was, 'Don't forget we're having a little farewell dinner tonight for Anthony, so this better be all forgotten about by then.'

I didn't see Anthony all day but in the darkness of the chalet I waited, terrified in case he came over for one of his little visits. All day I sat with my llama on my lap thinking about how I hated him. And my mum. And my dad.

I got into bed and pulled the covers over my head. If I could just go to sleep and never wake up again, everything would just stop. All of it.

When Anthony did arrive in the evening it was as though nothing had happened between us.

'Hello everyone!' Then turning to me, 'How's my lovely today?' Then came that smile. That beaming, nauseating smile and he bent down and kissed me. I felt sick at the thought of what he'd done to me the night before but I didn't want my parents to get suspicious about why I didn't like him. So I let him kiss me, I pretended I didn't mind. It was just another lie and I was getting used to those.

Anthony laughed as he picked me up from the veranda and swung me around. I wriggled out of his grip but then he picked me up by one arm and one leg, as you would a small child, and he was spinning me around and around. I was trying, desperately, to keep my legs together.

'Dad,' I screamed. 'Mum, Dad?' But they were laughing with him. In their eyes, Anthony could do no wrong.

He had bought a bottle of wine for Dad, some perfume for mum and some sweets for me – as goodbye presents. The sweets were in a big jar with bright, shiny wrappers with French writing on the side and they tasted overpoweringly sweet and artificial. I thought it was weird him buying me sweets given what he'd made me do. I couldn't help thinking about how Mum had always said you should never accept sweets from strangers.

I couldn't face the meal Mum had cooked and, anyway, she still wasn't speaking to me after our fight. Looking at Anthony made me feel sick and my food kept getting stuck in the back of my throat. I chewed and chewed, and I couldn't stop thinking about the way he'd made me hold his penis and rub it. Then I coughed, the food in my mouth was making me gag but I just couldn't swallow it, not with Anthony there, watching me and smiling. I wasn't sure if I'd imagined it but I could have sworn I felt his foot brushing my leg.

I watched Mum and Dad start bickering about who would do the washing up.

'Eat up, Jo,' Anthony whispered to me. 'I like a girl who's well nourished.'

I had a dreadful urge to pick up my plate and throw it all over his shining white shirt.

To go with the meal, Dad had proudly presented some wine he'd found locally but it tasted as sour as vinegar. Mum had already been drinking it in the kitchen but she held out her glass for more.

'Come on, Jo,' said Anthony, 'why don't you try some? All children drink in France, you know.'

Dad tipped some into my glass. The only way I could drink it was with my tongue curled up, knocking it back quickly. Very soon, I started to feel very queasy.

'May I be excused?'

My father scowled at me. 'Where d'you think you're going?'

'I'm really tired, think I need to go to bed.'

'But Anthony is our guest. It's rude to leave the table before we've finished.'

I looked around at the empty plates.

My dad saw what I was doing and added: 'There's coffee . . .'

'I really don't feel like any, I'm tired.'

Dad pushed back his chair so it made a terrible

screeching noise. 'I do apologise, Anthony, for my extremely rude daughter. And this your goodbye dinner, too.'

I stood up quickly, 'Goodnight.' And rushed to my room before Anthony tried to give me a goodnight kiss. 'But you haven't said goodbye to me,' he called, as I ran off.

I settled down in bed and kept my eyes on the door and pulled the covers well up under my chin. I could hear Dad telling one of his stories, and everyone was laughing.

I tried to get to sleep, counting the slats on the bed above me, again. The dinner was becoming particularly raucous; the wine was obviously going to their heads.

Listening to the chatter, I waited for the deep swell of sleep to overwhelm me. I could hear the clink of glasses, the boom of my Father's laughter. Then the voices grew fainter as I fell into sleep and silence.

I woke up slowly, not sure where I was or if I was still asleep. Then I smelled something familiar. A smell that made me hold my breath but I didn't know why. I was trying to remember where I'd smelled it before and my stomach was tensing. Then I recognised it – cigarettes. I felt a hand on my mouth, hard on my face, squashed up against my nose. I struggled beneath it.

'Are you going to miss me?'

I shook my head, writhing under his grip.

'Just do as you're told and you won't get hurt.'

Anthony's hands were all over me: under the bed-clothes, up my nightdress – strong hands that squeezed and rubbed. 'You like that, you little whore.'

I struggled to wake myself up but the truth was I wanted to slip into oblivion; it was easier. It was dark so I couldn't see what he was doing, but I could feel it. I couldn't call out for my parents because what would they say? Anthony was above me, he was all around me and he was strong.

He held one hand back as though he was going to hit me. 'Open your mouth!' Then he knelt down on the bed. I thought he was going to kiss me like men did with their tongues and I was frightened of him so I did what he said. It made no sense, but I worried he was going to call my dad and then he would find out how bad I'd been. I thought Dad would blame me for Anthony behaving like this and I'd be punished. I hoped, if I just did what he said, then maybe Anthony would go away.

I heard the sound of his zip and his belt buckle being undone. He held my mouth clamped open and suddenly his penis was right in my face. I struggled to push him away and managed to close my mouth. Then, with his hand prising open my top lip, he held my nose between his finger and thumb. I couldn't breathe. When I opened my mouth for air, he kept it open. I didn't understand what was going on, and my mind was racing. Suddenly, when I thought my mouth couldn't open any wider, he shoved his penis roughly inside and slowly pulled my mouth shut.

'Close your lips.'

I did as he said.

'Watch your teeth now, no biting.' Then he was right in, pushing.

I gagged. I had no idea he was going to do this. His penis was burning and it kept hitting the back of my throat. I didn't have any choice as he had both hands on my face, holding tight. He was pushing himself deep into my mouth. 'That good?' He moved his penis in and out, in and out, each time pushing my head deep into the pillow. This was far worse than Jan and his garlic French kissing, far worse than Peter and his slobber, far worse than when I'd had to touch Anthony last night. This was something else entirely.

Every time he pushed his penis to the back of my throat, it touched a part that made me want to be sick. My eyes were watering and stinging. I couldn't breathe. Again and again he thrust. He watched me as he moved in and out, one hand made into a fist. He was groaning now, he closed his eyes, his hands moving down over my body. He started to push my nightdress up roughly, touching me all over as he did.

It would have been easy to just clamp down my teeth

and finish it but it didn't work like that at all. It was the revulsion that stopped me biting him, the shock and fear of what was happening to me as I tried to convince myself this couldn't be real, tried to keep my mouth open and away. The struggle, for breath, for air, for life.

I was so scared. Scared of him, scared of my dad finding us. Then I heard a noise from outside the door – it sounded like someone was approaching.

Anthony pulled quickly out of my mouth, wincing as he scraped himself against my teeth. He froze for a moment and I saw my chance. I'd heard about how you could hurt a man by going for his balls. Quickly, I made my hand into a claw shape and went for him, squeezing as hard as I could, feeling the fragility of it.

I let go as Anthony reeled backwards, his mouth opening and closing soundlessly. I watched his mouth form a silent scream. Anthony zipped himself up and moved away, darting out of my room and down the corridor just as Dad must've been coming to check on me. I heard voices:

'What are you pacing around here for?' Dad asked Anthony. 'The bathroom is the other way.'

Anthony gave a hollow chuckle, 'I reckon I've had too much to drink. I totally forgot where I was,' he said.

Dad knocked on the door, 'You OK, Jo? Stopped sulking? Your mother and I wondered if you wanted to come back to the table and join in?'

'Yeah, I'm fine,' I said as I swallowed again, trying to get rid of the disgusting burning sensation at the back of my throat. 'I'll stay here. I'm just nodding off.'

I heard Dad sigh. 'Oh please yourself then. Can't say we didn't try.'

I held my breath as I waited for the footsteps to fade completely and then staggered to the bathroom just in time. I could hear the adults outside, laughing and joking. I was sick over and over again, until there was nothing left inside me. I retched and retched at the thought of what he'd done.

Mum knocked softly on the bathroom door. 'You OK Jo?'

My silent tears fell. 'I'm sick, that's all.'

'You know, I thought you were looking a little bit peaky at dinner.'

I looked at the yellow bile at the bottom of the toilet, thinking how I'd got rid of him, but no matter how many times I was sick, I couldn't get rid of what he'd done to me.

*

I was shivering when I got back into bed, finding my llama and holding it tight. I was glad my llama was blind now and couldn't see me. I felt dirty. I kept telling myself that I hadn't been raped, and so I could cope with it. Mum said if a man had done that to you, you were spoiled for ever, and no one would ever want you. But I wasn't spoiled, was I?

When I got up next morning, the dishes had been washed and put away and the small kitchen smelled of pine cleaner; there was no trace of last night's dinner. I sat in silence at the table looking at my hard-boiled egg. Mum's face was swollen and her eyelids were drooping.

'Are you still feeling ill, Jo love?'

I couldn't speak.

'Your mother asked you a question. Now listen here, young lady, in my book, if someone asks you a question at least you should have the decency to reply.' He turned to Mum. 'See how she is? She's been nothing but trouble since we got here. I don't know why I bother.' And then, to me, 'Get out of my sight.'

Anthony had gone. It was almost as though he'd never been there at all.

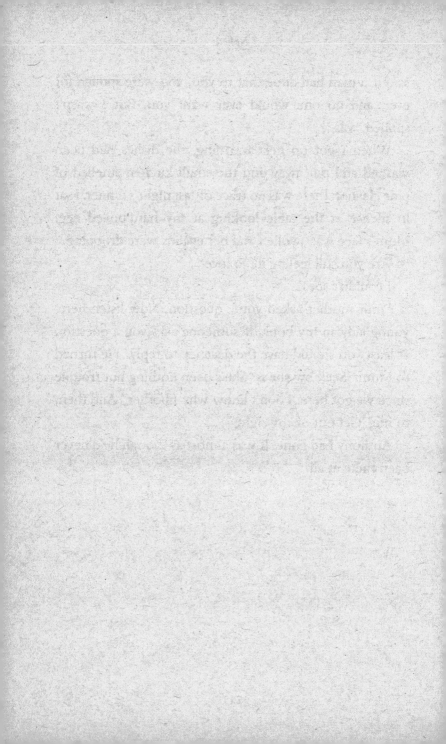

Chapter 22

Over and over again I told myself that I was lucky, that some other girls were far worse off than me. It was just that he'd . . . And I could never quite finish the thought. I knew that even though he hadn't pushed himself into 'that part' of my body, he'd still got inside me. I could feel the horror of him in my mouth, the way he'd grabbed my hair, his head back, teeth gritted.

It was like something hurting underneath my skin that seemed to burn from the inside out. It wasn't only about the pain of his rough hands on my hair, or the way he'd held my nose to keep my mouth open, or even the painful choking as he'd thrust himself in and out of my mouth. It was also the way he'd pushed in against my will – pierced me, put something inside me that I didn't want – and the weakness I'd felt when he did it. He'd taken something away from me. He'd left me with a memory I could never get rid of. No matter how many times I rinsed him out, I could never get rid of the bitter taste.

When I felt I was going to cry about it, my tongue

acted like a brake on my tears. Every time the memory of what Anthony had done welled up inside me, I'd push my tongue firmly behind my front teeth and, even when it wobbled, even when it juddered in my mouth with my whole body shaking, I could bite down hard on it until the pain blocked everything out.

Men's private parts were something I didn't want to think about. As far as I was concerned they were to be kept zipped up in their trousers. The worst thing was that I felt guilty about what had happened with Anthony. Guilty because somehow it was my fault I'd let him do that to me. There was anger too: when I thought about what he'd made me do I'd boil up inside. Thoughts of him would pop into my head at inappropriate moments and I'd find myself wiping my hand on my skirt, or feel bile rise into my throat and, when the tears stung, I'd open my eyes wide and focus on a point in space, forcing them to dry rather than shed them.

Anything might start me off, even something like the way Mum sometimes smiled – sweetly – would make me snap. She might, for example, be bringing me a plate of chocolate biscuits if I was refusing to come downstairs from my room.

'I don't want a biscuit,' I'd growl.

'I just thought . . . Sorry.'

I knew she was sorry. Then she'd do the smile. I hated that weak, subservient smile – the one that was there whenever Dad told her it was time to pack up for the weekend.

Mum called my mood swings my 'teenage tantrums', and even though I wasn't a teenager I understood a lot about those. The helplessness of wanting to be a grown up yet having to leave the child behind.

I missed my special times with my mum – sitting on her dressing table stool while she brushed my hair or watching her peel a potato man just for me.

Since we'd first gone to the nudist camp in Sussex, it had become increasingly difficult to relate to my parents – boundaries had been breached. There are certain things you shouldn't know about your parents, like how big your dad's penis is. But I did know.

Dad was starting to find me difficult.

'Take your feet off the coffee table!'

'Why?'

'Because I said so.'

'It's not like I've got my shoes on.'

'I said, don't do that.'

'But you do it.'

'Just do as I say, not as I do.'

I didn't want to do what he told me anymore and I certainly didn't want to go where he wanted me to go. He had to shout louder and louder to get his way. He was forever telling me to stop answering him back. I was changing, growing up – it was the beginning of a fight for dominance.

For fun, Dad would challenge me to an arm-wrestling duel. Facing each other across the table, I was charged up for battle. If only I could get strong enough to beat him, then I wouldn't have to do what he said any more. His hands were bigger than mine, his grip firm. I could feel the power of him as I pushed against him. Always pushing.

His face set hard. 'Is that all you've got?'

My arm juddering but not giving way.

His lips were taut. 'Imagine a broken glass, right there, under your hand . . . and push.'

Sometimes, to diffuse a situation, Dad would throw a cushion on the ground as a challenge, 'Cushion!' he'd shout like a hunting cry. Whoever could get the other to touch the cushion was the winner. We'd circle, like sumo wrestlers, and then make a grab, pushing and pulling at each other.

But what had happened with Anthony had knocked my whole life off balance. I withdrew – I spent more and more time alone, and if I communicated at all it was in the pages of my diary. I became diluted – people say, 'She's a shadow of her former self,' and I knew what they meant: there was something vague and shadowy about me.

I arrived at my secondary school looking like an outsider. On holiday in the Mediterranean sun, my hair had bleached pure white and my skin was tanned as deep as my new dark brown school shoes. Everything about me felt wrong.

At my new school, as I sat in the classroom full of strangers, I missed Sue's laughter and her company. And now, here was a whole new set of people from whom I had to keep my box of secrets safely hidden. That box of secrets was filling up, too – it was pretty weighty by now. Not only did my parents not get on, but my dad had made me a nudist plus I'd also been touched where I shouldn't have been and, worse still, I'd touched something I shouldn't have touched. I could hardly think about it.

That first day at school I'd wanted to fit in, it was a chance to start over. As we gathered in the cold assembly hall a girl prodded me in the back.

'Can't yer mam afford to buy yer a new blazer?'

'Sorry?'

'Oh, she's sorry is she? Been down the Oxfam has she?'

'Who?'

'Yer mam, yer silly bitch.'

We were all dressed the same in our navy uniforms but when I looked at the sleeve of my blazer I realised it was several shades lighter than everyone else's.

'Second-hand Rose, that's what she is,' and she shoved me hard in the back again.

After school, I hid in my bedroom so no one would see me cry but my dad must have overheard me.

'What's the matter?'

'Nothing.'

'Doesn't look like nothing. Come on . . .'

'They were laughing at me, that's all . . . doesn't matter.'

'What about?'

'Said my blazer was second hand.'

He looked out of the window and sniffed. 'Get in the car.'

He drove as fast as he could down to town and marched me into the department store that sold uniforms for my school. 'I want a new blazer for this young lady here, the very best you have,' he said. Back at home, as she sewed the school badge on Mum shook her head and said, 'I was just being careful, that's all.' I'll never forget the smell of that new blazer – it smelled just like school ink – and the stiffness of it, or the way my dad told me to stand up straight and be proud of the blazer he'd just paid for.

One day in class, the chair in front of me screeched back. A girl with a grey face and feather-cut brown hair turned around.

'You a wog or what?'

'What?'

'Wog, coon . . . whatever. Where yer from?'

'Warrington.'

'I hate coons.'

The teacher walked down the aisle and banged her book on the girl's desk.

'Carole, is there something you'd like to share with the class?'

She looked down at her desk.

'Look at me when I'm talking to you.'

Carole gave her a twisted smile.

'Come on, what were you talking about that was so interesting that it couldn't wait till break time?'

'Asked her where she come from, that's all.'

'Well, perhaps you could leave your conversation until after class?'

Carole smirked at the girl next to her. The teacher caught her look.

'Perhaps a spot of detention might encourage you to remember your manners? Report to me at break time.'

When the bell rang I made for the door. In the narrow

passageway Carole shoved into me, pushing me hard against the wall. 'You fucking wog,' she sneered.

Mum had always taught me to turn the other cheek. Here, that was the easy option as Carole was built like a brick house, so I just clenched my teeth and rubbed my shoulder. Carole shoved me again. When I didn't respond she put her face close to mine. 'Wog. Don't mix it with me!' I wasn't a wog, it was just a suntan.

When I followed the others to PE the sight of the changing rooms made my stomach turn over. I didn't want the other girls to see me undress. I hated the way I looked, hated the thought of people looking at me, so I kept to the corner with my back to them, making the swap from blouse to vest quickly. Big navy knickers completed the outfit and I managed to put mine on under my skirt.

I'd never been in a gym before. It was as big as a church and it smelled of salt and had worn wooden floors that squeaked under your plimsolls. The walls were made almost entirely of glass and wooden climbing ladders and knotted ropes swung down from the ceiling. Every sound echoed, so I could hear the bunch of girls with Carole in their midst, whispering something about a wog.

As we lined up in front of the ropes, two lads from the adjacent boys' school walked by outside the window. I looked up and caught the eye of the taller one. Carole poked me in the ribs.

'Here, wog! Don't be getting any ideas about him on the left. That's Mac. He wouldn't be interested in the likes of you.'

Mac walked with his hands in his pockets, with his back tilted and swaying casually like he owned the world. Every girl in that gym had noticed him pass by. He had bright blue eyes and sandy hair – the Carpenters' song about the boy with gold dust in his hair came into my head. His hair wasn't exactly gold but the rest of it fitted. I wanted it to fit. Mac . . . I was captivated.

The gym teacher put us in two teams and we were to race, girl by girl, up and down the knotted rope. The girl behind you was to steady the rope during your ascent. The girl behind me was Carole. Pair after pair scrambled up the rope with their team-mates shouting encouragement. When it was my turn, I ran at the rope and jumped onto the third knot, giving me an immediate advantage over my opponent, and up I went, leaving her way behind.

Close to the top, the rope jerked and I almost fell off – Carole was holding it at the bottom but instead of steadying it, she'd started to swing it around. Near the top, the motion was exaggerated so that the rope swung in a big arc. She was laughing as she did it. I held on fast, but could feel my fingers starting to lose their grip. I must have been around twenty-five or thirty feet up and all I had to break my fall was a thin rubber mat. The only thing that was likely to be broken was my neck.

I could hear Carole's voice echoing from below. 'Come on, jungle bunny!' and all her mates joined in making rabbit ears and sucking their teeth. The teacher was busy assembling a box at the far end of the gym and Carole had chosen her moment. 'Come on, wog! If you can swing from trees surely you can handle this?' she said, giving the rope an almighty yank.

I thought I was going to lose my grip. I looked down at the hard wooden floor and the upturned faces of the girls laughing. Carole swung the rope wider and I gripped as tightly as I could, my muscles tense like steel. As I swung – with my head buzzing, my small hands locked onto the rope – I discovered something. I had huge physical strength.

No matter how much she swung that rope, Carole couldn't make me let go and fall. I felt like an acrobat soaring way up in the sky. It was like flying. I was free! The jeers turned into slight cheers as I spun around and after a while Carole grew bored and stopped. Slowly and calmly, I placed one hand over the other and made my way down. The girls had stopped making any noise by the time I'd reached the bottom and were just looking at me as I enjoyed my victory. But it wasn't to last for long.

The teacher came to see what all the fuss was about and ushered us into the showers, standing like a guard at the entrance as she turned on the gigantic dial. 'Girls, get undressed! In you go!' The water hissed out of the nozzles and my stomach tightened as I realised these showers were communal – it felt just like being at the camp, totally on show for everyone to see. But the other girls didn't seem particularly bothered; maybe some were a bit shy under the teacher's stare but they all stripped off and rushed into the showers, squealing. The teacher directed her comments at me.

'Get a move on, we haven't got all day!'

By the time I'd taken off my clothes most of the other girls were out of the shower but Carole and her merry band were waiting for me. I cowered and stepped into the spray. Against the white tiles my skin was very dark, even through the steam. Carole pointed at me.

'You ain't got no difference. You're brown all over.'

I tried to cover myself.

'See . . . you're a wog, aren't you? Just like I said. You're darker than us.'

'I'm not. I . . .'

'Liar!'

'It's not what . . .'

'How come you're that colour without any lines then?'

But I couldn't explain.

'Stay away from us.' For good measure, Carole gave me a hard shove.

The tiles were wet and slippery under my feet, and I skidded into the far wall and hit my head. Then I felt a thump on my back, and another. They'd gathered round, naked girls, pushing, pinching, scratching, slapping. I kept quiet. They couldn't see I was crying in the showers but I wasn't crying because of the pain. I was crying because I felt so alone. The teacher put her head round the corner.

'What's going on?'

'She slipped, miss. We're just seeing if she's OK. We're all right.' Carole pushed her face right into mine and hissed: 'We hate your sort. Wash it off, you stinking wog.'

From that day, I was branded 'wog' for good. Sometimes I'd feel tempted to tell someone about the nudist camps, so I could know what it was like to live without a secret, but I never did. If you were different it mattered, so, like any young girl, I just wanted to be like everyone else. Wanted to fit in and be the same. Should I tell them that I went to a nudist camp, or should I just let them carry on calling me a wog? It was a no-win situation. Whatever I decided, they'd still hate me. And what Terry and the Rebels and Katherine and Jan and Anthony had done to me. There was a whole list of reasons for the girls at school to hate me – if they'd known. I was even more isolated from my classmates. I wrote that in my diary, too – that I'd been labelled a wog – next to the bits about being a nudist and a Catholic.

On the day of the shower incident, I came home from school and let myself in. The house was cold and quiet. Since our South of France holiday Mum had extended her forty winks to last most of the afternoon and was rarely awake to welcome me when I got in from school. That day, I wanted to talk to her about what had happened in the shower but she was asleep – and even when she was awake, she never seemed to have time for me. I wanted a mum like the one I saw on the adverts who was always cooking roast dinners with rich, dark gravy while the children gathered round and went, 'Ah, Bisto!'

I went into the kitchen and thought I'd help with the dinner while Mum slept. I peeled the potatoes, remembering – again – how she used to make me a potato man when I was little and sit him on the kitchen window. What had happened to my mum? What had happened to all of us? I cut the carrots into rounds, crossed the sprouts and laid them all ready for when Mum got up. By the time she emerged, her face puffy and crossed with sleep, I was chopping the potatoes, banging the sharp knife loudly on the chopping board.

'Had a nice day at school, love?'

'Do you really want to know?'

'Of course I want to know how it's going at your new school.'

I turned away from her. 'It was fine.'

'You don't mean that now, do you?'

'What d'you think?'

She shuffled closer to me. 'Jo, look at me, I can tell by your face that you're upset.' As she put her arms up to hug me, I could smell the stale alcohol on her breath and pushed her away.

'Don't.'

'What is it, Jo, what have I done?'

'You've been drinking again . . .'

'I have not.'

'Look Mum, I'm fed up with it . . . fed up with the lies.'

'I'm sorry.'

'Is that all you can say?'

She started to wring her hands. 'I know it's difficult for you . . .'

'Tell me about it. I've got a drunk for a mother and a father who insists we go to a nudist camp . . .'

'I know how you feel . . . I . . . I . . . Don't you think I know?'

But I couldn't answer her. I didn't have any answers, only questions.

Why don't you stand up for yourself? Why don't you stand up for me? Then, worst of all: Why can't I stand you?

Chapter 23

I thought about Anthony a lot and my stomach would tighten at the memory of him. I imagined him, driving down winding coast roads on his big bike, a girl hanging on for dear life. Who was he with now? Which families was he making friends with? Did they, too, have daughters just like me?

In biology at school, we'd started being taught about sexual reproduction. They'd started us off gently by dissecting plants, looking at stamens and talking about pollination, but now we were going to hear about human reproduction – the real thing. We copied drawings of reproductive organs from textbooks, including the penis. I felt Anthony again in my hand and gripped my fist hard, remembering how I'd crushed his scrotum. 'During ejaculation,' the teacher was explaining, 'the muscle walls contract, propelling the sperm forward.'

As I filled up a foolscap page with my drawing of a penis, marking the parts with arrows, I tried not to think of it in my mouth. Then the teacher looked over my shoulder.

'Think you're being funny, don't you?'

'Sorry?'

'I know what you're trying to do – make a joke out of a serious subject. Now do it again, properly.'

Then I saw what she meant. I'd drawn the male appendage so that it was huge, right down the length of the foolscap page. I could hear everybody laughing, but I wasn't laughing.

At our next biology lesson there was a buzz of excitement when the teacher switched on the huge television screen and a video came into focus. A cartoon of two naked teenagers standing side by side came into view. Everyone in the class started giggling as a deep man's voice went on about 'changes' and the cartoon characters started sprouting hair. I felt as though I was the only one in the class who wasn't laughing. I wanted to tell them that it wasn't really like that – that seeing people naked wasn't anything to laugh about at all.

Then, almost before the cartoon character had said 'hello', on screen was a cross section showing how a penis fitted into a vagina and moved up and down. All I could think about was Anthony's penis in my mouth. Then the video showed spermatozoa swimming, beating their tails and I felt the sick coming up from the back of my throat and I was hot and retching, leaning over the side of my stool, my head dizzy, trying to get up, to get to the door, and out to the toilets. But it was too late. I was sick on the floor of the biology lab.

Afterwards, a woman with a metal bucket came to cover the vomit with sawdust until it could be cleaned up properly. It was just more shame and humiliation. 'She's got no stomach for it,' Carole sneered. And she was right.

All naked bodies repulsed me – especially men's after what Anthony had done to me; but in particular, the hanging sexual parts, which to me looked as though they should be internal organs, like something that didn't belong on the outside of the body. I was repulsed by the penis – the enlargement, how it could grow into something mean and wilful. I thought of it like a weapon that had been used against me, and the thought took me back to the chalet, to suffocating, choking.

I took to spending even more time alone in my bedroom. I'd huddle under the candlewick bedspread, shivering in the dark and holding my llama close, wishing everything would disappear.

One morning, however, I felt physically ill and couldn't get out of bed. Mum brought me in a cup of tea and some toast. 'Come on now, Jo, your father's nearly ready to take you to school.' I put my head further under the covers, seeking the softness of the brushed Bri-Nylon sheets. Mum put her hand on my forehead, checking for a raised temperature.

'Jo, are you not feeling well?'

'I feel really sick, Mum.'

All I knew was that my throat had closed up. I tried to sip the tea but it wouldn't go down. Then my dad was in the room, opening the curtains.

'Up you get right now!'

I couldn't speak.

'Them's that lie abed, die abed.' He turned and stopped, then laughed. 'You're covered in spots.'

Mum laid a hand on my forehead again. 'Just stay right there.'

'Fiddle-de-dee, up you get, no daughter of mine misses a day of school.'

I struggled to get up.

'Get some breakfast down you,' Dad insisted. 'Waste not, want not – no point letting good food go to waste.'

I lasted until lunchtime when I collapsed and was rushed to hospital. There were blood tests and my dad looked at me, laughing. 'See, I knew you were putting it all on. Your spots have all gone!'

I hadn't realised at the time that the spots had gone because the blood was rushing to my face as I fainted on the floor.

The bout of glandular fever and a bad throat infection kept me off school for weeks. I looked at the white spots on my tonsils festering like boils and wondered if I'd caught this infection from Anthony when he put his penis in my mouth, and I worried whether or not the doctor would somehow know how I'd caught it. If somehow he would be able to read my mind.

I couldn't stay off school for ever, so after the third week, when I felt a bit better, I forced down some toast that Mum brought me. I washed and dressed and got in the car with my head spinning. I'd arrived at school after assembly had started, so I had to sit on my own in the classroom waiting for lessons to begin. The first person to stroll in, her cronies in tow, was Carole.

'Eee, look who's here! Got over your jungle bunny fever then?'

I looked away.

'Here, she's got paler – can that happen to wogs?'

And they all laughed.

I couldn't concentrate in class. I sat with my elbows on the desk, propping up my head with my hands. My head felt heavier and heavier as I fought to stay awake. Every now and again during the morning, a teacher would snap at me – then there were the incessant taunts from the back of the class, grinding away so that I felt totally worn down. Occasionally, I'd feel something hit the back of my head and then a ball of chewed paper would bounce on to the floor. I didn't want to go out at break time so I rested with my head on my arms trying to sleep. When lunchtime came I had no appetite and hid in the toilets so I wouldn't have to eat.

I struggled through the school day only to arrive home to find Mum sleeping off the booze with forty winks. By the time Dad came home in a temper after a bad day at work, I'd shut myself away in my room. Next day it all began again, and so the pattern continued. It was like some dreadful fairground ride that made me sick but I just couldn't get off.

At school there was a lot of talk about a visit from the local nurse. 'The bug explorer' came every year to check for nits – on your head and down below – and her visit was dreaded throughout the school: not least because inspection by her meant you had to take your clothes off. The very thought made me tremble.

'Bet you've got pubic lice,' Carole called at me from the back of the class. 'All wogs do.' Carole's elder sister had been checked over by the nurse the previous year and she was all clear. 'No lice in our family,' Carole said, combing her fingers through her hair and giving me a sideways look.

I was terrified of the visit of the 'bug explorer'. On the

day of the medical, we had to queue up in our vests and knickers and wait our turn. Carole stood a few places behind me.

'I'll be listening at the door,' she warned when I was about to go in. 'Don't think you can hide your nits from us. We don't want them.'

The nurse was a short stout woman with glasses and a flushed face. I was quaking, standing in front of her in just my underwear. It was as though I'd developed a kind of phobia about the thought of stripping off. I just couldn't understand why I felt like this.

'Stand still,' the nurse ordered, without so much as a hello. Then, with small fat fingers she searched through my hair, pulling and pulling. It made my head itch just to think of what might be lurking there. She lifted up my vest, checking for what, I wasn't sure, then pulled out the elastic of my pants.

Then, noticing something, 'What's that?' she asked me. I thought for one awful moment that she'd found some of those pubic lice crawling around down there, until she prodded my stomach.

'Oh,' I said, realising she was pointing at my scar. 'It's an umbilical hernia.'

'Right dog's dinner they made of that, didn't they? They do it all neatly round the navel now. Off you go now, all clear.'

I was so relieved that I didn't have nits, I was almost smiling when I walked out of the room.

'Found something, didn't she?' Carole taunted. 'I heard her asking.'

'No . . . well yes . . . I . . .'

'See, I told you . . . dirty wog.'

When I returned home from school I felt so weak that I could hardly walk. It felt as if there was something much more wrong with me than just getting over my recent illness. I could hardly put one foot in front of the other. And I didn't want to take any steps forward because whichever way they took me led to some kind of hell. All the girls at school hated me. Then when I came home there was no one who seemed to care about me either. I didn't even have Sue anymore. Then at the weekends I'd be back to the nudist camp and the horror of having to take my clothes off. In front of people like Terry. I tried to catch my breath but it was coming in short, stifling sobs. I was back in the pine woods on something that was supposed to be a holiday with Jan pushing me down on the ground. And though I tried to stop my mind from going there, I was there in the chalet again with the smell of ashtray all around me as Anthony forced my mouth open.

I was retching as though I was going to be sick. Then the sickness turned into anger as I let myself in through the front door, thinking about how my dad had made me go to these nudist camps.

I was almost shouting as I saw Mum folding his clothes and putting them into the cupboard.

'Do you love Dad?'

'What on earth's got into you?'

'Well, do you?'

'Never marry a man for his lovely hair or his lovely teeth,' she said, 'because he'll lose them both.' Then she laughed. 'Stupid advice that is, your father hasn't lost either.'

'But do you?'

'Love him? Of course I do.'

She was sure she loved him – she'd married him, hadn't she? In the eyes of God they were together. But I thought that what Mum wanted most was for Dad to love her. I was sure that she would do anything to make that happen, even if that meant going to a nudist camp and making me go, too.

Then I saw the bottle, tucked near the back of the cupboard by the sheets. I didn't say anything but I knew she'd hidden it there.

Perhaps he had loved her in the beginning, when they'd got married, before she'd started drinking and taking pills. She treasured the gifts he gave her. Those gifts were few and far between, mostly from the early days, such as her tortoiseshell powder compact bought on a holiday in Paris. Sometimes she'd take it from her crocodile-skin bag, open it and show me my face in the mirror, patting some powder on my face.

'Ladies should never have a shiny nose, just remember that, Jo. That is the mark of a true lady. Always appearing just so.'

I couldn't help but think that, like the powder, their marriage was all just a cover up.

Just when I thought it couldn't get any worse, it did. Mum had explained to me that one day soon the lining of my tummy wall would come off every month. She didn't use words like 'womb', but I knew what she meant because we'd done it in biology. It wasn't the detail of the process that shocked me; more the thought I would have to go through it so publicly at the camp.

'It's part of the burden of being a woman,' Mum said, her eyes raised heavenward. I was aged thirteen now and waiting for this 'burden' that I thought would save me from the nudist camp. 'But it means that one day, Jo, you'll be able to have a baby of your own. Not before you're married though. Remember that's a sin, a mortal sin.'

'You started yet?' The girls at school would ask as though whether or not you had gave entry to their exclusive club. Some of the girls who sat at the back of the classroom were members. Mum announced my transition to my father one day when he came in from work. 'Your daughter's become a little woman.' He flushed so deeply that even his ears went red. Wearing sanitary towels felt as if I was walking with a mattress between my legs. But under a pleated school skirt, a thick jumper and a blazer, at least it was hidden. I'd hoped in vain that my parents wouldn't make me go to the nudist camp when I was like this. No matter how much I protested, I still had to go.

It brought a whole new set of problems when I got there.

'Just wear something on your bottom half,' Mum coaxed.

So out I went, tucking my sanitary belt under my trousers. The gone-grey-in-the-wash ties that fastened at the back had a habit of poking out of my waistband and announcing my condition to the world. I might as well have strapped myself into a sandwich board reading 'I'M MENSTRUATING' in large letters.

It seemed more naked somehow. Older women walked by, with a sympathetic smile, nodding knowingly.

'Got a tummy ache?' Terry asked.

I shook my head.

'Time of the month then?'

I didn't want to talk to him about something so

private. It was like every single bit of me, inside and out, was on show. And period pains or not, I would get stomach cramps whenever I heard my parents packing up to go to the club.

At Edendale, there was always somebody organising events for everyone to join in. There was something of a holiday camp atmosphere about the place.

Mum and Dad had started to refer to where we went at the weekend as going to 'the caravan' rather than going to 'the club'. Perhaps the word 'club' raised too many questions, such as what kind of club? What kinds of activities took place there? Saying we were off to the caravan was far safer, lots of people we knew had caravans – mainly by the sea. When asked, Mum and Dad were always vague about where our caravan was – the question would be waved away with a laugh. It was a secret that was not to be found out, at any cost – although you could tell that some thought it a little strange not to keep a caravan by the sea.

People were becoming suspicious. What if anybody found out we were nudists? The neighbours would have a fit. Then there was Dad's job: his colleagues would never take him seriously if they knew he spent his weekends at a nudist camp. That was before we even started on what Mum's fellow-worshippers at the Catholic church would say. If they found out she was a nudist, she'd probably be excommunicated. I had visions of the local priest laying his hands on her head muttering Latin to drive out evil spirits. No, no one must ever know. It wasn't only me. We were all involved. All bound by this terrible secret.

So we carried on leading our double life. It was difficult living partially in a whole different world that we kept secret from those who were not nudists, a bit like being a double agent. I developed a considered way of conversing so that nothing to do with nudism or the club would ever slip out. The subject occupied a specific portion of my brain and I never talked about it, not even with my family.

Edendale was a place where you came to know people's bodies intimately, a place where instead of studying a person's clothes you saw, for example, their rounded stomach, sagging breasts and wrinkled bottom. You knew, too, their war wounds and puckered scars – appendix, caesarean – and, perhaps, whether or not they were natural blondes. You even knew when they were menstruating.

At the club every weekend, I had nothing better to do than sit in the caravan staring out of the window. I tried to distance myself from the horror I felt for it all by looking at the nudists almost in the scientific way that we studied things in biology at school. One of the things I passed my time doing at the club was categorising body parts.

I could recognise people by their bottoms: there were those wobbly bottoms that seemed to have a life of their own, often carrying on moving long after their owner had stopped; there were pinched bottoms with tight creases like pin tucks down their sides; there were perfect rounded bottoms and those that were overblown like balloons and there were bottoms with hollowed-out cheeks that looked as if they belonged in a museum.

I categorised breasts, too, which were as varied as the cakes on display in a baker's shop: flat and biscuity with hard currant nipples; pert and peaky like meringues or soft and doughy like freshly baked bread. Most of the older women had flat breasts, emptied from breast-feeding.

Then there were the penises. There was length – and that would change with the weather, just as a barometer would. On a hot day the penises seemed to stretch out, smooth as grass snakes, whereas if the temperature dropped, or if they'd been in the pool, the same penis would draw back like a tortoise neck. And had they been circumcised? The girls had talked about circumcision at school and I wanted to tell them how wrong they were – how they didn't cut it right down, they just skinned it – but I didn't want to show off my superior knowledge. It would only raise questions.

I also observed how the penis lay – left or right and how far over. Some looked like they were actively seeking cover, others seemed proud to be on display. Then there was the bend. I was sometimes surprised at how few straight penises there actually were, and wondered if it was the result of too many years of being coiled up in trousers.

If I looked at body parts like that and catalogued them, they didn't seem so bad. But no matter how much I tried to be scientific about it, I could never feel comfortable looking at naked bodies. As time went on I continued to wonder if there was something wrong with me. I was thirteen years old, I'd been going to nudist camps of one sort or another since I was ten, and yet it wasn't getting any easier.

I was often on my own pondering such matters. Dad would be busy painting, planting trees, helping around the camp in whatever way he could. Often he would join in with one of the many sporting events. He was at his happiest with other people, axe in hand and back to nature. Dad relished the camaraderie he shared with the other men when pitched against the elements – cutting, planting, building. When I saw him like this, I didn't think of him as a nudist, just someone who loved the freedom and the good things that it brought with it. Mum, however, would be stretched out somewhere on a sunlounger and in denial. I used to think that when she was naked she felt less visible when she was lying down because that's all she seemed to do. Perhaps she thought God wouldn't notice so much if she were horizontal. She was, after all, not standing up to be counted.

Mum was always tired. As her skin turned darker and darker under the sun, so did her mood. Often, her breath would smell sickly sweet and I'd wonder just how much she'd been drinking to anaesthetise herself to what was going on around her. She seemed to withdraw more and more into herself. It was almost as though the more naked she was, the more covered up she appeared to be.

Mum no longer talked to me in the way she did when I was younger. If she said anything at all it would be in a nagging sort of way about tidying up or helping, and if I answered her back, it would generally result in a crackle of abuse or a flurry of short, spiteful slaps. I hated her slapping. I never quite knew when it was coming or what I'd done to deserve it.

I spent yet more time in the caravan, simmering in the summer heat, getting hot and bothered, inside and out.

'Why don't you go and get some fresh air?' Mum slurred. I wouldn't even answer her.

I stayed away from the Rebels and their games, and tried to distance myself from Terry with those slithering hands and his seedy camera skills but he was always hanging around my parents. They liked him and they wanted to establish themselves at the club so, ready with advice on just about everything that they needed to know, Terry had made sure he was someone Mum and Dad couldn't do without.

As soon as I heard his whining voice calling 'yoo-hoo' outside our caravan, my fists would clench.

'What's he doing here again?' I snapped at Mum.

'Now don't be like that, Jo, he's just being friendly.'

'I don't want to be his friend.'

'Well, whatever has he done to deserve that?'

But I couldn't tell her. Where would I start? There was so much to tell but she was the last person I'd ever share my secrets with.

Sometimes, I wondered why Terry had done the things he had to me. I think I'd stopped wondering if I'd imagined it after all. It finally hit home that he was a bad man. It wasn't on anything like the same scale as what Anthony, or even Jan, had done, but it bothered me nevertheless. Whenever I saw him I was reminded of where it had all started, way back when I was ten years old in the swimming pool. So much had happened since.

Terry haunted me.

'Come on in, Terry', Mum called, 'I'm just warming

the pot. What about you, Jo? Have some tea with us?'

I read my book, pretending I was really engrossed in it so I wouldn't have to look up.

'Hello there, Jo,' and Terry smiled his yellow-toothed smile. 'Reading anything good?'

'Neh . . .'

'Always got her nose in a book these days, that's Jo. Move up now and make room for Terry.'

I moved along but I kept my feet up to stop him getting in right next to me. Terry seemed to know what I was doing and gave me a little wink as he squeezed opposite me on the sofa, his bare chest hanging over the table like women's breasts. Then, as Mum poured three teas in the kitchen, he turned to me, flushing pink, whispering:

'My, haven't you grown?' His eyes were all over me, while I tried as best I could to hide behind my book. He nodded in Mum's direction. 'Doesn't say much does she?'

I hated everything about him: the way he smelled, the way he slurped his tea, the way he nibbled around the corners of his biscuit. Most of all I hated the way he looked at me. And Mum couldn't see it. I looked at Mum and then back to Terry – she was oblivious. But could I blame her? My parents didn't know what he'd done to me and I didn't know how to tell them. They'd brought me here, after all. It would devastate my parents to think that they had subjected me to such a terrible environment.

I still found it difficult to be anywhere near Terry. If it was possible, it was even more unnerving facing him across the caravan table. I tried to cover myself up with my hair while he sat opposite me, his bare bottom on the seat, sweat matting his curly hair.

'How about if I showed you how to play miniten?' he asked.

Miniten was a similar game to tennis but played on a smaller court. As far as I knew it was only ever played in nudist camps, where tournaments were fought with a zeal worthy of Wimbledon champions. For some reason nudists took the game really seriously.

'No thanks,' I answered. I'd seen miniten players in action and there was something about the wobbling of the men's penises when the game sped up that made me feel I could never watch for long. I didn't want to play, and I especially didn't want to play with Terry.

Mum plonked two pieces of date and walnut loaf in front of us. 'Oh go on, Jo, you're always cooped up in here.'

'I'm not in the mood.'

She turned to Terry. 'You know what they're like, these moody teenagers.'

Terry smiled his yellow smile. 'Come on, Jo, I've just passed the court and it's empty.'

As a teenager, it's hard to say 'no' sometimes. After all,

it wasn't as though I was going into the woods with him.

Terry downed his tea and stared at me. 'I'll be all offended if you turn me down.'

He said it in a whining little boy voice, which made Mum laugh.

'Go on, Jo, out with you! Get some sun on your back.'

Terry stood up. Perhaps it was the sight of his genitals at eye level, far too close to the dining table, that made me get up too. I moved, half to get away from him, and half because I didn't know what else to do.

'There's a good girl. Glad you changed your mind. I'm a good teacher', he said, adding in a low voice, 'I'll be gentle with you.'

I stumbled out of the caravan into the white light. Terry turned as he talked, placed a hand on my shoulder and herded me towards the court. He picked up some bats and tennis balls from his caravan as he went. His wife looked at me through the window and I wondered what she was thinking.

The bat that Terry gave me was made of two circular pieces of wood, angled like bellows with a handle in between. I grasped it like a shield and tried to walk in a way that would cover me down there. Terry smiled and I felt my skin prickle. 'You've nothing to be ashamed of, nice little body like yours. You're growing up, that's all.'

He looked hot and sweat was forming in pools all over

his skin. Perhaps he really did understand how growing up felt? Perhaps he was right and I was feeling awkward because I was growing up. Terry wasn't at all uncomfortable with no clothes on and he walked next to me with his chest pushed out. I looked sideways at his penis. It was hardly there at all. With all that hair down there it was virtually hidden from view. If I looked at it that way, it didn't seem half so scary.

The court was empty. I shuddered. Terry put his arm around me and rubbed my shoulder. 'Don't worry, I'll soon warm you up.'

I soon found out that miniten was a painful game. The home-made bat banged hard on the top of my wrist every time I hit the ball. And to hold the bat firmly, it hurt quite a lot. Big red weals started to form over my wrist but I played on. Terry grew hotter as we played and a great red blotch like a map appeared on his chest. He was sweating all over and his curly hair was clotted together. He kept licking his lips all around with his fat small tongue which looked like it was tied at the bottom of his mouth.

He came over to my side of the net and stood close behind me so that he could show me how to stand and hold the bat properly. His hands were hot and clammy and when he smiled that sickly sweet smile, I felt ill.

The Rebels sat nearby, on the swings. They were laughing but I didn't know if it was at me. As always, I disliked having them watch me naked when they were dressed and, again, I shivered at the memory of Peter's kiss.

On the way to her sunlounger, my mum walked past and waved to me. At that moment I wanted to be with her, to tell her what was going on: that I didn't know what to do about men like Terry and that I wanted it all – Terry and attending the camps – to stop.

I pulled my hair down as far as I could. 'I have to get back.'

'D'you want to go to your caravan and play some cards?' Terry asked. Alone in the caravan with Terry? I started to get that sick feeling again, deep in my stomach.

I wished he'd stop looking at me. 'No . . . no thanks, I really have to get going.'

'We could play strip Jack naked?' He snorted through his teeth. 'Just joking.'

I put the bat down carefully and thanked him. He was saying something about being a spoilsport in his whining, childlike voice as I turned.

'Hang on a minute, Jo!'

But I was off.

Terry broke into a sweaty run trying to catch me up, but there was no way I was going back to the caravan with him alone. I ran faster.

'Where are you going?' he called.

I wasn't hanging around. I ran past the Rebels on the bench. I didn't know where to go: I didn't want to be with the Rebels, I was afraid to go back to the caravan, I didn't want to join my mum and the others by the pool. The only thing I could think of doing was to run to my dad. Perhaps, if he saw Terry chasing me, he'd see what was clearly going on. Even I had realised that this was not something that I had started or could control. Dad and I hadn't been getting along but he was all I'd got and he wasn't scared of anything. He would sort Terry out, just like he'd sorted out Mrs Gilmore when her dog killed my guinea pig. I wanted my dad and I knew where to find him: in the nursery.

'Dad! Dad!' I called, my screams lost in the dense wood.

I shot around a bend and a twig or a thorn on an overhanging branch caught the corner of my eye. I stopped, holding my head in my hands as my vision blurred. Then I went to take off again and I stumbled, rolling over onto my knees into the brambles. It was only a moment and Terry was there, panting over me.

'You all right?'

I shrugged away from him.

'Here, let me help you.' And he reached down a small fat hand.

'I don't need your help.'

'But you're hurt, there's blood on your face. Let me see.'

He moved towards me.

'Just keep back, or I'll get my dad.'

'I was going to take you to him, Jo. Don't be like that . . .'

'I'm going to tell him about everything . . .'

'Tell him what?'

'About the pool . . . you know . . . and the photos.'

'We were only playing, you know that . . . come on,' and he reached to help me up.

I saw my chance. I lifted up my hand to him and watched him reach out, then I sprang to my feet and took off.

'Jo, where're you going?' he called.

I ran down the muddy path towards the old lake, hearing Terry's feet behind me, pounding the ground.

'It was our secret, remember?' he shouted.

I looked behind me. His face was wet and his whole body red and sweaty.

'Wait, Jo, wait!'

I ran deep into the wood where the trees were dense. I kept looking back, saw the strain on Terry's face and kept on.

Through the woods I heard Terry's voice. 'Coming, ready or not!' he sang. I jerked back into a run. My chest was aching. 'Dad!' I called. 'Dad!' I knew he was a way off. 'Dad!'

Terry's feet were pounding behind me, faster and faster. I could hear his breath coming in short rasps. I crouched in the bracken and waited, listening to the thump, thump, thump of my heart. I listened for a snap underfoot, a rustle. I hoped Dad had heard me.

'Jooo, where are you?' he sang out loud.

I went completely still. I kept as still as I could, willing my breathing to calm down.

'Where are you?'

I held my breath.

'Come out right now!' He was shouting, almost screaming.

A centipede started to make its way up my leg. I watched it move its legs in a ripple and I started to shake.

He looked, apparently, straight at me. 'Come out or you'll be sorry!'

I don't know how long I waited. I was aware of the centipede marching onwards further up my leg and it took all my willpower to keep still. My arm was throbbing from the tennis game, and my legs and back ached.

Eventually he left. My legs had pins and needles from crouching. Slowly, I followed the path, checking all around in case he was lurking somewhere. Then the feeling came back into my legs and I quickened up. I ran down the path, following the sounds of men working. And there was my dad, thrusting his spade deep into the raw earth. At the sight of him, I felt tears rise from deep inside my chest.

Chapter 24

I still led my double life, keeping my secret safe. Not that anyone at school ever asked me to go down to the town with them on a Saturday to share secrets over a cup of coffee. Very occasionally, I would still do that with Sue and we'd talk quickly, trying to make up for lost time. She liked a boy called Mike and was always trying to see if she could bump into him in the town. And when we did, it struck me how normal it was to meet boys like this: normal boys who wore clothes.

But my friendship with Sue was slipping away – now that she was at a different school, and she was making new friends. One day, we drove past her on the way to school – I almost didn't recognise her among the sea of grey and maroon uniforms – she had her arm linked through another girl's, head back, laughing.

I banged on the car window, 'Sue! Sue! It's me.' But she hadn't heard me. I couldn't blame her for making new friends. I'd rarely been free to see her at the weekends anyway – so she was bound to find other friends to spend time with.

'Is that your silly friend?' Dad asked. 'You want to stay away from her, hanging around with that lot.'

It was winter now and my suntan was fading but, at school, I seemed stuck with the name 'wog'. I'd told my classmates that I had a tan-through swimming costume and that's why I was brown all over. I'm not sure whether they believed me – it was, after all, yet another lie. It seemed like a day never went past when Carole and her cronies didn't find an excuse to push past me with a dig from a hard shoulder. And in class they turned a cold shoulder, sitting at the back whispering so that every now and again I would hear, 'wog'. I could feel their eyes upon me wherever I was, but I just kept my head down and kept quiet.

So it was a real shock when, one day, the teacher told me that I was to give the reading in assembly the following week.

'But, miss . . . I . . .'

'I don't want to hear any excuses, Jo. Public speaking is something we are all required to do from time to time. It's character building and will make a stronger person out of you.'

The girls at the back of the class broke into laughter.

I was given a passage to read and told to practise it at home. It was some modern take on the Bible in which a point was being made by a leather-clad teenage biker called Dennis Tucker. At home in the evenings I went over and over it, standing in front of the mirror speaking out loud as the nerves in my stomach tightened. How could I stand up there on that big stage and face the whole school? I felt so battered and down that I just didn't have the courage.

As the day grew nearer, I started waking up in the night, worrying about it. Night after night I'd get stomach cramps imagining walking onto the stage and facing everyone. Then the big day arrived and all too soon I found myself in assembly waiting by the side of the stage, ready to go up.

The headmistress nodded at me and looked towards the podium. It was a long walk; the piece of paper with the passage on it was rattling in my hand, and my stomach was so tight that I thought I'd be sick. I could hear my shoes echoing on the wooden floor as I took my position behind the podium and looked down briefly. Six hundred faces looked back at me. I felt exactly the same as when I was naked.

I looked at the words, then back again at the girls. It seemed like an eternity as I tried to pluck up the courage to speak. Then there was a cough – a disguised cough – that to me sounded like 'wog'. I looked over to where my class stood and there was Carole slowly sliding her hand up her face in a 'fuck off' sign, ending in the pretence of a scratch.

I started to speak, my voice squeaking. 'Dennis Tucker was a rocker . . .' And that's as far as I got. A huge great sob rose within me, and no matter how hard I tried to push my tongue behind my teeth to stop it, I couldn't. I was shaking, sobbing uncontrollably in front of the whole school. I was so alone on that stage, so broken.

I heard the sound of shuffling feet, then muffled giggles and then laughter. I stood with my head bent over the podium, the words on my piece of paper blurring together. All those people watching and not one friend. I felt the hot shame of it, feeling worthless in such a public way. I'd never heard of 'low self-esteem'; all I knew was that I hated myself just as much as Carole and her cronies hated me. And then a teacher had her hand on my shoulder and was leading me off the stage.

I was completely and utterly humiliated and, from then on, along with 'wog' I also got the 'Dennis Tucker was a rocker' taunt – which crescendoed into hysterical wailing. It seemed like everything I did gave the girls at school a new reason to hate me.

In class, I'd stare out of the window thinking about anything other than the group at the back of the room. I'd hope for a glimpse of Mac and think of the fairy stories I used to read about the prince on the big white horse who would come one day. It didn't seem very likely in Warrington.

Sometimes, I'd see Mac hanging around on the edge of the playground and I'd watch him walk up the path to where the boys' school joined with ours. I'd write his name in fancy patterns all over my jotter and my satchel, even on the back of my identity bracelet – though only in nail varnish in case I changed my mind. Every now and then I thought he'd caught me looking at him from the corner of my eye. Occasionally I even thought he winked at me, or at least I told myself he did.

Every Friday we were herded over to the ballroom for dancing lessons. There, we'd line up facing the boys and be pushed towards a partner then we'd shuffle around trying to learn the waltz and the Dashing White Sergeant. I felt awkward putting my left hand on a boy's shoulder and holding his hand in my right, and I kept my arms stiff so that he couldn't get close. I liked Mac, but the thought of being up close to him made me feel really weird. Would he have to touch me? Would it feel like it had with Terry and Anthony? 'He won't bite you, you know,' said the teacher.

But I knew differently.

'Here, I'll show you how it's done.'

And before I had time to protest, he'd whisked me

away to the music and, much to my surprise, I was dancing, really dancing, gliding around that room as if I was floating. I soared past Mac, caught him looking at me and, for the first time in ages, found that I was laughing.

I'd been waiting for the invitation to arrive, then in November it did. It was the first real invitation I'd ever had, on thick card with squiggly gold edges and it looked like it'd been dipped in Ribena. The school social was the highlight of the year. All those dancing lessons would finally be put to good use. I was so excited. I could think about only two things: that Mac would be there, and that I had absolutely nothing to wear.

The girls at school were talking about their new outfits and who they were going to dance with. 'And you can keep yer filthy mitts off Mac,' Carole had snarled at me. 'He won't want to be dancing with the likes of you.'

I worried and worried about what I was going to wear. Mum knew I'd been feeling a bit down and suggested we go and spend some of her 'just in case' money – money she kept back from the housekeeping, 'just in case'. I was almost skipping as we went around the shops. Mum picked out lots of different outfits for me to try on, telling me, 'Don't worry about the price, Jo, this is my treat.'

Then I saw it – a dark blue paisley crop-top that tied at the front and a matching wrap-around skirt. The material was thick cotton and Mum rubbed it expertly between her finger and thumb. 'That's lovely, Jo. Go and try it on,' she said. When I looked at myself in the mirror, it was the most grown up I'd ever felt. I walked coyly out of the changing room.

'What d'you think?'

'It's super, you look lovely in it,' and Mum smiled and gave me a big hug. 'My little Jo, all grown up.'

'I'm still only thirteen.'

And she looked at me and put her head on one side.

Sometimes, on my own, I'd try on my outfit, wondering if Mac would like me in it. When the day of the dance came around, I spent ages getting ready: washing my hair, putting on pale eye shadow and mascara, trying not to smudge it even though it felt like sand in my eyes.

I walked into the kitchen slowly to make my grand entrance. Dad had his back to me and turned suddenly, looking me up and down and fixing his eyes on my bare midriff.

'What d'you think you're doing, dressed up like a trollop – is that bare flesh?'

I couldn't understand why he was bothered about a bit of stomach showing when I took all my clothes off at the weekend.

'It's . . . it's . . .' I looked at Mum for support.

'It's a belt,' she blurted out, 'nothing wrong with that.'

Dad looked slightly puzzled and then sniffed. 'Just get that muck off your face.'

'I'll see to it,' said Mum and made a 'hush' face. She hurried me off to my room and smoothed off some of the eye shadow and gave me a little hug. 'Off you go now, quick.'

And I rushed out of the door before Dad could stop me.

I was so excited when I arrived at the hall. We all had to join in the dances and time after time I looked around to see if Mac was there. Then, for the Dashing White Sergeant, we were in threes dancing in sets of six. Around and around we danced in a circle, then our threesome would duck under the other and move on to dance with the next three. Mac's threesome was getting nearer. Surely with the next move I would be his partner? I was holding my breath, he was looking at me. And then the music stopped.

I never got to dance with Mac that night, but it didn't matter, in one small corner of my heart, he was looking at me.

As well as the school dance, another thing that cheered me up was being selected for the hockey team – I'd found something I was good at. Carole was in goal – and padded up she looked even nastier. The rest of her gang were dotted around the team and I was in a key attacking position, right inner. Even though Carole and her gang didn't want to be friends with me, we all had to play in the same team. And I could score goals, deliver victory and with that came their grudging respect.

I was thirteen and I was changing; I was getting stronger and I could outrun most of my teammates. The rigorous training routine meant I developed some muscle and, unusually for a girl, I had a six-pack stomach. I prided myself on my press-ups and started to really enjoy keeping fit. I was beginning to feel proud of my body, instead of ashamed.

Sometimes, after a match, I used to challenge my team-mates to a bout of arm-wrestling. At first, I'd let my arm give a little, judging their strength, letting them tire a bit, then I'd breathe in deep and set the angle of my arm firm. I'd fix my eyes on my opponent's and feel her start to falter. Her arm would begin to shake and I knew that signalled the end. It was a mental thing; concentrating, holding on like you'd never let go – like when I'd held on to that rope in the gym. I was starting to use my anger to fight back.

Dad hated the fact that matches were on Saturdays. 'Splitting up the family,' he'd shout, when he realised he couldn't stop me, that it was important as I went off to a match on a Saturday morning. But as far as I could see, our family was already split and anything I could do to keep away from that nudist camp at the weekend was fine by me.

On match days, we'd stand shivering on the cold frozen ground facing our opponents and I'd feel the anger rise up in me. I was lethal on that hockey team – and mean. I didn't care if I hurt anyone. I wanted to hurt them because that's the way I felt myself and sometimes, if I could just get rid of it, just a tiny bit, I'd feel better. But the angry feeling always came back.

Mum would plead with me not to be so difficult – she couldn't understand this sudden change in me. We'd been close during all the outfit buying for the dance, but now I didn't want to talk to her.

'You're impossible,' Mum would say when she tried to make conversation with me.

I didn't want to talk.

I watched her at the ironing board as she banged hard on Dad's shirts, using her weight like he was still in them. It was as though if she took that iron to him, she could smooth out all the roughness. She jammed her teeth together as the sweat glowed on her face, lighting her up. Bang. Bang. Bang, the iron went as the old board creaked beneath Dad's shirt. Sometimes I imagined she was searing his skin.

It was almost as though my silence at home had infected my parents. I wondered if they'd given up talking to each other, as if after all those rows they'd finally blown themselves out. I'd disappear off to my bedroom whenever I could.

'You're growing away from us,' Mum said, her head peering round the door, her speech slurring. Yet again, she'd had too much to drink, and I was sick of it.

'What exactly do you mean by us?'

'Well me and your father.'

'It's not exactly "us", is it? I mean it's not like I haven't noticed that you hardly talk.' I saw her eyes glaze over and flash. She was as angry as me.

Mum came at me then, with her fists up. But I was ready, and every time she tried to land one on me I fended her off.

'Is that the best you can do?' And I saw the tears in her eyes. 'Tell you what. Why don't you go and lose yourself in a bottle or pop some pills?'

She ran from my room, crying and I heard her banging cupboards as I sat on my bed, staring out of the window.

When I'd calmed down, I went to find her. The curtains were drawn in her bedroom, casting a purple light on where she lay in bed, and the air was thick with that familiar sickly sweet smell.

'Mum?'

'I'm having a little lie down.'

'Mum . . . I'm sorry.'

She didn't answer. I moved close to her and smelled the alcohol strong on her breath.

'Mum, why can't you stop . . . please, Mum?'

'Stop what?'

'Thing is, I know you drink . . . have been drinking for some time. You know I know, don't you?'

'Sh . . . want to get back to sleep.'

I knelt by the side of her bed and touched my hand to her hair. 'Mum, please stop, do it for me. Just try.'

She half opened her eyes. 'I don't even like the taste . . .'

'It's getting . . . you know . . . bad . . .'

Her eyelids flickered as she struggled to keep them open. 'I only have the occasional glass . . .'

'You know that's not true.'

She rolled over, turning her back to me. 'Just leave me alone . . .'

'I was just trying to help. Come on, Dad'll be home soon, you've got to get up.'

'Do you love me?' she asked, quietly into the pillow.

'You know I do.' But I couldn't say the words she really wanted to hear. I couldn't say, 'I love you'.

It was getting late. I looked at my watch – Dad would be home any minute now. I kept going to her room, trying to persuade her to get up, but she wouldn't move.

It was dark by the time Dad came home and I'd done my best to put a meal together with the bits and pieces I'd found in the fridge.

'Where's your mother?'

'She . . . she's having a little lie down.' It was another one of those lies.

'What d'you mean?'

'She's not feeling well . . . she's . . .'

And he stormed off to find her in the bedroom. I followed, peeping round the door.

I looked at my mother's bloated face and, next to it, my father's – red and deeply lined – and suddenly I saw what they'd become. Dad started shouting, telling Mum she was drinking too much, that this was no way to live. As usual, Mum just cried. That was always the way she reacted when she was drunk. It was almost as if she couldn't see or hear any of what was in front of her, couldn't see it all unravelling around her. Dad stormed out, slamming the front door in a rage and soon Mum was snoring again. Back in her own world.

I ran to my room and shut the door. I picked up my eyeless llama and held it to my face, grating and grating it against my skin until I thought it would bleed. And, still, the more I tried not to think about my horrible memories, the more they just came flooding back: Terry, the Rebels, Katherine, Jan and Anthony. Always Anthony, hot in my mouth.

Nowhere was safe – not this house, not school, not the club, not even anywhere we went on holiday.

Chapter 25

My insides twisted as Mum excitedly announced another holiday. Somehow, she thought that the fact it was abroad made it exciting. Italy felt so foreign to me though, we didn't even get to learn the language at school.

Hidden beneath shady pine trees and tall security gates this camp was on a completely different scale from any nudist camp I'd ever been to before.

Residents there were numbered and tagged. We had everything we needed in this utopia. There was a supermarket, a cinema, a disco, food stalls, tennis courts and mile upon mile of sandy beaches. There we roamed, free in this huge pen away from predators. Or so they intended.

We walked along duckboards to get to the beach, past security guards who checked our tags, where we lay like walruses all day long. However, it wasn't a private beach, which made a mockery of all the security tags and the solemn-faced guards. To the south was access for any Tom, Dick or Harry who might be taking a stroll with his friends and a long lens camera.

I was thirteen. And this place in Italy was to become our summer holiday destination for the next four years.

It wasn't easy to get to from Warrington. It took days in the car, with the nauseating smell of petrol emanating from the back of the car. Because petrol was so much more expensive abroad, Dad would insist on taking along a full container of fuel and it would wobble about, leaving us only enough luggage space for a toothbrush. But then we didn't need clothes.

By the time we finally arrived, I would help to put up the tent for Mum and Dad and then make my own camp in the car. With the car seats down and some towels slung over the windows I had some privacy. It was better than sharing the small bedroom compartment with my parents but, away from the mother ship, it had its own set of problems.

Each day, we'd make the long haul down to the beach, past the checkpoint and over the dunes. I remember that tedious walk in the high, hot sun, a towel around my waist. Up over the top we'd trudge to take in the full vista. The waves crashed mercilessly down on the long straight stretch of sand and the sky was a watercolour blue. Behind us rose endless dunes and a thatch of pine trees. In many ways it would have been a perfect beach holiday, except, down there on the beach, everyone was naked.

It wasn't that I was shocked any more by seeing people

with no clothes on. Rather, it was something about the mass of them; the brown writhing mass of skin, all merged into one.

There were the very old and the very young, the beautiful and the disfigured: pretty teenagers wearing sarongs and towels huddled around a radio; amputees struggled with one leg, or part of an arm. They were all saying that they didn't care, that they didn't mind if you looked at their beautiful, ugly, old or maimed bodies. They were saying, 'Look at me!' There was too much of it. Too much skin. I felt I was the only one saying, 'Look away! Please!'

People did care how they looked, though. The men sucked in their stomachs as they strutted past each other and the women held back their shoulders. They weren't liberated at all. They weren't free. They were just like anybody else on a beach and they all looked at you – especially the men. When I got to know some of the teenage boys, I came to understand about those times when they had to lie on their stomachs. The deep holes in the sand. Their reluctance to go for a swim right now. But that was to come later.

In the beginning, on that first visit to Italy, when we went to the beach I had to stay close to my parents. They were worried, they said, about me wandering off on my own, so I dug myself a deep hole in the sand and tried not to look as they sautéed themselves under the sun, covered in Ambre Solaire and pure olive oil. We spent the day just lying there. They passed me juicy peaches stuck with sand and sandwiches stuffed with melted cheese, sweating from the heat. We roasted all day until it was time to go back to our tent where we'd cook up tinned ravioli and talk about tomorrow, which would be just the same as today. I hated those holidays in Italy.

Down at the far end of the beach was a sulphurous mud stream. The locals would sometimes go there and use it for medicinal purposes but I had another use for it. Covered in rich, dark green mud, I could hide from the world. I could walk the beach, 'clothed'. I even covered my hair. I must have looked like Medusa with my hair in snakes and my skin flaked all over. After a while, the other beach-goers ceased to notice the green girl. I would bake by the sea all day, until the mud cracked and dried. At the end of the day, I'd wash it off and emerge like a butterfly from a cocoon.

In my green armour I wandered further and further from the main beach, as my parents very quickly gave up trying to keep a close eye on me. Sometimes I'd get so hot in the caked-on mud that I'd feel like I was roasting in a chicken brick. It would tighten on my skin and crack and then I'd have to wash it all off in the sea.

On one of those occasions, I'd wandered way off. I'd

been washing off the mud in the sea, rinsing my hair over and over to get it all out. I stretched out on the wet sand where the sea could just touch the tips of my toes and I stayed there feeling the water dry on my skin, leaving just the tickle of salt. When I looked back at where I'd come from, the bare bodies were all a blur. When I looked the other way, the distant figures appeared so faint they were almost not there at all, like a mirage. If I looked at them they would flicker like candle flames and almost disappear.

I was tired after my long walk. I made my way up into the dunes and dug a nest out of deep, white sand. Underneath was cooler. I stretched out on my tummy. It felt good to be far away from my parents and their never-ending striving for an all-over tan, lying in embarrassing postures, angled to the sun.

It was almost completely quiet. All I could hear was the whooshing of the waves on the shore, the hum of the breeze through the grass above my head. I hadn't been sleeping well in the car, waking up early each day to the smell of hot plastic car seats as soon as the sun rose in the sky. I was tired. Listening to the swell of the ocean way down on the beach, I could feel my eyelids getting heavier. I would close my eyes just for a moment. Then I had drifted off into a doze.

Bzzzp . . . bzzzp . . . bzzz, bzzz, bzzz. An insect

buzzed around my ear. A persistent insect, faint at first, then louder. I wished it would go away but it wouldn't. Sometimes it came right near to my head, at other times it was further away. Bzzp, bzzp. If I just stayed still, then maybe it would realise I had nothing on offer. There was nothing of a flower about me, it was probably the smell of the sulphur from the mud attracting it, I thought.

Bzzzp, bzzp, bzzp. Then it was going crazy. I had a horrible feeling I was about to be swarmed, so sat up with a jolt. A large camera lens was pointing right at me. Behind it was a man wearing a hat and shorts. He took a few more snaps and kneeled up, fixing his sunglasses quickly in place. It took me a moment to come to. When I did, there was only one thing I was thinking – I was far from anyone who could help.

As I curled myself into a ball, I saw from over my shoulder that the man wasn't alone. There was another man with him, who had a bald, shiny head and sunglasses. They both stood over me. Despite the sun, I started to feel cold. Very cold.

The one carrying the camera looked around. The other one made a 'hush' sound with his finger to his lips but I couldn't have made a sound if I wanted to. I was paralysed with fear. Then the man with the camera held it up again and started to shoot.

I grovelled about in the sand. I didn't want to get up

because that would have left me more exposed than I was. I remember putting my hands over my face. Then I did something else: I started to call out for my dad. Not in a shouting, screaming kind of way but in a pleading, little girl way, like when I used to call out in the dark, after a bad dream.

I was crying when the bald man reached out for me and held me. I was still crying when he stretched me out for the camera. I thought if I did what he wanted then they would leave me alone and go away. But I couldn't stop crying. I thought of the stern faces of the security guards. Where were they now? Where was my dad? I whimpered for my dad over and over. But he didn't come. No one came, not my dad, not a single person up on those windswept dunes. No one came when I called out as the two men held me down, the sand grating on my body, their hands probing.

They took turns, one holding me with my face in the sand to photograph and touch me. I wanted to bury it in there, where I didn't have to see what was going on. If I got in deep enough I couldn't feel either. Then came the bzz, bzz, bzz. The weight of heavy bodies. Older men who ought to know better. Older men who liked little girls. They stretched me, unwound me, trying to keep me still. I was still crying for someone to come.

I was sinking, deep, deep into the sand, as if it was a

grave that would swallow me up. Soon it'd all be over. There'd be nothing here – just the wind blowing over the grass, playing a sad song and the sand blown back as it had been, covering up what had taken place. There'd be no hint of a struggle. No footprints even. Nothing.

Then deep down inside, I felt my fist clench hard. My arm moved to its familiar angle – set. I started to push up from the sand, muscles tense and I was thrashing. This wasn't just a fight in the school playground. I didn't care if I hurt his face. I didn't care if I ripped all the flesh from his body. This was for real.

I snatched the glasses off the bald man and threw them away, hurling handfuls of sand at his eyes. I was kicking now and screaming like a wild cat. I was up on my haunches, lunging for the man with the hat. Nails clawing. Scratch. Hiss.

The man was backing away. He was shouting something at me in Italian. I was growling now, from somewhere deep and dangerous.

'Don't mix it with me!' They were Carole's words.

The bald man had gone, staggering away up the dunes. I was snarling now at the other man, grabbing for his camera. I was charged, electric. It was like the cushion game I used to play with my dad but there was nothing playful about it. I felt a beat pulse through me. I went for his face again and again, nails like scythes.

The man turned, holding his face, dragging his camera. I went for it, kicking it into the sand and grinding it down. He was shouting but backing away. A coward suddenly, on his own. I chased him up the sand dune, scratching at the back of his legs as he puffed up those hills. I watched as he tumbled down the other side, righted himself and with a final shout was gone – off down the beach, limping.

I watched until they'd merged with the other people in the far distance. From a long way off they didn't look like people at all, and they weren't.

Chapter 26

'Hey you, beautiful doll!' Mac called down from an upstairs classroom window.

I looked around but there was no one else there – only me.

'Yes, I'm talking to you,' said the voice from above.

I looked up quickly, and away.

'Yes you, beautiful doll!'

Me? I never thought I was beautiful. How could I be? I was a 'wog'.

Mac leaned on the windowsill with his arm in a white plaster cast. 'Will you go out with me?'

'What?'

'Go out with me! Please! Or I'll fall from this window and I've already broken one arm.'

'I er . . .' We never express ourselves well at such moments.

'Just say "yes".'

'I . . .'

'It's only one, small word.' He held his finger and thumb just so.

The bell rang. 'I've got to go.'

He climbed on to the ledge and framed in the window, holding on by his one good arm, leaning right out, he called, 'I'm falling . . . I'm falling . . . for you . . .'

'Mac!'

'So you know my name?'

Know his name? It was inscribed on just about every surface I possessed. 'I . . . er . . .'

'Meet me at dinner time, under the sycamore tree.'

There it was. All my secret messages had finally been answered. Mac and me. I couldn't believe it.

So I started to see Mac. We'd meet at lunchtimes under the tree and talk, and after school he'd walk me part-way home. Never all the way as I didn't want my parents to find out. He was older and they wouldn't like that. He wore two-tone parallel trousers that changed colour like magic as he walked. *He* was magic. Just being with him, with my arm linked in his, made me so happy I wanted to sing. In fact, I did sing – the song that had popped into my head when I first saw him – but I only sang on my own in my bedroom as the Carpenters weren't cool. They were brother and sister, so how could they be? I told my diary all about Mac, singing away as I wrote.

Mac swung around the lampposts as he walked me home from school. 'I'm so lucky,' he said. 'I can't believe

that I'm actually going out with you. My beautiful doll.'
I couldn't believe it either. Whatever did he see in
me?

He stopped to write my name on the bus stop. 'Jo is a
beautiful doll' it read, in letters etched deep into the green
paint so it showed through to the red. I often wonder if
it's still there, under all those years of new paint.
Someone liked me and not just someone, but Mac. I was
so happy. I didn't care about the girls at school. I didn't
need to be their friend – I had Mac. Everything was
different now he was around.

Even having to go to the club at the weekends seemed
more bearable. I could cope with it better when I thought
about Mac. He was a lifesaver.

News soon got around school that I was seeing Mac.
People had seen us under the sycamore tree and no one
could keep a secret. The girls at school looked at me in a
different way.

'She's going out with Mac.'

There was a bubble around me but the trouble with
bubbles is that sooner or later they burst.

Carole was not pleased. 'My sister likes him,' she
snarled.

But I knew it had nothing to do with her sister.

She stuck her tongue through her chewing gum. 'He
was hers.'

'She wasn't even going out with him. He doesn't even like her.'

'How do you know, you evil bitch?'

'But . . .'

'You've ruined it for her, yer stinking wog.'

'I only . . .'

'Don't mix it with me, girl!'

'I . . .'

'Fine . . . I'll fight you anytime.'

She spat her gum on the floor. 'Good.'

'Good.'

I tried to keep away from Carole and her cronies but it was difficult as we were in the same class. Whenever she bumped into me, she'd make some mention about the fight and my stomach would clench. Soon, all she had to do was look at me and my stomach would go into spasm.

Isolated by my classmates, I sought refuge in my work and, with no one to distract me, I concentrated on what the teachers were saying. Following chains of numbers that organised themselves into solutions. Drawing layers of sediment that changed into rocks. Tracing perfect diagrams of body parts and plants. I soaked it all up. Filling the space that should have been filled with friends.

We weren't a literary household. I grew up on Dad's discarded paperbacks. Apart from *The Science of Life* that Dad had directed me to, mumbling something about the facts of life. There was a book on the shelf that was covered in brown paper and because of that it made me even more curious to know what was inside. I stood on a chair and lifted it down. When I pulled the brown paper off, I could see the cover read *Lady Chatterley's Lover*. It was only later, much later, that Dad explained.

'Didn't want you reading rude books, did I? I knew you'd never pick it up if I made it look boring enough.'

At school I discovered writers such as William Golding, Laurie Lee, Wilfred Owen and even Shakespeare. I read them well ahead, swot-style, and, because I loved them, wrote essays that got A grades.

'Jo,' the teacher said, 'can you stand up please and read your essay?'

It was just another reason for my classmates to dislike me. Around the same time, one of Mum's friends suggested she should go for a job advertised in the local paper – it was selling make-up and knick knacks: a bit like that job as an Avon lady she'd tried out. She'd go door to door and sign up as many customers as she could. I was pleased – it might help her meet people and she'd be her own boss. Mum took to making an effort and wearing smarter clothes and piling her hair up high in a bun. When she was sober, she wanted to look professional and in control. As Mum started to enjoy the freedom of her job, I decided to do as she suggested and send some of my essays off to the local paper. They had a monthly slot for individual writing. It was the final nail in my coffin.

'What's this?' hissed Carole, sliding the newspaper over to my desk. 'Jo's column?'

There I was with a photograph heading one of my school essays about fire.

'You fucking poser.'

It was a bad moment.

'Who the fuck do you think you are?'

The thing was, other than what Mac thought about me, I thought I was nothing. Nothing at all.

The tension between Carole and I was mounting with every look as we passed, every shove, every comment. I tried to look hard, like Carole, but I wasn't at all convincing. Carole started to spread rumours about how I looked down my nose on her house – I didn't even know where it was but suspected it was somewhere in the sloping streets that stacked up at the back of town. I couldn't change any of the things about me. I wished I could but I didn't know how.

I came in one morning to a sign written in large chalked letters on the wall.

'Jo is a poser.'

I felt my stomach churn. It was such a public display of hatred. Carole and her gang were giggling at the back of the class. One by one, my classmates came in for the morning, saw the sign, looked at me and then away. Some put their hands to their mouths. Some laughed. Some just pretended not to notice. I'm sure all of them were glad it was about me and not about them.

I took deep breaths trying not to cry.

It wasn't so much the words themselves that were upsetting but what was behind them. It's hard to be disliked at school. Your world is those people in the classroom and suddenly I couldn't see beyond it. Everything was so complicated. Then there was Mac. He loved me. He'd told me that. I kept the thought of him in my head like a light. Mac. Everything was all right because of him.

The classroom was filling up. I couldn't bear the stares of the girls around me. It felt like a physical pressure. I lifted the lid of my desk up to fend it off, as though I was searching for a book, and inside was a note, folded up, with my name scrawled on the top. I knew who it was from.

'You think we all want to go around with you . . .' it read '. . . but we don't. We know you're a wog. And you bleach your hair to try and hide it.'

On and on the note went about how they hated me, how I had to stay away from them, how I looked down on them. How just everything about me was wrong. I stared at the word 'hate' written in pen with hard, downward strokes. They hated me all right. I'd got the message. They'd told me enough times.

I folded the message back up and put it under my books and closed my desk. They were laughing loudly now, calling me wog, banging their desk lids. The space next to me was painfully empty. Julie, who normally sat next to me, was always late. I saw her come in now, look up at the sign on the wall, then at me. She threw her satchel on her desk and stared at the girls in the back row. Then she walked to the front and got the duster. She climbed up on the desk and rubbed out the message.

I'll never forget what she did. The row at the back went quiet. She'd shamed them.

Chapter 27

One of the curious aspects of nudist-camp life was the organising of fancy dress events. It always seemed a peculiar thing for nudists to do. I could go along with, for example, the idea of body painting in, say, some tribal warrior way but dressing up seemed quite bizarre. All the trouble naturists go to being naked and then, given a choice, they decide to dress up.

At fourteen, the attraction of fancy dress had long since passed me by. Especially fancy dress in the context of a nudist camp. It was decided at the club that there would be a lads and ladies parade, which particularly seemed to contradict their striving for the freedom and equality everyone being naked was supposed to give them. The last thing you'd think they'd want to do was bind themselves up in corsets and breeches. But that was the way they were. It wasn't as if it was being done for any great purpose – not a fun run, or a charity event – it was just to amuse themselves.

A couple at the club were antique dealers and they offered to provide some of the costumes. They had a tiny black dress covered in heavy piping and embroidery, with a matching bonnet lined in black silk. The finishing touch was a pair of tiny buttoned-up boots. Everyone wanted to wear that outfit but no one could fit into it. It was like the quest to find Cinderella as it passed from person to person and they squeezed and puffed.

Mum looked at me. 'I bet it would fit you.'

'But I don't want to wear it.'

'Oh please, Jo!'

'I don't want to take part in your stupid parade.'

'Why must you always spoil things?'

She looked at me so pitifully that I agreed to wear the outfit. At least it was wearing something. I led the procession around the camp, hating every step.

Terry stood by his caravan, taking photographs. I could face him better with clothes on and stared at him hard. Then he walked towards me and handed me a red rose.

'Just stay like that. A picture of innocence. That's right. Yes.' He pointed the camera at me and flashed. 'I like the way you didn't smile. That would have spoiled it.'

Soon the dressing up became a weird fixture, and it didn't stop there, next it was a pyjama party.

Mum was so excited that for once she looked animated. 'What shall we wear?'

'I'm not going.'

'Don't be like that, we're going in pyjamas – think of it as being like a sleepover party.'

'The pyjama thing is fine but why can't I just wear them in bed?'

'What about the teddy bear ones we bought you for Christmas?' Mum tried, nodding at Dad.

I shook my head. 'I'm not going.'

Dad removed his glasses so his eyes looked small and mean. 'You'll just do as you're told, young lady.'

'I've never heard of anything so stupid in my life. A pyjama party? At a nudist camp?'

They both went quiet. I'd mentioned the forbidden word.

Mum bounced up her hair. 'Stop being silly now and choose something to wear.'

'I just don't get it. All this time you've been dragging me here, trying to get me to take my clothes off and now you're telling me to put them on.'

'Stop being so difficult,' Dad cut in.

'I just can't win.'

'It's not about winning.' His tone sounded final.

'No, I can see that, all right. It's quite the opposite.'

It seemed to me that dressing up in pyjamas for a fancy dress party was dangerously close to the thought of bed, and what went on there, excluding sleep or snoring. A nudist pyjama party is on a whole different scale because there are no boundaries. There were people dancing in different stages of undress because, what the hell? We were all naturists so it didn't matter.

But somehow it did. Seeing them partially covered up made the look of their bodies take on a whole new meaning. There was a woman wearing no knickers and a thin, see-through negligée and a man doing the Highland Fling with a hot water bottle tied round his waist like a sporran. There were women clutching teddy bears and rag dolls, and a man in a long silk robe, open at the front, swinging a tasselled belt seductively.

A naked woman raised a feather boa in the air and I wondered who, if anyone, took one of those to bed with them unless it was to tickle someone's fancy? With the flashing disco lights, they were a ghoulish collection of individuals. They may as well have arranged a group of beds in the middle and just got on with it.

That was even before they started on the dancing. There's a certain age when grown ups should definitely stop doing disco dancing – probably the right side of twenty – but disco dancing partly clothed takes on a whole new dimension.

Then there was Terry. He had nothing on but a soft, crocheted blanket draped around his neck. He looked like a big fat baby with his special cuddly.

'Come and join in,' he whined, thumbs up, wiggling his fat bottom.

'No.' It was enough. I didn't do thank-yous anymore.

Standing there in my pyjamas, watching Terry turn and join them, gyrating in the disco lights, it felt as if I'd been woken from a dream, or a nightmare. I saw my parents drinking wine in the corner and decided to leave them to it.

It was time for bed.

The night was cloudy and a mist hung between the branches of the trees, lying in swathes like shrouds. I pulled my dressing gown around me. It was just a short walk to the caravan, through a small copse. The music behind me was fading and I tensed at the snap of a twig, the dying hoot of an owl, howling at the night.

The cold night air gripped my chest and I coughed. I could see my breath, the life of me, swirling in front of my face. Beyond that, the bare shadows of the trees cast grotesque shapes in the undergrowth like naked, wizened old men. I hurried on, trying to keep my eyes on the path and rubbing my hands together for warmth.

I looked behind me and went inside the caravan. Closing the door I searched for the key before remembering we didn't need locks at Edendale. I felt my way in the dark, trying to remember where we kept the matches.

I found them, struck one and the caravan was

suddenly alive with shadows. I cupped my hand over the flame and lit the calor gas lamp, watching the moths flutter towards it. I shuddered and, suddenly aware that our caravan was lit up like a Halloween lantern, I started to close the curtains. Shutting the blackness out there, closing the staring, dark eyes.

Then, from behind the curtain, I heard a scratching noise, hardly there at all. It seemed to come from the far side, bordering the woods. I flattened my back to the side of the caravan and edged towards the door. The noise on the window changed to a high-pitched squeal, like something was being rubbed against it, eeek, eeek – hitting a pitch so high that every nerve vibrated inside me. Eeeek-eeek.

The noise came first from the far window, then round to the next, then the next, getting nearer and nearer, closer to the door. I reached out and held the handle fast. I felt the handle turn as I gripped hard, holding with all my strength.

I could feel something pulling on the other side. Something, or someone, stronger than me . . .

'Boo!' Dad burst in through the door.

I held my hands to my face, drawing air in a gasp. 'That's pathetic, it really is!'

He laughed. Mum was behind him, giggling from the wine.

I took a deep breath, trying to steady myself. 'Tapping on the window like that. How childish!'

Dad ran his fingers through his hair. 'I was nowhere near the window. Don't be so silly. What's got into you?'

'But I heard something.'

'Fiddle-de-dee.'

'There was someone there!'

'You're just letting your imagination run away with you. Who on earth could possibly be tapping at the window at this time of night?'

But I couldn't tell him. Because if I did, he would never believe me.

Chapter 28

One day at school, as Carole passed me with her usual shove, I tried to call her bluff.

'You ready for me then?'

Unfortunately she was. 'I'm just waiting for me dinner to digest. Then I'll have you out by the prefabs. Say your prayers, wog!'

'I'm not religious,' I said, but I hoped right there and then that the great hand of God would scoop me up and put me on a fluffy cloud right away from all this.

I couldn't back out now even though a fight was something I'd rather put off for eternity. The excitement of the fight gathered like storm clouds. I tried talking all through class so I'd get detention but it didn't work. Sooner or later I knew that it was going to happen.

On the way to the prefabs, I kept swinging my arms, practising my right hand jab – like Cassius Clay. 'Fight! Fight! Fight!' the crowd was chanting as I walked up. They must have been ten deep. A fight always drew the crowds.

The large porch area in front of the double doors to

one of the prefabs acted as a kind of stage. With the closed doors to the back, the brick walls to the sides and the crowds in front it was completely boxed off. I felt my chest close. Suddenly it was difficult to breathe. The crowd parted, jeering, and there was Carole standing with her feet apart, her arms swinging at her sides. I noticed she was wearing rings. She was prepared.

We faced each other in the porch. Her lips were turned down like a dog before it bites and her face was pure hatred. At that moment all I felt was, why? Why had it come to this? I certainly didn't feel the same way about her despite having every reason to. But I just didn't. I couldn't summon it up. I felt immune to what she'd done to me.

'Ready for me?' Carole clenched her teeth as her fists came down on my head, thrashing fists, in a windmill action, over and over.

I knew I was strong. Very strong. I could have easily dragged her to the ground, like I was playing the cushion game with my dad. I could have stamped on her or screwed her miserable face into the wall if I wanted. But I didn't want to. There are times when you realise certain things about yourself. It wasn't that I was a rubbish fighter because I knew what I had, but I couldn't bear the thought of hurting her. I particularly didn't want to mess up her face. Didn't want to make her worse than she was.

So I let Carole batter me. I pushed her a bit, yes, but I didn't hit her once. I took it – the rings, the nails. I understood why she hated me and, in a way, I hated myself, or at least my situation. So I let her come at me, over and over.

The crowd was screaming and then: 'Stop!' It was a loud, almost grown-up voice. Through blurry eyes I focussed on Annette Smith, one of the older girls at our school. I'd never spoken to her before as she'd always kept herself pretty much to herself. She'd not be the sort to speak to someone like me.

'Leave her alone!'

The fists stopped. The crowd went quiet.

'Leave her alone, you bitch!' Annette reached for me, putting her arm around me and pulling me close. I couldn't see much as she led me away through the crowds. I watched her shoes as we walked, her great muscled calves in tight white socks.

'All right then, Jo?'

It was her kindness that made me start to cry. Something soft underneath her hard voice. I cried for all the things that were wrong: the girls at school who hated me; the colour of my skin; what my parents made me do; what those men had made me do. I cried for my own weakness; for the helplessness of not being able to do anything about it; for the fact I hadn't been able to fight

Carole back.

Annette stayed with me until my face went dry. She didn't say much but she'd taken a stand. I had someone on my side and the very fact she was with me made a difference. Now there was her and Mac.

Sometimes I wondered about whether or not I should tell Mac that I went to a nudist camp and that was why I was the colour I was, and that's why they called me a wog. But, so far, I'd never quite summoned up the courage. What if he let it slip? It was difficult enough keeping the secret myself and I couldn't risk the whole school finding out. I'd never get over it.

But, still, I thought I should tell him. He'd said he loved me and it said in *Jackie* magazine that there shouldn't be any secrets between you and your boyfriend, particularly if you'd used the 'L' word. I hadn't told him I loved him yet either. I was working up to it but I wasn't comfortable using the word 'love'. Dad always said that love is need. I knew I needed Mac so I must have loved him. So, after much agonising, I decided I'd tell Mac my big secret.

We were in the kitchen. His mum was in the front room. The telly was blasting away. How would I put it? Perhaps just blurt it out. My heart was thudding against his chest as we leaned entwined next to the cooker, the smell of fried eggs in his hair.

'I've got something to tell you.'

'Don't tell me, show me.'

I think he thought I was going to say I liked him. If only it was that simple.

Show him I went to a nudist camp? How would I do that? 'What d'you mean?' I asked him.

He put his hand on my breast.

I thought I might go half way. After all, I loved him and I wasn't showing him something I hadn't showed before to loads of people I felt nothing like 'love' for. I listened for sounds of his mum and then started to unbutton my blouse. I'd show him what I did at the weekend.

Looking back on it, it was perhaps not one of my wisest decisions. But I didn't have the same sort of feelings about undressing as most young girls should. I was totally confused about it.

I had on a thin lacy bra with painful under-wires that pushed me up like dumplings and made me look more than I was. I was fourteen and I wanted to look more. I wanted to be older.

He looked down. 'You're very developed.'

He cupped my breasts gently, glancing quickly at the door.

'Mac, I've got something to tell you,' I repeated.

But his mind was on other things. I can't really blame him for what he did next. Looking back, I can see it's what any testosterone-fuelled adolescent would do with a young girl in a lacy bra who was looking deep into their eyes but, at the time, I wasn't expecting what happened next. I heard the now familiar sound of a zip. Mac took my hand in his.

I froze. It was all coming back to me. Was it the only thing that men wanted from me? He wound my hand around his penis, showing me how to do the action.

'Just keep rubbing.'

We did it together, to the distant sounds of *Coronation Street* on the telly. Occasionally he winced as I caught him with a nail. I wasn't a natural, couldn't catch the rhythm, the right beat.

I may as well have been milking a cow for the degree of passion in the act. Faster and faster we went. He could have been getting on with it on his own for the contribution I was making but I suppose there was the bra. The real thing I was worrying about was how I was going to tell him about the nudist camp. He didn't seem in a particularly receptive mood.

He could see I wasn't really getting into the spirit of it. Then, at the crucial moment, he reached for the tea towel. Years later I'd wonder about that tea towel and how many dishes it wiped up before it went into the wash.

Soon after that, Mac finished with me. I never did tell

him about the camp. I don't think he was very impressed with my technique. Perhaps the learning curve was too great. He hadn't really loved me. He'd only seen me as a kind of plaything.

Chapter 29

'I want it all off. Short.' The woman at the hairdressers shaped her mandarin-lipsticked mouth into an 'O'. 'You sure, love?'

'Yes.'

She held the weight of my hair in her hands. 'It's beautiful. So thick. How can you cut off such lovely hair?'

Because I hated it. Hated everything about me. I couldn't do anything about myself but I could do something about my hair.

'Just cut it. Please.'

'Sure now?'

I nodded.

'OK, love, but it's such a shame.'

She brushed my hair through, divided it into three strands and carefully bound it into a thick plait. It reminded me of when Mum used to do that when I was little and she'd put an Alice band on afterwards, scraping all the hair from my face so I felt nice and neat, then she'd kiss me on the top of my head. I missed those old times with my mum. Recently with her job and her frequent afternoon naps, I'd become a latch-key kid, letting myself into the cold house where I would scrape potatoes and peel vegetables, following hurried notes from her about when to put which pan on to boil.

They say you 'lose touch' and it's exactly the touch that goes. I couldn't remember the last time Mum had touched me, unless you counted the few times she'd tried to slap me. She certainly didn't hug me, or run her hand over my hair. I suppose I'd become difficult to touch. I'd built a wall around myself, higher even than those walls around nudist camps. It was so high that no one could get through to me. The hairdresser fixed two elastic bands around my hair, one at the nape of my neck, and one at the other end. Reaching for the scissors, she stopped.

'I can't do it. Just can't.'

'I want it off.'

'But you'll regret it. I'm sure you will.'

'Just do it . . .'

She reined in her bottom lip with her teeth. 'OK . . . OK, give me a minute. You sure now?'

'Sure. All off. Short.'

She held up the scissors, looked at me in the mirror, closed her eyes quickly, opened them wide and cut. As she cut, I felt something close to pain although I knew that was silly. There were no nerves in your hair.

It took a couple of chops with the scissors. 'Heck, it's so thick!' Then it was off.

Good riddance. I didn't need long hair and all that came with it. All those stories where women had enticed men with their hair in some way. I didn't need that kind of attention. It was time it all came off.

The hairdresser held up the shining plait like a trophy for me to see. 'You've sure got lovely hair.'

Had lovely hair. Everything about me was going to change.

With the weight of it off, I felt light headed, almost dizzy. I saw that I had a long neck and sharp, elfin features. They would need some work too. The short hair changed the look of me completely. I wasn't a soft little girl any more. I was hard.

I looked at my plait lying like an amputated limb on the counter top. The hairdresser snipped away, shorter and shorter, cutting the hair close to my head like a convict. She cut it in jagged layers that were rough and unfinished. It was darker underneath where the sun hadn't bleached it. I looked really ugly. I smiled, then I ran my fingers through the roughness of my new barbed hair. Spiked it up. Even the texture of it seemed different – coarse.

The hairdresser went to the till and handed me some money. I looked at her, puzzled.

'It's for the hair. It'll make someone a fine wig. No charge for the cut.'

I'd never had that much money before. Sometimes on my birthday or at Christmas I'd get a note. Or recently I'd got the odd bit of pocket money, but this payment for my hair was a fortune. For the first time in my life I had real cash and together with my saved up pocket money I knew exactly what I was going to do with it all.

Next stop was the beauty salon. There the beautician asked where my mum was but I knew I looked a lot older with my hair short so I told a lie.

'I'm sixteen. Don't need my mum.'

Even my voice was changing, getting rougher, deeper. I liked the new sound of it. I was leaving that little girl way behind, like the cuttings on the hairdresser's floor.

The beautician frowned at me as she showed me the rows of earrings.

I chose plain gold hoops with small crosses. 'Can you take one of those off?'

'What, the cross?'

'Yeah.'

'But then they'd be odd.'

I nodded. I wanted them to be odd. I liked the idea of a cross in one ear and not the other, in a kind of heaven and hell statement. Like me.

She dabbed my ears with methylated spirit, and put the stapler in place.

'This is going to hurt a bit. You haven't got much of an ear lobe. Ready?

She squeezed.

It was how I imagine torture. I clamped my teeth down hard and didn't make a sound. I knew about being the silent child.

She removed it to check her handiwork and gasped. 'It's not gone through. I'm gonna have to try again.'

Twice more she tried to staple a hole in my ear. I could feel the blood trickling down my neck. Each time I tensed, ready.

Her hands were shaking. 'I just can't do it. It won't go through.'

On the fourth attempt she made the hole and secured the sleeper through the bloody mess.

'I think you'd better come back next week or something for the other one. You've had enough for one day.'

'No. I want them both done.'

So she tried, again and again with her stapler, to get through the tissues of my ears. They were tough, I thought, like me – or at least how I would be. I was shaking, too, by the time she'd finished. My ears were burning.

'I'll never pierce anyone's ears again,' she said as I handed her the money. 'That was awful.'

I checked myself in the mirror. My ears were bright red and wouldn't stop bleeding. The beautician gave me some tissues to take home and instructions about methylated spirits. I had never felt pain like it, not even when I'd been beaten up by Carole.

From there I went to the market where I bought white tights, a pair of black platform lace ups with large stack heels and a coat with patch pockets. Black Rimmel eyeliner and thick lash mascara were also on my shopping list and I bought a black scooped-neck cardigan and two fists of large cheap rings. I had plans for the finishing touches, which required a ball of black wool, some knitting needles, black material and a pattern.

I couldn't wait to get home.

Dad was washing the car. He didn't recognise me at first and just carried on polishing with his chamois leather. Then he looked up. He put down his rag and stood with his hands on his hips, biting his lower lip.

'What the hell've you done?!'

'Got my hair cut.'

'I can see that, young lady. But why?'

I scowled at him. Why? Because I never wanted to look like a little girl again. I kept walking past him.

'Your hair, Jo? Your crowning glory? Well, all I can say is that you look a sight. A bloody sight. What have you got to say for yourself? Going off and doing a thing like this? Without my permission?'

I shrugged.

'How dare you!'

'It's my hair, I'll do what I like with it.'

'Now listen here, young lady . . . and what's that blood? Oh God, what have you done?'

'Pierced my ears.'

'You . . . you look like a common trollop.'

I nodded. That was exactly the look I wanted to create. I pushed past him.

He didn't speak to me for a week.

Mum held her hands to her face as I came in through the door.

'Mary-mother-of-God. What've you done?!'

'What d'you think?'

'What did your father say?'

Slowly now. 'He said it looked really nice.'

'Heavens above! I don't know I . . . Jo . . . ?'

I shut myself away in my bedroom. I couldn't wait to get started. I looked in the mirror at my cropped, dark hair and saw two rivulets of dried blood running down my neck, like a bride of Dracula. That was my inspiration. I would create something from hell.

I put some of Dad's Brylcreem in my hair so it looked even darker, edged my eyes in black and smudged it in well under the lids like dark shadows. Then layered mascara on my lashes so I looked like a grotesque doll, or one of those puppets that comes to life with a turn of their head in horror films. The hair and the make-up made my skin look paler. I turned the sleepers that were already starting to scab up. My ears bled fresh blood. I tried on the white tights and the shoes, put the coat on top. It was nearly there.

Over the half-term week I worked to perfect the look, practising a certain expression in the mirror with my head down, angled to one side

I decided I'd make my own clothes to complete my new look. We'd been doing sewing at school and I'd quite enjoyed it, although I'd made a blouse and managed somehow to sew up the armholes so a skirt was a major undertaking. All week I worked on it. It was in six sections, slightly flared and it stuck out because the material was thick and cheap. I made it short and tried it on with the black jumper and my school shirt. I wouldn't bother with a blouse. Then I spent some time knitting a perfect skullcap. Knit one purl one, reducing it row by row so it fitted perfectly to my head.

It would be a good look.

The only bad thing about cutting my hair was going to the club. I missed my Lady Godiva locks but overall I liked my new look, which made me feel angry and mean.

I wasn't vulnerable anymore. Everyone at the club hated it, particularly Terry.

'Your hair!'

'What about it?'

'It's all short!'

'Ah, top marks for observation.'

'But how could you?'

'Easy really. You take a pair of scissors and go snip, snip, snip.'

'What's got into you?'

'I've changed.'

'I can see that all right. You look like a boy. Well . . .' looking down at me . . . 'not quite.'

'You know something?'

'What?'

'Just stop looking at me like that, you pervert!'

'Jo . . . ?'

I would have flicked back my hair as I walked off but I didn't have any so I scowled instead. I loved my new look. It said I was dangerous.

Everyone stayed away from me – Terry, the Rebels, even my parents. The distance between us widened to a huge chasm, particularly with Mum.

'Take off that make-up,' she hissed, her unsteady hand coming up, as if she was going to slap me. These days, it seemed to be the only way she could communicate how disappointed in me she was, despite never having hit me much when I was small. It was as if the drink made her feel invincible.

I caught her hand mid-air, held it there as we struggled.

'Jo . . . Jo, let me go!'

I twisted it round to her back.

Her eyes were pleading. 'For the love of God, what're you doing?'

I put my face up close to hers. 'You will never, ever raise your hand to me again.'

She tried to get her arm free. 'Lord Almighty, you're hurting me.'

But I was too strong now. 'Say it!'

'What?'

'That you won't . . .' and I tweaked her arm at her back.

'Aaah. God forgive you, child.'

'Say it.'

She held my gaze. Then looked away. 'I . . . won't . . . ever . . .'

'What?'

'I won't ever hit you again.'

I let her go, stared her down and away.

Mum didn't say anything when she saw me in my new look school uniform. Instead of the knee-length navy blue pleated skirt and V-neck jumper, now we were older, we started altering our uniform any way we could without sending the teachers into a total spin. I was dressed all in black with white tights and clumpy platform-soled lace-ups. At the top was dark spiky hair and black eyeliner.

Her eyes focussed on the cross hanging down from my left ear. I wondered at that moment if she was saying a mental prayer to God. I think even if she could have spoken, she wouldn't have known what to say. She couldn't bring me back – not from the dead.

Even my walk had changed. I'd learned something from my time at Mac's side and now I too, could arch my back slightly and sway. I put metal segs on the heels of my shoes so they clicked loudly when I strutted along. Now everyone would know I was coming. I had become the kind of teenage monster that every parent dreads but that most kids at school respect.

Sometimes I'd get sent home, get told to come back when I was properly attired in school uniform. I might wear my navy jumper for a day or two, then I'd be back to my personal style. Eventually the teachers gave up on me and, with that, I gave up on my work. Or rather, on what showed.

I'd hand in my essays late or not at all. I'd make them so bad, that I never had to read them out in class. They'd certainly never appear in the local paper again. I was fourteen, I was learning and the gang at the back responded. Soon they were inviting me to sit with them.

I didn't need teachers or work. I had friends. I had street cred. I learned to talk like them, copying their flat vowels and missing the ends off words. I had a whole different language at school that my parents knew nothing about. The girls at the back stopped calling me a wog. I was still a wog but I was all right and even Carole started to leave me alone. With that, so did her cronies.

I winked in the mirror. 'All right.'

I belonged.

I upped the ante and soon became the naughtiest girl in the class. Once I had started, I couldn't stop. It was like all the time I'd been quiet I was storing it up so, when it came out, it was unstoppable.

I baited and baited the English teacher until I made her cry. I got myself sent out of class every music lesson. The list of bad behaviour was endless and I had detention most weeks. We'd sit doing Chinese burns on each other, seeing who could take the most pain. I'd take a compass in there with me, etching crosses deep into the back of my arm and filling them in with ink to make crude tattoos. Or I'd sneak in a nail file and eyebrow tweezers and we'd do beauty treatments on each other. We plucked our eyebrows to fine hard lines to look expressionless. Filed our nails to points.

I had found a way through. I was hard. It wasn't real, of course. It was a coat I could put on every day. I was in with them but I would never let them get too close. I could choose, I had some control now, and with that came a whole new life.

I started to go out with my new friends in the evenings. There wasn't much choice in Warrington for fourteen year olds and we'd usually hang around bus stops or outside the chippy, sharing splits – chips and mushy peas, or chips with onion gravy. We'd hold our hands around them for warmth in the cold. We'd buy cigarettes in packets of tens and pass them around, huddling in gangs, talking about boys. There were rival gangs of girls and sometimes they'd come at you, with bottles or chains. Even then, despite my rings like knuckle-dusters, I could never quite follow through. I was a sham. I tried to keep it from the others, but I couldn't crumple another girl's face with my fist or kick her when she was down.

One evening I came home in a police car, my face slashed with chains.

'What's been going on?' shouted my dad, horrified, while Mum wept silently in the chair.

The policeman's radio was buzzing. 'Picked her up by the park. There's been a fight.'

My parents' faces blank, exhausted, wondering what

I'd do next. After I'd had a good talking to from the policeman and my dad had read me the riot act, we prowled around in that police car, past the rival gang who'd found their mark.

The policeman caught them in his headlights. 'That them, love?'

I shook my head. 'Never seen them before.'

There was a mutual respect amongst the gangs. We understood each other. You didn't tell tales.

'Just goin' down the youth club,' I'd slur, then remember I wasn't supposed to speak like that at home.

'You mean going down to the youth club,' Mum would correct.

Then my father would add, 'And I expect you back by nine o'clock or else, young lady.'

The youth club had actually closed down a year before. I'd get changed in a phone box and join my mates in a cavernous dance hall. There, we'd perform perfectly synchronised formation dancing, the girls in neat lines dancing with dainty sideways steps while the boys would peel off to demonstrate their prowess at backdrops and spins. I could do them as well as any lad in the hall. I would practise all the newest moves in my bedroom and could knock spots off anyone.

I'd found a place. I was still pretending, but at least I could do it with my clothes on.

Mum had taken to trying to be my ally on those nights out. I think she hoped it would bring us closer together, that we'd be like a secret team, us against the world. Despite her drinking, she was alert enough to work out that I'd never get back for a nine o'clock curfew, so she'd wait until Dad fell asleep after their evening meal, then turn the clock back an hour or so to give me more time. One evening I was late. Dad had sussed out where I was. Or maybe he'd known all along but just hadn't said anything. The first I knew that he was there in the disco was when a spotlight swept over the crowded dance floor.

Then his booming voice. 'Is that my daughter?'

Dad stood in the middle of the dance hall, pointing an industrial searchlight right at my eyes.

'Jo?'

The light burned into my face.

'It's time you were home. It's well past your bedtime, young lady.'

It took a while to recover my street cred after that one.

After that, Dad was always turning up unexpectedly. Perhaps deep down he was trying to protect me. Whatever the reasoning, sometimes his methods were extreme.

I'd been being my normal self at the school film society. Disruptive. I sat at the back with my mates as we watched a crackly version of *Love Story*, trying to spoil it for everyone else. The rest of the audience were enjoying a good cry in the bit where Ryan O'Neal climbs on the hospital bed to hold Ali MacGraw one last time as she's dying but I was singing along to the theme tune, waving my hands in the air. We were all laughing on the back row.

The religious education teacher, however, didn't see the funny side of it. He struggled along the back row and caught me by the shoulder.

'Get out!'

'Wha'?'

'I said, "Get out!" You're ruining it for everyone.'

'No, you're ruinin' it for everyone. Shoutin'.'

We all laughed. We were always making fun of him because we could see he was weak. But he didn't seem that weak as he clutched my shoulder and tried to drag me out.

I shrugged him off. 'OK, OK, I'm going.'

We all walked out.

'You'll be hearing from me in the morning,' he shouted.

We decided as we had time to kill we'd all go back to my house. Dad wanted to know why we'd come home early. He listened carefully, his fists getting tighter and tighter.

'Nobody manhandles my daughter like that.'

Apparently, Dad stormed into the film society just as *Love Story* was finishing, and gave the RE teacher what for.

When Dad told me what he'd done, all I could think was, if only he'd been there all those times when I really needed him.

Chapter 30

I was fourteen now and my relationship with Dad had all but broken down. I'd dyed the front of my cropped hair pink. That, he'd said, was the final straw.

'Straw-berry,' I'd retorted, rather pleased with myself.

But he hadn't seen it like that. 'Don't ever answer me back again!'

He saw red. Not pink. Not strawberry. But red.

'I don't know what's happened to you. Ever since you got that hair of yours cut and maimed your body, you've been a nightmare.'

'I'm not a little girl anymore.'

'Just watch it.'

I stared at him without blinking my eyes. 'I'm watching.'

I hadn't been on the receiving end of one of his rants for a long time. We just kept out of each other's way.

'Watch your lip, young lady!'

I pulled my lip out, let it go and turned on my heel.

Something had to give and when it did happen, it

was as these things always are – nothing very much to do with what was going on at the time. It was lunchtime and I was carrying in his plate to the table. It was a variant of what we always ate: meat, vegetables and boiled potatoes. I'd put slightly too much gravy on his plate, so I was concentrating, my tongue out. I'd almost made it to the table when I tilted the plate as I was putting it down and the gravy spilled out onto the white cloth.

'Sorry . . . I . . .'

But Dad's fists were tightening.

As I went to sit down, he started shouting at me for being careless. I don't know why, but something just snapped in me.

Without thinking, I grabbed Dad's watch that lay on the dining room table and threw it at him. It was heavy, stainless steel with round cut-out circles on the strap. It hit him right in the mouth and I heard it clang against something. He raised a hand, checking.

'Holy-Mary-mother-of-God!' Mum clasped her hands in her face.

Dad was shaking his head, with his hand in his mouth. 'She's chipped my tooth! That . . . that . . . she's chipped my tooth!'

I stood up, ready, but he stayed seated, looking back at me. We stared at each other for a moment, breathing hard, hands raised. Then he looked away.

*

I was sitting at the station thinking about what I'd done in losing my temper like that.

I stared at a brick wall. I was just fourteen and all I had was a bit of money, a small suitcase with a few clothes and my llama. I'd thought about leaving llama behind but he'd just looked at me with those long-gone eyes of his and I'd felt guilty. He'd been with me through it all and I couldn't leave him behind now so, even though he'd taken up most of the space in my case, just knowing he was there made me feel better.

I wasn't sure exactly where I was going. I just waited for the train,

When I'd announced I was leaving home, I'd just got carried away with the thought. What I'd meant to say was that I wanted it all to stop – the arguing, the fighting, the drinking and, most of all, going to those nudist camps. It had all come out in that unstoppable train-screaming-down-the-tracks way.

'I'm leaving,' I'd announced half way through lunch.

Dad had looked straight at me. 'Good riddance.'

I don't know what I'd expected, perhaps some pleading to stay.

Maybe 'Please don't go, Jo. We'll work it out.'

Then Dad's arms round me. 'Come on then, enough of all this nonsense.'

I'd felt stupid storming off to my bedroom with much door slamming.

Mum had come in, holding her face in her hands. 'Jo, what's going on?'

'I'd have thought that was obvious.' I pulled open a drawer.

'What d'you think you're doing?'

'What does it look like, spring cleaning?'

'Don't be like that!'

'What?'

'Oh you know, difficult.'

'What d'you want me to be like then? More like you? Just not saying anything? Keeping the peace at all costs? I don't think so.'

Mum tried to put her arms round me but it was the wrong time.

I crossed mine in front of me. 'Oh for God's sakes, Mum – leave me alone.'

She stood there, with her arms out-stretched, hugging the empty space between us. Then she started to cry. 'I don't know what I've done to deserve a daughter like you. All I've ever tried to do is what's best for you.'

'Have you? Have you, Mum?' I screwed up my clothes, throwing them roughly into the case.

'I'm just staying out of it. I'm not coming between you and your father.'

'No. Why change the habit of a lifetime?'

I turned my back, busying myself with my packing.

I sorted some trousers, a few shirts and jumpers. My stomach was tight. Where was I going?

I zipped up the case, kept my eyelids lowered.

I pushed past them both.

Mum was standing in the hallway. 'Mary-mother-of-God, you're not serious about this, are you?' She turned to my dad. 'Do something! Make her stop!'

Dad was behind me with his arms folded.

'Leave her alone. Let her go if that's what she wants to do. We can't stop her.'

I hadn't turned around as I'd walked out through the door, hadn't let them see that my face was wet. I kept my shoulders still so they couldn't see them shaking. I had it all under control.

The train was appearing as if out of nowhere, screeching and raising goose pimples all over me as it came to a halt. It stopped and I opened the door, stepping in, checking the platform in case Dad had turned up. The guard rushed to secure the door and blew his whistle.

I kept looking out at the platform as the train pulled out but the station was empty. I clutched my small case to me. Where would I go? I had a sick feeling deep in my stomach.

I longed to stay on that train for ever, just keep going and going, listening to the steady beat-beat of the train, comforting as a heartbeat, and watching the world go by in a blur. Everything was distant, almost unreal. If I stayed on the train I wouldn't have to take part anymore. I looked out at the rows of houses; all those people out there, did they ever feel like I did now? I took out my llama and looked into his unseeing eyes that still seemed to watch me quietly.

I didn't get very far on that train. Just to the next station, then over the bridge to the opposite platform and back on the first train home, I knew I had nowhere else to go but, as I approached the house, I was dreading the confrontation with my parents.

Dad was mowing the lawn – he didn't even switch off the lawnmower, didn't even look at me. It was never talked about, that little episode when I left home. I wasn't really sure that it even counted since I'd barely got out of the train station. At home, we were back to how we'd been: covering up.

By going back home I knew I was accepting the world as it was, that the arguments and fights would continue, even the silences. I also knew that, despite having tried to make a stand, I would carry on taking off my clothes as required.

Chapter 31

The school term was almost finished and it was coming up to the summer. Everyone except me was looking forward to going away on holiday, because I knew we were going back there, to Italy.

It was like a recurring nightmare: the long car journey, the stink from the carboy of petrol in the boot, my mum and dad arguing all the way. Then, when we got there, more rows and sulks.

I hated it all, especially the mass of sweating, naked bodies, browning on the beach – like sausages.

We pitched our tent and I set up my camp in the car which, as usual, would be my home for the next two weeks. Mum was too tired to cook so she sent me shopping for something to eat.

'What shall I get?'

'Oh, use your imagination,' she said as she handed me some money.

One of the incongruous images I have from that time is of nudists carrying shopping bags and going from stall to stall, pondering over the produce, looking like they'd forgotten something other than their clothes. A collection of huts a fair distance from our tent served a variety of ready-cooked food – cauldrons of simmering, unidentifiable slop, slimy casseroles of aubergines and tomatoes, and cartons of freshly fried calamari with sprawling tentacles. It was a bemusing place for someone raised on meat and two veg, and a hazardous place for a nudist with all those spitting-hot sauces.

And it was here that I met Marco and, just as I had with Mac, I fell instantly in love with him. We were each waiting in separate queues that ran at right angles towards the servers. Suddenly, we were next to each other at a corner post, his face – in profile – close to mine. I gave him a quick glance and a smile.

They say you 'fall' for someone and that's how it felt – unsteady, as though I was falling into those soft, angelic, eyes, or the promise of them. He had a beautiful face, full lips that turned down at the corners, and hair that swept like clouds around his face. Around his neck he wore a delicate gold chain.

He was truly breathtaking.

'Hello,' he said softly.

'Hello.'

'Are you English?' He had the most perfect mouth when he talked.

'Yes.'

'I speak only a little English . . . and I am sorry but it was very, very bad.'

'I think you're good . . . I mean your English is good.'

'Thank you.'

We stood talking for another twenty minutes or so, before he just came out and asked if I'd like to go to the disco that night with him.

I said yes right away.

There is something really odd about talking to someone you really like, having just met them, when you are stark naked.

He took my hand and kissed it, telling me he'd see me later.

I was skipping, floating back to the tent.

'You look flushed,' Mum observed.

'It's a long way.'

'Hope the food hasn't gone cold.'

I divided the sludge up on to plates but I was thinking about Marco's eyes. 'Eat up,' said Dad. But I wasn't hungry. As the time drew closer to eight o'clock, I became more and more edgy. We were allowed to wear clothes to the evening discos, so that meant an outfit dilemma. I dressed in what I had which, unfortunately, were sports clothes.

Mum was washing up plates in a small plastic bowl with water left in the sun to warm.

'You all right, Jo?'

'Yes.'

'What's up?'

'Just going to get some fresh air.'

'But you're already outside.'

'I mean proper fresh air.'

'I'll come with you.'

'No!' Kinder now, 'I just want some time by myself.'

Despite everything that'd happened to me in the camps, I felt a weird sense of calm as I set out for the disco, which was just a short walk from the food stalls at the far end of the camp. It was in the woods, so I walked quickly, guided in by the music then focussing on the glow from the disco ahead. The building was hexagonal and lit up like something that had arrived from another planet.

In fact, inside it was also like something from another planet because they were all wearing clothes; and far from committee-approved sportswear. There were a lot of French and Spanish kids staying here too, that helped as I'd started learning some French at school and so I could get by with a few words here and there. The boys wore well-cut linen trousers or jeans with pastel T-shirts, and light-coloured sweaters draped casually around their shoulders. The girls wore dresses, mini skirts or tailored shorts. I looked down at my baggy tracksuit with go-faster stripes down the sides and the only place I wanted to go fast to was back to the tent.

I stood for a while watching the dancers. They clutched each other in amorous grips as they slow-danced. It had long gone eight but I waited as the minutes ticked by on the face of my luminous Timex, hoping to catch a glimpse of Marco. But then I decided I couldn't face him, not dressed like this – I would almost have preferred to face him naked. So I left.

I walked outside, back into the woods away from the disco. Some of the dancers were peeling off in pairs, disappearing into the woods for a cuddle. I kept hidden. A couple came close to me, whispering, as he was holding her hand. They didn't see me in the dark. They stopped and started to kiss. Then they 'got busy'.

I didn't want them to know I was there. I felt a bit of a gooseberry as they carried on.

I couldn't tell whether it was because they were on holiday or because they were nudists, but in no time at all they started undressing each other.

I didn't know what to do, so in the end, I did what I'd grown accustomed to doing in woods – I crouched down, kept still and hoped for the best as they started having sex. I tried not to look, terrified that they might see me. I closed my eyes but the noise was difficult to ignore. It was another bad introduction to the world of sex. Fortunately it didn't go on very long and soon the couple got up, dressed and went back to the disco.

After I'd calmed down, I picked my way silently through those woods. Everywhere there were couplings going on. I tried to walk past them with my eyes blinkered.

The teenagers would meet up on the beach during the day to recover from their nocturnal activities. When I was walking past with my parents a couple of days after the disco debacle, Marco called me over. I looked at my mum and dad and they nodded. Of course I could go and join a bunch of naked teenagers, there was nothing wrong with that. We were naturists.

I was cross with myself for not being brave enough to go into the disco. I apologised to Marco for not showing up. He said he'd been convinced I'd think he was weird for asking me out when we didn't know each other. He seemed a bit shy and unsure. I guess I knew how he felt.

I was accepted into the gang. We lay on our stomachs all day around a radio, or someone would pick up a guitar and sing. It was the closest I'd ever been to feeling right at a nudist camp. The others were all so beautiful, they didn't have anything to feel ashamed of. They had nothing to prove.

I was in love with Marco, my angel. Hands entwined

all day on the beach and, in the evenings at the disco swaying to love songs with Marco trying to translate the words.

'It's a romance. It's a beautiful story.'

And so it was. I learned something from those naked teenagers on the beach in Italy. That you could feel comfortable there, lying naked in the sand. That it could seem natural. I saw how relaxed they were and, although I never attained that nirvana – for me the damage had already been done – I saw it was possible. I realised that that was how my dad felt – totally comfortable in his own skin.

I became even more distant from Mum and Dad. I'd see them, sometimes, lying on the beach working on their suntans, communicating the only way they could without rowing: silent and naked. One day my dad did something really heroic, which impressed me. The sea was notoriously dangerous, plagued by rip tides and you always had to check by the colour of the safety flags on the beach whether or not it was safe to swim.

Dad was just lazing around when he saw a woman wave from the water. She kept waving so he waved back but he soon realised that she was in trouble, the tide was taking her out to sea. Dad was a strong swimmer and, straight away, he was on his feet, dived in and swam out to her.

Later, he told us how funny it had been when he'd got to her. He couldn't actually reach out and clasp her in a firm body hold because she was naked so he'd just held her hand and dragged her out of the current. The woman was so happy she cried and cried, and she obviously didn't have the same etiquette concerns as my dad – Mum said it was unsettling watching him being hugged by a completely naked woman.

Dad had seen me with Marco and didn't seem to mind. I could never understand why he was so protective towards me at home with my clothes on but didn't care when I was with a teenage boy, completely naked.

Picture the scene – a typical day, lying naked next to someone you find extremely attractive. Perhaps more than once it enters your head that they might feel the same way. Later, at the disco, following an intense bout of kissing glued together to the strains of various foreign love songs, all that smooching music gets to you. Marco and I had gone into the darkened area outside the disco where couples in lust were accustomed to going.

It had been hot on the dance floor but out here it was even hotter. His lips were cushioned and soft. I was caught up in the beauty of him, running my hands through his long hair, feeling him all around me. Marco was sensitive, and tender; he also had the additional advantage of being Italian. I had no idea whether he would have bored the pants off me if he were English, but he was certainly getting into my pants now.

His eyelashes brushed gently against my face. He was moaning as he gently caressed me. Then I felt a stirring from him way down. I began to understand an equation that they didn't teach you at school, which was that starting size has little to do with full potential. He undid his zip to release the pressure and pulled me further into the woods.

I don't know if it was the zip thing or the woods that made me stop and go rigid. Then I started to shake and any flame of passion that might have been burning was doused by a bucketful of dirty memories. Terry was there, somehow between us, his eyes glinting in the moonlight, then there was Jan and his insistent tongue and Anthony in the dark of my bedroom. I felt my bare feet on sand and the two men who'd attacked me in the dunes were with us, too, taking photographs.

Memories crowding. Black memories in a dark wood. 'No . . .'

Marco's soft eyes looked up at me, confused. I pushed him away and started to run. In all my nightmares I'm running through woods, their branches whipping my face, blocking my path. I ran and ran back to my den in the car, wriggled into my sleeping bag and pulled the zip up high. I reached for my torch in the bottom of the bag and switched it on, safe now in the glow. I lay curled up like a foetus until my breathing slowed.

Then I heard a knock on the car. I sank deeper into the sleeping bag, hoping whoever it was would go away. Then the knock again. I shone the beam of my torch at the sound. A white face was looking back at me. I didn't register at first it was Marco. When I did, I could breathe again. Slowly I unlocked the door and placed my fingers to my lips – my parents were asleep in the tent just a short distance away.

Marco wound me in his arms, knowing that I was frightened. I stepped out into the night and we walked over to where the sand was soft, and lay down with our backs on the ground watching the mass of stars fizzing above us. Every now and again, a shooting star would burn briefly in the sky and he'd point it out. He didn't try to get to where we'd been earlier. He knew something had happened.

'You are a good girl,' he whispered.

But I knew it wasn't that I was good – I'd just lost the ability to be bad.

I was so confused by the feelings I had for Marco in relation to everything bad that had happened with the others. I felt dirty because I found Marco attractive. I didn't know how to be normal.

Chapter 32

Back in England, I thought about what had happened that summer with Marco, and it worried me. Not that, at fifteen, I was ready for a full-blown sexual relationship but I had lost the ability to even feel comfortable kissing someone – it all made me feel sick and uneasy. There were certain things that started a closing down operation within me, and once the process had started, it just couldn't stop.

But I couldn't tell them that what I really wanted was a boy just to be my friend – that I needed someone much more mature and understanding to take it a lot more slowly. They were just young boys doing what young boys do.

I had quite a few boyfriends at that time but whenever they tried to get close in that way, I'd start to feel sick. It was maybe just a kiss, that would start innocently enough and then it would turn to something slimy and horrible and the memories would start slithering back. Worse still was anything more than that. Once the closing-down process had started, there was nothing that could stop it.

I just couldn't enjoy it. There were too many memories – too much revulsion. If the shut-down could happen with someone I really liked, like Marco, then it could happen with anyone.

All through my teenage years, I was stuck. While my school friends would tell stories of their sexual exploits, I kept quiet. It was as though a button had been switched off somewhere in me. I did meet boys but I couldn't give them what they wanted. I was a misfit. While the others in the gang I hung around with were doing what they did around the back of the bike sheds, I was telling anyone who came near me to get on his bike.

Eventually my friends turned on me and started to mock what they thought were my high-minded principles. And despite my tough front and the fact that everyone had been following me round for some time, it soon got around at school that I was frigid and they gave me a new nickname – 'Tightknickers'. I tried to shrug it off, to look as if I couldn't care less, and just see it as something else that made me different. I didn't like losing my tough-girl status though.

We were all getting older, I was nearly sixteen. The skinhead culture was being overtaken and groups of girls with bad fashion choices no longer roamed the streets. My friends were peeling off and pairing up with boys. Once again I found myself set apart.

It also didn't help that most of my weekends were still spent going to a nudist camp with my parents. Even if I'd wanted to, I couldn't sustain a social life. Occasionally I'd still get invited to parties and discos but I never knew if I could go.

'Are we going to the club this weekend?' I'd ask.

Silence.

'Well are we, because there's this party and . . . ?'

Dad would sniff and turn his back. We didn't talk about what we did at the weekend.

I had to find a way to get out. I took a long hard look at myself and decided I had to change. Without the distraction of friends or boyfriends to impress, I guess I just drifted into filling my time by starting to work again at school. It wasn't a conscious decision, it simply happened as both at home and at school, there wasn't much else to do. It was the start of my O Level year and after I'd done a few essays, I thought that this could be my chance to get out. At school, I kept a low profile; not that anyone noticed as there was a new class joker. Because I was good at keeping secrets, no one ever found out. I never handed my homework in, as I didn't want to look like a swot, but I worked really hard at home.

I also took a long hard look at my surroundings and decided that they had to change too. There had to be something more on offer than Warrington and a campsite of nudists. But to get it I would have to work. I wanted my independence, my freedom. That required an education but it also required money.

My first summer job was certainly a strange one – working during the holidays as a receptionist in a funeral parlour. I had to wear black and be quiet all day. It was already quiet in there with only the corpses next door. I'd take my knitting to work and all I would hear would be the clickety-clack of the needles. It smelled the same as our biology lab at school and the highlight of the day would be a visit from the embalmer.

My job was to show grieving relatives their loved ones; the man who owned the place had shown me how to take the handkerchiefs off their faces as I did so, and to look away respectfully.

I'll never forget my first customers. A highly distressed couple wanted to see their Auntie Mabel. There were three bodies in the room next door. I showed them the first and they shook their heads. Then the second and they turned away. Then the third. Each time, the woman's weeping got louder and louder. Then the man had to put his arm round his wife. None of the bodies was Auntie Mabel.

It turned out that Auntie Mabel wasn't even in this funeral home. She was somewhere else at the other end of town. I only found out later that their names were inscribed on brass plates on the lids of each coffin standing up at the side but the funeral director hadn't told me that.

From that job I learned never to send flowers to funerals. The parlours couldn't cope with them and more often than not they just ended up on the tip. Far better to send flowers to the people left behind, to remind them that life still goes on.

When I finished my shifts, I invariably took with me huge bunches of Arum lilies, or white carnations, or stephanotis. I'd remove the black edged cards and give the flowers to Mum – she knew where they came from but it was better that, than to see them thrown away.

I also wore black for my next holiday job at the Hillview hotel, which was mainly a restaurant for business travellers. Donning a little white apron on top of my black dress and waiting on tables I was always polite, sharing a joke. Most of the visitors were American and sometimes they'd tip 'the little English waitress'. The tips I got were often more than I was paid for a whole evening's work.

I spent a few weeks of that long summer holiday working in an off-licence, too, serving everything other than cigarettes and alcohol. I'd stack the shelves full of confectionery and then play shop. I loved it. It was like being a child again and I remembered how all that time ago Sue and I had wanted to run a sweetshop together. I never saw her now.

I could help myself to anything I wanted. I'd cut slices of ham for the man who owned the place, who was always in the back room watching telly. He'd never eat them though, or drink the coffee I made him. Far easier, he'd say, to help himself to a drink – he had a barrel on tap for this purpose.

One day, fortunately not on my shift, he left a note telling the other girl not to come in. He'd hanged himself. I wondered how bad you'd have to feel to do that. What on earth could happen to give you the strength to commit that final act? What a terrible way to end things.

My various jobs provided what I needed; I opened a bank account and watched my money grow. One day I'd have enough of my own money so that I could get away.

I became increasingly independent. Perhaps that's how it should be as a teenager. Mum was slipping away from me too – out pounding the streets selling her stuff. She had taken on more and lines and had branched out to towels, sheets and other household essentials. Always neat and tidy – hair and make-up perfect and her over-powering Estée Lauder perfume – I liked to see Mum working – with a purpose. I think it showed her what she could do when she was sober and not full of pills, that life wasn't all about drowning her sorrows. Mum grew

further and further away from my father. He didn't
approve of his wife working – the fact she enjoyed it
didn't help either. There were more and more rows, but
although she appeared OK on the outside, to be in
control, as time went by I'd come home from school and
with increasing regularity Mum would be home early
from work, or wouldn't have been at all. Bottles of Dad's
home brew started disappearing until one summer his
total stockpile of fifty-eight bottles of homemade beer
had vanished. Mum got worse, going to neighbours'
houses to borrow a half bottle of wine, going down to
the pub to fill a carafe. Soon she was banned from pubs
altogether

Alcoholism makes you desperate. Sometimes Mum
would talk a neighbour into getting booze for her. I'd
come home from school and she'd be in the bedroom
sleeping it off, so I'd go round to a friend's for a cup of
coffee and try to pretend it didn't bother me a bit that my
mum was a drunk. But it did, I didn't understand it and I
wanted to make it all better. I thought that she could just
stop drinking. I didn't realise that it had her in its grip and
like a big fist it was squeezing the very life out of her. I
can't remember how many times Mum took the pledge,
kissing the Holy Book and promising me and my father
that she would never, ever touch another drop.

At the weekends we'd still go down to the club. Dad

was making a name there for himself and there was talk that he might be invited on to the committee. He worked so hard at that place. He loved it and nurtured it as though it were his own child and I could feel his pride in what he did as he showed me around, talking of all the changes they'd made and the part he'd played in helping. It was his empire, his little piece of England. He had found his place. With a wife who was often drunk and distracted, that club, more than anything, was his home.

Chapter 33

I was sixteen and it would be my last holiday at the Italian camp. In some ways, it was a holiday I would rather forget, not because of what happened to me but because of what happened to someone else.

My hair had grown longer again, to just below my shoulders. Though I was small, I was toned from years of hockey training and had the kind of body I should have been proud of, but never could be. That was lost for ever. I was always tanned as though my skin had been permanently stained by years of all-over exposure, although I worked hard to create strap marks so I wouldn't get teased at school. When no one was around, I wore a swimming costume in the sun, stretching out at the back of the tent whenever I could. My dad had given up trying to tell me to take my clothes off. I liked to think that, at last, perhaps he could see how difficult it was for me.

I remember one evening I was standing on the lookout tower by the beach with Dad, watching the sun sink slowly in the sky. Recently, we'd developed a new kind of truce, an understanding with each other. I came here with him at the end of the day and we watched the sun set. That night we seemed to meet half way. It was easier because in the evenings we wore clothes.

We watched for the green flash, which is a relatively rare phenomenon that occurs on the horizon at the moment when the sun sets or rises.

There was a small group of us gathered on that tower. The wind swept over the sea as we waited, our faces still burning from a day in the sun, our hair blown back by the wind from the sea. The wind was so strong it felt as if we were moving. Dad's face was lit up with a red glow.

'Watch now! Watch, Jo! Don't blink or you might miss it.'

I strained to see the green flash.

As we concentrated on the horizon, I saw something in the distance. What appeared to be a cloud was heading our way and, as it came nearer and nearer, I could hear a buzzing.

'Duck, Jo, duck!'

But I was too late.

A swarm of large insects was caught in my hair.

'Keep still, keep still, they're mayflies!'

Huge thick bodies of insects buzzing and buzzing. The more they struggled, the more entangled they became. Dad tried to free them and as he did they squashed in his hands, their large bodies popping like boils. I started to panic with the buzzing close to my ears. More than anything it was the sound, bringing back memories of those buzzing cameras on the beach. The men who'd attacked me. It was as though they were here again, all around me. I couldn't disentangle myself from them.

I started to cry and once I'd started I couldn't stop.

'Don't worry, Jo. Hold still now! Hold still!'

I was sobbing and sobbing.

'Don't cry now! Soon get you sorted.'

I remember Dad pulling and pulling those buzzing bodies out of my hair.

It was a bad omen.

The times we had visited Italy, I had formed some strong attachments with other teenagers, including Marco. We'd meet up and take our places in the same spot on the beach, chatting together like old friends in a mixture of broken French and English. In between holidays, we'd write to each other. It was as though we shared a secret (although they had always been much more comfortable at being naked than me) and it was a relief to be able to communicate. It was as if, with age, we'd stopped rebelling and had accepted it.

One day, we had gathered as we always did, huddled around a radio, by the duckboards near the entrance to the beach. But the atmosphere was different. It wasn't the usual, lazy relaxed crowd of teenagers – there was tension as they spoke in quick, angry voices.

I tried to find out what was going on but it was difficult because at first nobody wanted to explain. They kept looking away as I pressed them.

Then one of the girls started to cry. It was her friend's sister, she said. She was only eleven. A chill crept through me. Not from the sea, or the wind whipping up the beach but from somewhere deep inside. It started in my stomach and went right through to the ends of my fingers.

'What happened?' I asked.

But I already knew the answer. The girl carried on crying. The others tried to explain to me in quiet voices, in snippets, so I had to translate it in tiny pieces when I could. They were angry. Someone threw a fistful of sand at the grass in the dunes and spat.

'Shit!'

I listened hard, trying to piece the story together as my friend explained. It had happened in the grass, up among the sand dunes, way down at the far end of the beach.

I didn't want to hear anymore, but then I knew I must.

The others in the group carried on the story, each supplying a bit of information. I don't know why one of them described the girl to me but they did. I could see her clearly – small with long, dark hair and large bright eyes.

She had been with her parents and then wandered off from the main beach, up into the dunes, shouting something about hide and seek. He put his hands over his eyes to act it out.

The girl's parents had searched for her, calling her name. They searched but found nothing so they gave up on the dunes, thinking she'd gone back down to the beach to find them. Surely she knew they were there? Surely she could hear them? The girl's parents had listened but heard nothing. They'd climbed the dunes and looked: they were empty. I remembered how the wind had whipped over those dunes, the man holding on to his hat.

It was getting late, and the sun was sinking in the sky. The girl's father continued to search the dunes. Her mother stayed on the beach, scanning the sea, terrified that the current had taken her daughter and she'd drowned. Then, from the dunes, the mother heard a scream.

It wasn't the scream of a little girl but of a man. I was shaking now, my skin turned to goose pimples. Even though she was frightened, the mother ran up the steep dunes. Her husband was carrying their little girl. Blood was dripping from between her legs. The mother rushed to them and she and her husband fell to their knees.

Someone made a sign then. A circle with his thumb and forefinger. Then he pushed his index finger roughly into it. I didn't know the word for rape in French.

I asked about the police, wanting, needing some form of justice.

He shrugged and shook his head. She was just a little girl. They didn't want to involve the police.

That little girl haunted my dreams. I wondered if it was the same two men who'd attacked me and felt guilty because I had never said anything. Now I was to carry the weight of it like a gravestone. I see that little girl, still, calling out to the wind. Did she call out, or whimper quietly like I had? I resolved right then and there that I would have no further part in this disgusting place; that this would be the last time I took off my clothes at this, or any other place like it.

What had happened to that little girl was going to have a big impact on my life.

Chapter 34

'I'm not going.' I was over sixteen and I knew my own mind. They couldn't make me. I stood my ground.

'Come on, Jo, get in the car.' Mum's face pleading.

'No.'

I couldn't stop thinking about the little girl with the dark hair – couldn't help but remember what had happened to me in the woods. I certainly couldn't tell my mum any of that or about the photographs, the probing hands and tongues. I couldn't tell my parents anything – like, I could still taste their friend Anthony's penis in my mouth.

Dad clenched his fists. 'Suit yourself, young lady. I'm sick of trying to reason with you.' And they drove away in a gust of dirty exhaust fumes. And I couldn't believe how easy it had been to say no.

I liked my weekends now. I lived off Smash instant potato and Heinz baked beans, sometimes mixed together with corned beef – we called it corned dog hash. Or I'd have tinned peaches with evaporated milk. Mum might leave me a Dairy Cream Sponge and I'd pick it up whole and take big mouthfuls, all by myself. They never called – but I was fine on my own. There were always neighbours if I needed them but, in any case, I liked to be alone.

My parents would come back on Sunday evening as though nothing had happened, as though they'd never been away at all. We never spoke about where they'd been or what they'd got up to at the weekend. We had never spoken of the nudist camp so it didn't make any difference. Why should we start now?

I used to bring my schoolwork home with me at the weekend and lose myself in it. I read and read my set books for English because I'd read everything else we had in the house. I knew great passages of Shakespeare that I would quote just for fun. I was rediscovering what I had missed.

Although they spent their weekends together, my parents seemed to be growing still further apart. When they talked it always ended in a row and there was even talk of my dad having an affair. I was sure if there was another woman, it must be someone at the nudist camp.

Mum seemed controlled about her suspicions on the outside. I suppose that was because, in her eyes, once you were married you were married for life: 'through thick and through thin,' she used to say.

More and more I'd find her losing herself in booze and

pills. At those times I'd find more and more pins in the voodoo doll.

Mum still had her work – that was until the company went bust and all the women were let go.

Suddenly she went back to having nothing. Her job had gone and so, it seemed, had her husband. Her world was tumbling all about her. She could hardly look after herself and she certainly couldn't look after me. She was in a black hole.

I wrote long passages in my diary. I didn't need anyone to talk to if I had my pages to confess on. I still have them now. Though the ink has browned, my thoughts are still fresh. I used the pages to work it all through.

But the nightmares continued. I'd see the dark-haired girl, naked, with her blood dripping into the sand. I'd be holding her and crying. I'd never seen her face but I could see it now, pleading for them to stop. I'd wake up in the dark with the wind howling at the window, put the light on and bury myself deep under the candlewick bedspread. I never knew her name.

I tried to tell myself that it didn't happen. That I hadn't understood the teenagers when they'd told me. So I coped in the only way I knew how – I underwent another metamorphosis. I wanted to be someone different, to leave what I knew of myself behind. I wanted to emerge with iridescent wings, light and airy as a butterfly, and fly away.

I was tired of crowds, fed up of pretending to be someone I wasn't and watching my back. But who was I?

I knew one thing – I was someone who wanted to cover myself up. I took Mum's old business suits and restitched them, fitting them tight to my body. I wore cowl hats down over one eye so I only had to look at half the world. I remade pencil skirts and wore high peep-toed shoes. I wanted to be alone so I dressed to ensure it.

No one was like me and no one liked me. I was too different. I wanted them to keep away. I even wanted to keep away from myself. I blamed myself for that little girl. I blame myself still and can't shake the feeling that she took the fate that was meant for me.

I hadn't realised that my parents' relationship breakdown would hit me as hard as it did. I thought I could handle anything but I wasn't as strong as I thought I was . . .

The strain started to show around the time I was sitting my O Levels, when I started to collapse with the stress of exams and my parents' marriage breakdown. Their endless arguments that were now raging, left me sleepless and anxious. My mother took me to the doctor for a quick-fix remedy and he prescribed anti-depressants, which worked in a way. They left me so relaxed that I didn't seem to care about anything. I fell asleep in my maths O Level and I missed one of my other O Levels completely. They'd taken the will out of me, left me flat so I didn't care what happened. I was on the same slippery slope as my mother.

Fortunately I saw what was happening. I took that bottle of pills and threw it in the bin. Even now, there has to be something seriously wrong with me to make me take a pill. To me, there's just no quick fix. I have a mistrust of pills with their shiny two-sided coats, their easy-to-swallow promise of hope. I don't believe you can prescribe happiness, particularly if it's torpedo-shaped. Pills like that are an assault on the nervous system. They need an early warning system attached to them.

The ailment I had needed much more than a few milligrams of chemical to fix it. It needed those things you can't prescribe for your children but you hope come naturally, like nurturing and love.

About that time I met a boy who was like-minded and who went to the same school as me. He told me about universities, about courses I'd never heard of. I was discovering that there was a whole world out there where people could think for themselves. In that world you could choose to go to university if you wanted and you could choose a career. He was there for me, not just when my parents were away at the weekend, but for the real absence in my life. He helped to give me a direction. He was kind. He was the friend I'd been waiting for.

After a time, naturism and nudists became confined to that box on the high, high shelf of my memory. I never went near it by choice but sometimes it came to me in my dreams.

I became absorbed in my work. My relationship with my new boyfriend made me even more isolated from the girls at school, but this time by choice. I kept graphs of my school marks, watching my performance in each subject. There was no one but me to care how I did, so I made the graphs my judges. They judged me harshly. I followed the thin biro lines staggering upwards, striving for perfection.

It was a way of making right what had happened to that little girl and I wouldn't waste it. Not now. I had escaped and she hadn't. She would never have the chance to get her life on track.

So I tracked my life. With no one to distract me, the lines were left to grow upwards, seeking the light. My marks on the left hand side, up to a hundred; the names of all the subjects colour coded. They rose up like a rainbow. I monitored my progress, working hard when they slipped. I was going up. Up and away. But then something brought me back down to earth.

I came home as I always did at around four o'clock. My boyfriend had walked me to the bus stop and his face, in profile, was still with me. Mostly, he looked straight ahead when he was with me. I'd traced an imaginary finger down his forehead, thinking he couldn't see me watching. Down over the perfect straightness of his nose, then down his lips as he was talking, settling my finger in the dimple of his chin that I knew was there but couldn't quite see. So when he'd turned, it had been unexpected. That quick, shy kiss. He'd gone for my mouth and missed, landing somewhere short of my left nostril but it had been a kiss nevertheless. A first kiss that I wanted.

'See yer then.'

'See yer.'

I was thinking that I couldn't remember when exactly we'd got together as I turned the stiff key of the front door. When was it I'd let him in? Except now here he was kissing me, sort of, and all I knew was that the house didn't feel so cold anymore when I unlocked the door.

Today was Tuesday and Tuesday was Scouse. That was easy, just mince, carrots, onions and potatoes served – if that was the right word – on a slice of white bread. It wouldn't take me long to make it. So I wasn't expecting the smell of burning, or the high-pitched squeal of the pressure cooker as I opened the door.

As Mum wasn't working anymore I thought that she must have been cooking for a change and forgotten about the pressure cooker. Maybe she'd popped round to a neighbour's. Or maybe she was in bed having her usual forty winks? Except that the screeching pressure cooker would have woken the dead.

The noise was as loud and jarring as a fire alarm. That piercing sound that penetrates every pore of your body, leaving your muscles taut and your face screwed up. I dropped my satchel and rushed into the kitchen.

Mum was lying twisted on the floor as if she'd fallen from a great height. The room was full of steam, coming from the pressure cooker on the gas. The noise went right through me. I stood for a moment, staring at the impossible angles of her crumpled body, trying to push myself into action.

It was as though I was watching something that I wasn't part of. I couldn't see her clearly but her eyes were closed and blood was pouring out of a cut over her right eye. Broken plates were scattered like shells about the floor. I was holding my breath as you do at times when you want to stop the earth spinning on its axis.

Then I was back in the world.

'Mum! Mum! You all right?'

I rushed to her, heaving her up, heavy as a sack. As I lifted her, her teeth jangled loose in her mouth. At first I thought she'd fainted and banged her head.

'Mum, wake up!'

I couldn't get her to come round. The pressure cooker

was still screaming as I cradled her head in my lap and bent down to listen for her breath.

Nothing.

'Mum? Mum?'

I put my face to hers to check for some sign of life. As I held her close it wasn't breath that came to me but a strong smell. Acrid. One that even today makes my stomach twist.

I pulled back from her and noticed that among the broken shards of plates there was glass. I picked up one of the pieces that still held a liquid dark as stagnant water and smelled it. Whisky.

I pulled Mum into a sitting position and started to slap her face. Her skin was cold as a fish, and wet. Her eyes flickered open, glazed, moving independently as though she were a thing possessed. Then she started to shake.

'Holy-Mary-Mother-of-God. Virgin Mary. Ha. Blessed Virgin.' She started to retch.

The vomit shot out all over me, hot, stinging. She pulled away on all fours, rocking and dribbling, the vomit mixing with the whisky and the blood. She turned to face me, pounding her fists on the shards of glass and broken plates. Growling like an animal in a pit, she was somewhere where no one could reach her.

'Leave me alone! Get away, bitch!' She veered to one side and fell.

I switched the gas off, moving the pan over to the back of the cooker. I dabbed at the blood on her forehead, listening to the dying screams of the pressure cooker. All over the kitchen units the steam had settled, streaming like tears. I rocked her there until the pressure cooker was quiet and there was no sound at all.

This was to become the way of things. I got used to finding her on the floor after one of her drinking sessions. She'd cry and promise me she'd never do it again – until the next time.

The neighbours got to know about her drinking bouts. Sometimes when I'd settled her in bed I'd go round for a cup of coffee with them and stay there for hours until she'd slept it off and it was safe to go home.

Something had changed for ever. It was as though I'd seen the demon that lived in the house. It had been let loose.

Chapter 35

More than anything, I felt so removed from my parents: the demon that was sozzled so many times when I came home from school, and the father who screamed at me. I wanted nothing to do with their life at the nudist camp. I was my own person now. It was time to grow up.

I also wanted to be like the other girls in the class who'd crossed the 'great divide' and lost their virginity.

'Have you lost it yet then?'

I'd smile and look away. I didn't know how to lose it, I had nothing much to lose. To lose something meant you had to have something you valued, and there was not one thing I valued about myself. So as one by one each girl in the class joined this secret society, I found myself wanting, as ever, to be included. And when you're a young girl on the lookout for 'that', it doesn't take long to find someone up to the task.

My parents, of course, were going away regularly to the club at weekends. 'While the cat's away,' I told myself as I led my boyfriend into the spare room, 'the mice do play.' There was a sofa in there with a secret button that magically transformed it into a bed. Suddenly, it was down, and he was down, lying on top of it, and I was on top of him.

He looked scared. Did it matter that I wasn't feeling very much? I was sure that if I could just keep going, it'd come to me. I'd seen the way people did it on films, and in the woods at the camp, where they got on top of one another with lots of gasping and hair thrashing around. I could do that, couldn't I?

'I've got something in my coat pocket,' he said.

Then he was up and away, heaving on his coat, shaking his head. 'I just don't think you're ready yet.'

I didn't realise he was being nice, that not all men were like the ones I'd met. We didn't have sex and I was glad. After that, I went back to concentrating on my school work. Careers advice at school was limited to a couple of choice phrases: 'Have you thought about being an ophthalmic optician?' and 'Have you thought about being a nurse?'

I decided to make up my own mind. For most of us in Warrington struggling to do this, the path was obvious – a few years down the chippy wearing a blue gown and sitting in the rarefied atmosphere of vaporised crisp fat, then into an early marriage and kids.

I wanted to see what else was on offer. I wanted to do something with my hands. 'Save that for extramural activities,' the career adviser said when I told her I was interested in textile design. I looked up the long word in the dictionary. If no one was going to help me, then I would have to help myself.

I was on a path that I'd identified as the way out. I would get the best exams I could and go to university. I was on course to get away. I would be my own person and no one would ever make me do things I didn't want to do again.

I was totally focussed, knowing that keeping my head down now would mean I could hold it high later in life. I became even more of a swot, if that was possible. I didn't care. It was a way to get up and away. Not only did I work as hard as I could but I poured over manuals of university entry requirements, cross-referencing subjects. I was on a mission. It wasn't exactly mission impossible but it was mission bloody difficult. To study textile design you had to have A level art.

'That's not a proper A Level,' my dad said.

'But I like it.'

'You're not going to art school and that's the end of it.'

'But why?'

'Hippies and drugs.'

That was the end of that.

So instead I concentrated on those subjects that scored highest as entry requirements for university. English, maths and biology. It was a science so Dad would probably approve. I hadn't passed O Level maths as that was the one I'd fallen asleep in, so it was a struggle making a case to sit the A Level. But I worked so hard, they couldn't really say no.

When she wasn't drunk, Mum would bring me tea and biscuits when I was shut away in my bedroom. 'You're working yourself into the ground, Jo.'

'I'm all right.'

Her sweet face smiling. 'Here, have a little break.'

I wouldn't stop. 'Thanks, Mum.' She'd stand there for a moment by the door while I kept my eyes on my work.

There weren't many of us who went on to sixth form college and even fewer who got A Levels. In fact, there were just two girls (not including Carole, which was satisfying) who got into university and I was one of them.

My dad made it difficult for me to leave for university and he took a lot of persuading. But I went in the end.

From time to time I'd come home and witness the further disintegration of my parents' marriage and the steady increase in my mother's drinking.

Whenever I was home, she'd ask: 'Do you love me, Jo-Jo?' and I would reassure her that I did. But although she became even cleverer at hiding the evidence, I still knew what was going on and that it was worse than ever.

'It's just one,' she'd say pleadingly.

'But it's never just one, is it? Can't you see what it's doing to you?'

'I promise, I promise on my life! Never again.'

That was until the next time. She had lost all sense of herself, of her sense of purpose

One term, when I was away at university, Dad rang to say that Mum had been admitted to hospital, so I rushed home. It was where they locked people away who had lost their minds. I'll never forget visiting her there. With its jumbled Gothic turrets and dark windows it looked like a haunted house. The patients rocked in corridors or slumped, as if folded, in chairs, waiting to be put away.

I followed a nurse down a long corridor, stepping around a girl with hair as wild as brambles who was sitting, gently rocking on the floor. The girl looked at me from bruised eye sockets, and flinched as a woman shouted 'bitch' from her room. A man opened his dressing gown to me and proffered a withered penis.

In a room in the midst of this place was my mum, her eyes glazed and shifting independently of each other.

'My little Jo, you came.'

Her tongue was thick with drugs.

But all I could say was: 'Mum.'

I held her hands but she wasn't with me. I tried to

remember her dressed in her smart clothes, her hair all neat and arranged. I just felt so sad for what she had become.

'Your mother's a manic depressive,' the doctor told me. Before adding, 'Don't worry, it's not hereditary.'

'I . . . but what does it mean? Will she get better?'

'Let's put it like this. Your mother knows highs that you will never experience. And the lows . . . well . . . that's the other side of it.'

I struggled to remember her highs. A distant voice singing in the echoing kitchen. Her own special lullaby that she sang just for me.

'My Jo, my Jo, my Jo darling girl . . .'

Once, when I came home, I even agreed to go back to Edendale. It had been more than two years since I'd last visited the club. I was eighteen so technically an adult, and somehow that realisation made me want to face up to it. I'd like to say it was to bury those ghosts but I suppose I was still trying to please my dad.

It was late autumn and, driving there, I still got the same sick feeling I always had when I was a child in the car all those years ago. As we approached the gate, I felt the same tightening of my stomach. Would Terry be here? What would I say if I met him?

It was smaller than I remembered it, like the feeling

you have when you go back to your first school. I kept my clothes on as I wandered past the volleyball court, the Rebels' caravan, the clubhouse, the miniten court, the swimming pool all covered up.

I looked everywhere for Terry. Then I caught a glimpse of him, bare shouldered, in the gloom of his caravan. I stared long and hard at him but he stayed where he was. I carried on walking, pulling my jacket around my shoulders as I took the twisting path to the woods. Then I heard a car drive past close to the perimeter and I saw Edendale for what it really was. Just a little field, Somewhere in England.

I had a new life now and it had nothing to do with Edendale. In the holidays I worked to earn money for my next term at university. One year, I went over to France to work on a farm where I castrated maize – which involves cutting the flowers off the male plant – for a summer. Then I went down to Pau University to work in the kitchens, which meant helping to feed 800 students and mopping the vast dining hall. I helped French chefs prepare perfect meals. Having to peel all those potatoes at home had finally proved useful.

Sometimes when I was peeling, my hands stiff with icy water, I'd think of Mum. She was in and out of hospital, on and off the bottle.

But Mum was scared of being alone. What would she

do without Dad? He was her life. She'd never really lived on her own, having gone straight from her parents' home into marriage, and she wasn't sure she could handle it. I just didn't know how to advise her. I didn't know what to think about it all.

I worked to fill up my mind so I wouldn't have to think and so that when I had finished my studies, I could move to London, away from home for good. As students, we'd somehow scrape together enough money to go on holiday to Greece. Taking the ferry over from Piraeus, baking all day in third class at the top of the boat, we'd stop off on Mykonos and rent cheap rooms with dodgy toilets from ladies dressed in black. We'd go to Paradise and Super Paradise beaches, the tourists at a further stage of undress on each one. I never told my friends I'd seen it all before.

When we were bored of Mykonos, we'd hop on the next boat and go to another of the islands – Syros, Paros, Tinos. I liked that feeling of taking off whenever you wanted to, of carrying all your earthly possessions in one bag. It was surprising just how little you needed.

In Greece all the tourists went topless. Some even went bottomless too. It was different somehow, from seeing them in a camp. They were free to bare themselves if they wanted to. Some did, some didn't. Adult naturists had a choice. While I could never feel comfortable baring my breasts, I did feel the freedom of not being harnessed by clothes in a way I wished I could have had as a child.

Chapter 36

'Jo's got a fucking two-one!' That's how I heard the news about my degree results. We were all crowding around the board. Three years at university had paid off. At the graduation ceremony, I clenched the scroll that was my degree certificate as though it were my actual ticket to freedom. I would get a good job. I would go and work in London. I was on my way.

In the marquee after the ceremony I raised my glass to my dad. After all the years I felt he hadn't supported me, he did turn up to celebrate my big day.

'Thanks for letting me go.'

He laughed. He knew he'd been difficult but I think at that moment he felt proud. I was the first in our family to go to university.

'Where's Mum?'

She was nowhere to be seen. We hunted all over for her on that sunny afternoon among the gowned students and the suited parents but she was nowhere to be seen. I was beginning to worry when I spotted her: she was standing near the used glasses pouring the dregs into her cup and drinking them down. People were laughing at her in the way they might at an old tramp in a park, with a bottle in a brown paper bag.

I looked away. It would be so easy to pretend I hadn't seen her. Far more difficult to go up to her in front of my friends.

'Mum?'

Her eyes were chameleon-like, not focussing.

'Jo. I'm so proud!' She staggered towards me, went to hug me and collapsed.

Dad gave me a hand to carry her to the car. We skipped the rest of the celebration, driving instead to a lay-by where we sat while she slept it off. Over the sounds of her snoring, Dad told me a little of how things were. I saw that no matter how hard it was for her, it was hard for him too. It was one of those situations that had become untenable.

Over the coming weeks and months, he struggled to stay with her, to do his duty by her, but it was already too late. Alcohol had her in its grip and wouldn't let her go.

I had found my freedom. I got a job in the city and bought a small flat in Shepherds Bush. It wasn't much but it was enough for me. I'd stay up all night just for the joy of looking over the rooftops and the feeling that, at last, I had something that was mine. I still had more money going out than coming in but in a fair wind and with an expense account I could just about manage.

I'd found my own way of escaping. For Mum it wasn't quite so easy. Her relationship with my dad was almost beyond repair. When I'd left home, the last thing that was tying them together snapped. She'd taken more and more to drinking and sleeping pills, filling in the gaps of loneliness with self-induced, drugged sleep. Alcohol was her friend, but it was a bad friend. It would cheer her for a short while and then leave her alone so the only thing she had left was the hazy view of the world through the bottom of an empty bottle.

When she was well and going through a detox phase, she'd come down to London and I'd book us into a show. At times like this, I'd remember the mum that was in control when I was small and I'd have hope she might get well. But when I came home from work the next day it was the usual story. The 999 call, the ambulance men arriving, ready with a joke. The stomach-pumping and her promises afterwards that it would never, ever happen again.

Mum joined Alcoholics Anonymous when I was twenty-two. For the first time in her life she actually admitted to herself that she had a problem. She talked about it as one step at a time.

Mum wrote poems about her struggle. No matter how

many times she told herself she might leave my father, she couldn't get her mind round it. She knew that the only path forward she had to take was alone but she was too scared to set foot on it. She was so tired of it all – she didn't have the strength to take that first step and I wasn't there any more for her to lean on and help her take it.

Occasionally Dad would come to see me when I lived in London – always on his own – always heralding the visit with the same conversation.

'You're probably busy, Jo, but I was just thinking that I might be in London next week. I have to be back by Thursday for a dentist appointment though.'

'Oh when? I'd love to see you.' I meant it. 'We'll go to a show . . . the opera . . .'

'Not on my account – no use wasting money on that sort of thing . . .'

'But I'm working now. I . . .'

'I'll pop down maybe Tuesday . . . if you haven't any plans. Then I'll be off the following day.'

'Dad, why can't you . . .'

'Bye, Jo, bye . . . see you next week.'

He'd bring his tool kit, fix the sash windows, or the door that wouldn't open properly.

'Who'd have thought it,' he'd say. 'Jo's own little flat in London. Horrible place . . . wouldn't give you tuppence for it . . .'

One day he took me shopping.

'Choose anything you want, Jo, anything at all. I want you to choose something for the flat and any time you look at it you can think, my dad bought me that.'

Eventually, I chose a glass paperweight with a glazed bubble inside. When I held it up to the light, I could see another bubble with a surface cracked into prisms of soft pastels. It was a fragile thing – a bubble within a bubble. Like our relationship, all made of glass.

Chapter 37

I was in Bermuda, staying with some friends in their own patch of paradise. They had a private jetty leading out from their house. Each evening I'd watch the sun set, and each morning I'd get up and run along the warm wooden boards to dive deep into the sparkling sea. I'd swim around the bay. Just me, the rising sun and a few boats chugging along the horizon. Sometimes, I'd lie on my back, looking at the gulls circling overhead and feel as small as a drop in that ocean.

As I breathed the salty air in deep, I'd wonder whose life I was living. It was a long, long way from the choking factories and warehouses of Warrington, from those grey, wet pavements. Swimming in that ocean, I felt light as sea spume. Free.

I was twenty-six and was doing well. I had a job I loved, my own flat, a boyfriend who doted on me, and here I was, swimming off the coast of Bermuda. At that moment I thought that things just couldn't get better.

I pulled myself up on the wooden steps at the end of the jetty, trying to avoid a spiteful little fish that guarded his territory there with ferocious nips. The sun was stretching into the day. I grabbed my towel and laid out to dry off. It was strange, I thought, all those years throughout which my father had tried to offer me freedom through naturism, that had nothing whatever to do with my own concept of freedom now.

Freedom for me was right here in this moment: knowing that I could choose how long I could lie here in the sun; knowing that if I wanted to dive back in that water again, I could; knowing that I worked to pay my own way and that rewards such as these were part of what made it all worthwhile. Freedom to me was knowing that whatever I chose to do, I could do it. And that, to me, was worth a hundred fortunes.

I was thinking just this as I slung the damp towel around myself and walked back to the house. My boyfriend was standing on the veranda and as I got closer I realised he was crying. He was shaking his head, his arms folded about his chest.

'I don't know how to tell you.'

'What's wrong?'

'Your dad's been trying to get hold of you.'

'Why?'

'I . . .'

'What is it?'

'Your mother . . . She's dead.'

Everything went quiet, as though I was underwater. I could hear a buzzing in my ears.

'Mum? Mummy?'

'Your dad's been trying desperately to get you at work and . . .'

I tried to listen but it came in fits and starts. She'd been drinking. There were pills, lots of pills. No, he didn't know what sort.

'No . . .'

They'd found her dead in my bed at home in Warrington. That's when I took off.

I ran and ran, up and away. I couldn't stop. I ran until my lungs were screaming with pain and my face was wet with tears. When I stopped, I realised I couldn't hear myself crying. It was that deep crying that has no sound, like the crying of your soul.

Next to me some crimson hibiscus wound up around a hedge. I took a flower and twisted it between my fingers. Mum. But I couldn't picture her, couldn't even hear her voice. Not even the last time she'd said goodbye.

I took the flower and ran on up the hill, everything a blur. At the top was a small white chapel alone on the headland. I remember it was called the Chapel of Ease and it felt somehow that God had put it there for just this moment. I struggled against the wind towards it and opened the door.

It was calm inside, dark and cool. I sat down in a pew with the flower and, twisting it around and around in my fingers, looked deep into its centre, trying to remind myself of something living. This delicate flower already withering here in my hand. There in that emptiness I offered it up.

'Mum, Mum, Mum, Mum . . .' I called out over and over again, like a wailing child, knowing that she would never be there any more to answer me. I don't know how long I stayed in the chapel. It was all time. No time. The time that stands alone.

I wished I believed in God; I had never felt like I needed him so much. I bowed before him and prayed and prayed for all the times I hadn't prayed before. I prayed that he'd bring her back; that we could do it all differently; that I had been a better daughter; that I had been there to catch her when she fell. There, in that empty church, I prayed for all the things that I knew could never be. I placed the flower carefully on a bible as a gift to my mum and left.

Chapter 38

I told my dad I loved him as I stepped from the train. Although he wasn't one for showing emotion, I felt he needed to know. He looked away, not knowing what to say, grabbing for my case, holding it like a barrier between us. We took the road home.

Dad looked straight ahead at the road as he spoke. 'She didn't mean to do it. It was an accident.'

I saw, once again, the pills in their velvet box, smelled the alcohol on her breath, felt the weight of her as I pulled her up. The words formed in my mouth but I couldn't voice them. It was too late.

Dad talked about practical things – how marvellous the funeral people had been, what would happen at the service, the flowers he'd chosen. I could choose some too, no expense spared, whatever I wanted. Then we were home.

I looked at the charcoal sky, the trees almost black against it, a single silver birch broken down by the wind. There was not a person or a living creature in sight – no birds swept the sky – only the clouds, pressing down like palms. It was that half-light you get some days, when you know the sun won't break through and the air lies thick and heavy.

The simple lines of the house seemed like a drawing done by the child I had been long ago. For a moment, I saw Mum there on the front step, her arms outstretched to me. I thought of her dream to have a cottage in the country, with roses around the door, and I felt for her, living in that stark place.

Dad dropped me off at the house, as I'd asked if I could clear out Mum's clothes. He had lots to arrange and wanted to keep busy. I half expected to hear her singing as I opened the door, 'My Jo, my Jo, my Jo darling girl . . .'

I followed the silence into the kitchen. The house felt damp and unlived in, with every surface shrouded in fine dust. I saw Mum's hands arranging the ornaments just so, polishing the silver until it shone. In the kitchen, everything had been put away. I heard the scream of the pressure cooker somewhere in my memory and saw her crumpled body on the floor.

I knew I had to go into my room to see where she'd died. I opened the door slowly, like I used to when she was having her forty winks and I didn't want to wake her. The bed was made up, hard and stiff. I touched the familiar softness of the candlewick bedspread, saw her slumped to the floor. Had she tried to call for help? Tried to write a note? Then I lay down on the bed and reached out to her over the distance, saying over and over again, 'Why?'

My parents' bedroom was unbearably quiet and cold. I opened the wardrobes. The smell, the life of her was there for an instant and then gone. I sorted through her life, remembering.

I put away her glittering cocktail dresses that smelled of Estée Lauder and the stiff ball gowns I'd dressed up in when I was a child. I folded them neatly, seeing her again. Clothed. The way I wanted to remember her.

Her life was arranged in a row of black dustbin bags. As I sat down at her dressing table I looked in the mirror and tried hard to create her face from my own. I saw the half-child, half-adult I had become – an odd mix of vulnerability and strength – and I knew then that I would forever be swinging between the two. I knew that at times some men would take advantage of the child in me, at other times I would find some inner strength and put it to good use.

Strength was something Mum had strived for. At the funeral, I stood in front of her shiny coffin and faced a crowd of faces. My voice quivered as I read from one of Mum's favourite poems. I made my way back to the pew where my father gripped the rail in front of him.

*

I never wanted to get married. I never wanted to have children. As it turned out, they came upon me unexpectedly, later in life. And that's why I found myself walking down the aisle at thirty-two, five months pregnant. Life sometimes has a way of sorting these things out for you.

The man I married couldn't have been more different from my dad. With my husband I felt safe, and together we built the home with roses around the door that my mum had dreamed of, with children who played fat-cheeked in the garden and a cat curled contentedly on the sofa.

Over time, I have come to understand my dad more – maybe you can only do that when you are an adult. I can appreciate his quest for freedom away from the prison of his marriage. Dad has mellowed and I have grown older. We meet, now, somewhere in between, though the great unsaid still stands between us in all its nakedness. We cannot talk easily about it. Dad has his own box full of secrets – his naturism lies in there, as still and as cold as my mother. Certainly his answer was somewhat off the wall when, years later, I asked him why he had made me go to nudist camps.

'You were just at that age,' he said, sniffing for emphasis, '. . . of discovering boys. I wanted to take away all that curiosity.'

That he'd achieved with aplomb.

Dad has a new wife now, and has his happy ever after. I see now that having an alcoholic wife brings its own challenges and remind myself that you cannot be fully responsible for another human being, unless it is your child. Where there is a vulnerable child, there will be a certain type of adult waiting to abuse it.

I don't want to fall into the cliché of having had an unhappy childhood. At the time I had nothing to compare it with, it was as it was. Like it is for any child, there were times when it was good and other times when it was bad. But perhaps it was an unusual childhood.

Chapter 39

As I wrote earlier, being a nudist stripped me of so much more than my clothes. It made me lie; it made me scared; it made me different. It stripped me of the joy of discovering the opposite sex and made me ashamed for ever of my own body. But most of all it made me frightened of a certain kind of man: one who will be always lurking in the woods – somewhere in the shady recesses of my memory.

Strangely, I often feel naked when clothed, as though, even after all these years, everyone can still see me bare.

I will always question the wisdom of my parents in joining a nudist camp. As parents we never mean to put our children at risk but, sometimes, in doing what we believe, we make terrible mistakes.

As a child, my mistake was that I never spoke up. For that I will always feel naked. Like I've been spoiled, unwrapped too early and enjoyed by others, inappropriately.

Let me tell you about my dream.

I am in a garden, a lush garden where the boughs on

the trees bend with the weight of blossom. The scent fills the air so you can almost taste it. Golden apples hang from trees. Vines wind in intricate patterns and through their woven leaves frosted grapes glint like jewels. The grass is soft and lush and when you sink back into it, it holds you more gently than the finest goose down.

I breathe slowly, in and out, in and out. I lie on my back, naked, with not a care in the world. I know, somehow, that I'm not in the world. It hasn't even occurred to me until this moment that I am naked. It feels as if I am floating. From the distance I catch the whisper of a brook trickling past. I could be drifting on that stream, letting the current take me wherever it will.

I close my eyes and let my breathing beat to the rhythm of the world. In that special place between breathing in and breathing out, I am almost not there at all.

A shadow wavers over my face and I wait for it to pass. A coldness chills my bare body as I will the sun to return and shine its warmth on me.

I open my eyes and pull back, feeling the air scream into my lungs.

The garden is shrinking. In fast-forward fruit withers on the trees, flowers burst open and brown. The smell of rot is in the air. I retch. The kaleidoscope of colours dims and, looking down I see that my skin is grey. Everywhere are twisted shapes of blackened trees and then among them I hear a soft buzzing sound, like a hiss.

Round the stumps of trees snakes rise, twisting and coiling around and up. I try to stand but my legs are weak. The trees are moving with snakes, blocking out the light. I'm gasping now. Heads of snakes are darting at me with split tongues. I can feel them on my face. Then down my body, slithering, searching. Everywhere is dark. Monochrome.

Then it starts to rain. But as I put my hands up to my face, I draw them quickly back. The sky is raining blood.

I cannot stop the dream. I wish I could say that it is just that – a dream. But from a dream you wake up and know it never happened.

I need a chink of light at night, even if it's just beneath the door. Between the dreams I have a whole other life at night. Technically, I suppose I must be an insomniac. I never know what wakes me at that time, shortly after three a.m. I read somewhere that three in the morning is Satan's time, the opposite time of three in the afternoon when Jesus died on the cross. I like to think it's just a coincidence. After all these years, it may just be a habit or maybe I don't need much sleep, but I've given up fighting against it, of lying awake in bed and thinking.

I try not to think about those dark memories when I wake up. They are in that box, in a box on a high shelf.

Instead, I think of all those other things that aren't important at all – the trivia of life: have I taken out that chicken to defrost? Mustn't forget to write that thank you note to Jackie; that doctor's appointment at ten past ten tomorrow . . .

There they are, like a jostling crowd, pushing and shouting, vying for attention, getting louder and louder. I know they're not big, earth-shattering worries. They don't even deserve to be called worries at all but they're all running at me, screaming. Only I can't see that the really big thing, the King Kong of all worries that is coming right behind them.

Often, my thoughts will wander back to those dark places in my memory. If I stay in bed, they have to take their course so I have learned to make friends with my insomnia. Instead of lying there going down some path in the darkness, I get up. I clean the kitchen, tidy up, get out of the way all those chores that normal people do in the daylight. My husband calls them my nocturnal scurryings. Then I pick up a book, or turn the television to Sky movies and fill up my mind.

A psychologist would probably have a field day with such behaviour but it's my way and there's a lot you can get done in those dark hours when no one is around to bother you. I have even come to enjoy those hours when the world is still.

Sometimes I go and watch the sleeping faces of my children. I sit on the ends of their beds following the rise and fall of their chests. I see the softness of their faces, the innocence there and hope, for them, they can hold on to it.

What haunts me are those things I can't remember. Maybe that box is on a shelf too high to reach down after all these years. Or maybe there are some dark corners inside that, when I open it, I can never quite shed light on. We all have mechanisms to survive. Some of us block things out in order to get on, otherwise we'd be forever stuck on some macabre roundabout of childhood memory. But what I will never know is what is in those dark places or how I've made sense of those things I've brought to light.

I started to write this book to rid myself of demons – demons that have been following me around for too long. I wanted to colour my demons in, so that everyone could see them – to give them a face that other people could recognise – otherwise I would have kept them in the pages of my dusty diaries where they have lain for more than thirty years.

But when I started to research this book, I realised that it wasn't just about my own demons; search the Internet for any length of time and they're there. Trawling on the Internet I found instances of little girls just like me, little girls who have had their photographs taken – to be distributed around paedophile rings. There are little girls – boys, too – playing in nudist camps with no idea that the wrong eyes are upon them, for the wrong reasons.

Sometimes I wonder if there are photographs somewhere, of a little girl with the frightened eyes of a foal, making her way through the dark thicket of a wood. I see the twisted shapes of the trees and feel them closing in on me. I get lost in the maze of pathways, the darkness pressing in on my chest. I listen for their sounds, their whispers – the wail of an owl, a snap underfoot. I sense them watching, hidden eyes, shapes hiding in the shadows. Waiting for something to block my way. Waiting for what might come from out of the dark.

My demons still come to me at night, or at twilight when the light is fading, and often in a wood when a shadow or a crackle underfoot reminds me of what was. They say memory is what's left over after we've forgotten everything else. Some of what happened to me I've wanted to forget but I write it down to remember. Then perhaps I can see the wood from the trees.

For me now, I seek out the light places in life, away from the trees – and laughter, always laughter.

A little girl walks along a twisting muddy path, padding her bare feet on the cool earth. She doesn't know where the path leads. She is as naked as the day she was born, she is free. The sun seeps through the young branches of the trees overhead, making puzzles on the floor and she skips through them, placing her feet carefully on the light patches. The leaves on the trees are just starting to bud. Carefully, she holds one between finger and thumb. It is a fragile thing, delicate. Held by a brown sheath like a hand. She traces the whorl of it, ready to unfold, tender, green, fresh and new to the world.

The wind blows gently, murmuring through the branches, whispering of secrets long ago. She knows she must leave them behind on that path, in that wood. She throws her long hair back over her shoulders and strides on. As she comes out of the dense wood, she feels the sun on her bare skin and reaches for her mother's hand.

Acknowledgements

To my husband and children for showing me how it could be.

Also: Thanks to Susan Smith of MBA for her belief and for helping me to write in real sentences. Also huge thanks to Carly Cook of Headline for her agile mind and endless patience. And lastly to friends for their support and numerous cups of coffee.

The National Association for People Abused in Childhood

Set up to help provide support, training, information and resources to persons and organisations supporting people who have experienced ill treatment and/or neglect in childhood, this charity offers a range of services, from a free advice line, to guides to local and national support groups.

http://www.napac.org.uk/

0800 085 3330

More Non-fiction from Headline Review

DADDY'S LITTLE GIRL

JULIA LATCHEM-SMITH

Julia's family was a picture of respectability. To the outside world it was middle class, decent, loving. But her mother didn't love her enough. And her father loved her too much.

Between the ages of eight and thirteen, Julia's father sexually abused her. Loyal to her family, and desperate to keep it intact, the abuse had to become their little secret. Even as Julia struggled to come to terms with her ordeal, she knew that revealing the truth would rip her family apart.

When she finally cried out for help, she was encouraged to retract her allegations and branded a liar. In her teenage years, she began to doubt her own sanity. Had the abuse really happened? Her father couldn't have done that . . . could he?

This is the harrowing story of how Julia's father abused her trust, and cheated her of her childhood. But it is also the uplifting story of how, years later, Julia successfully confronted her painful past and began to carve out for herself a meaningful future.

NON-FICTION / MEMOIR 978 0 7553 1638 0

DESTROYED

JAYNE STERNE

When eight-year-old Jayne left bomb-torn Northern Ireland, her family stayed with relations and a distant relative began a campaign of abuse so horrifying that her world was shattered for ever.

And when the family moved again – her relative came too. Raped repeatedly, beaten, abused and battered, Jayne's life was a living hell.

One thing kept Jayne sane: the love and care of her older brother, Stuart. But he had demons of his own, and Jayne watched in despair as the boy who had always protected her turned into an adult consumed by rage. Out of control, Stuart went on to commit the 'Barbecue Murders', one of the most terrible crimes of recent years . . .

Destroyed is the heart-stopping true tale of an innocence stolen and a family torn apart – told by a woman who has finally managed to confront her harrowing past.

Someone she knew
Someone she trusted
Someone who betrayed her

The devastating true story of a shattered childhood

NON-FICTION / MEMOIR 978 0 7553 1799 8